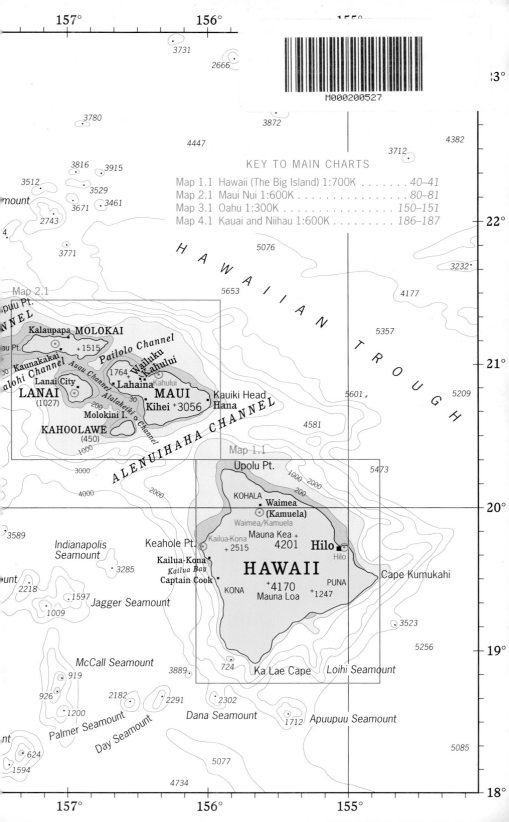

157°　　　　156°　　　　155°

3731

2666

M000200527

23°

3780

3872

4447

4382

3712

3816　　3915

3512

3529

mount

3671　　3461

2743

22°

3771

KEY TO MAIN CHARTS

Map 1.1 Hawaii (The Big Island) 1:700K *40–41*
Map 2.1 Maui Nui 1:600K *80–81*
Map 3.1 Oahu 1:300K *150–151*
Map 4.1 Kauai and Niihau 1:600K *186–187*

5076

3232

H A W A I I A N

5653

4177

Map 2.1

T R O U G H

puu Pt.

5357

au Pt.

Kalaupapa **MOLOKAI**

Pailolo Channel

Kaunakakai +1515

alohi Channel *Auau Channel*

Wailuku
Kahului

1764

21°

Lanai City **Lahaina**Kahului

200

LANAI 30

MAUI Kauiki Head

(1027) *Alalakeiki Channel* Kihei +3056 Hana

Molokini I.

KAHOOLAWE

5601

5209

(450)

A L E N U I H A H A   C H A N N E L

4581

1000

3000

Map 1.1

Upolu Pt.

5473

1000 2000

4000

200

2000

KOHALA

3000 **Waimea**
⊙ **(Kamuela)**

3589

Waimea/Kamuela

20°

Indianapolis
Seamount

Keahole Pt. Kailua-Kona

Mauna Kea +

+ 2515 **4201** **Hilo**

Hilo

3285 **Kailua-Kona**
Kailua Bay **HAWAII**

unt **Captain Cook**

2218 **KONA** +**4170** **PUNA** Cape Kumukahi

.1597 *Jagger Seamount* **Mauna Loa** +1247

1009

3523

5256

19°

McCall Seamount

919 3889 724

926 Ka Lae Cape *Loihi Seamount*

.1200 2182 2291 2302

Palmer Seamount *Dana Seamount*

1712 *Apuupuu Seamount*

nt

.624 5085

1594

5077

4734

18°

157°　　　　156°　　　　155°

Diving Hawaii

AND MIDWAY

By Mike Severns and
Pauline Fiene-Severns

Photographed by Mike Severns
Edited by David Pickell

PERIPLUS

Published by Periplus Editions (HK) Ltd

Copyright ©2002 Periplus Editions (HK) Ltd
ALL RIGHTS RESERVED

ISBN 962-593-064-7
Printed in Singapore

Publisher: Eric Oey
Series editor: David Pickell
Photo and text editing: David Pickell
Cartography: David Pickell
Interior design: David Pickell with Peter Ivey

DISTRIBUTORS

ASIA PACIFIC	Berkeley Books Pte. Ltd. 130 Joo Seng Road #06-01/03 Olivine Building Singapore 368357 Tel: (65) 6280-3320 Fax: (65) 6280-6290
INDONESIA	PT Wira Mandala Pustaka (Java Books–Indonesia) Jl. Kelapa Gading Kirana Blok A-14 No. 17, Jakarta 14240 Tel: (62-21) 451-5351 Fax: (62-21) 453-4987
JAPAN	Tuttle Publishing RK Building, 2nd Floor 2-13-10 Shimo-Meguro Meguro-ku Tokyo 153 0064 Tel: (81-3) 5437-0171 Fax: (81-3) 5437-0755
USA	Tuttle Publishing Distribution Center Airport Industrial Park 364 Innovation Drive North Clarendon, VT 05759-9436 Tel: (802) 773-8930, (800) 526-2778

COVER Whitetip reef sharks (*Triaenodon obesus*) at Molokini. This harmless and (usually) shy species is common in Hawaii.
PAGES 4–5 The commensal shrimp *Periclimenes soror* living on a crown-of-thorns star.
FRONTISPIECE *Rhincodon typus,* the whale shark.

Contents

Part III Oahu

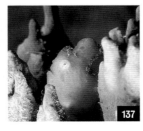

Part IV Kauai and Niihau

Part V Midway

Part VI Practicalities

Preface
and Acknowledgments

Mike Severns and Pauline Fiene-Severns

WHEN THE SUBJECT OF DOING THIS BOOK came up a few years ago, our main reason for saying yes was the opportunity to work with editor David Pickell. His intellect, charm, and talent for his craft made us forget that this was a writing project involving 74,500 words, and that we would be required to write almost all of them. When it finally came time to actually begin writing, it became obvious that this was a much bigger project than we had ever imagined. Although we had lived and dived in Hawaii for more than 30 years, and had dived off of all the main islands and Midway, we realized that writing a guidebook is not something that we could do on the side. At the beginning of May we sat down for four months, getting up only to run a few miles, feed our animals, and make sure we were still in business.

Of course, the other reason we wanted to do this book was our love for diving in Hawaii. The discoveries, the once-in-a-lifetime animal encounters, and the solved mysteries have brought us almost daily inspiration and incentive to keep learning more. We know this feeling is shared by divers throughout the islands and we wanted to share some of their stories as well. We spent months revisiting the islands and talking to divers and dive shop employees. Personalities in this business are varied, to say the least, and there are many different passions for diving. After a while we began to get a sense of each island's unique flavor.

This is what we have tried to do in this book: show you what diving in Hawaii is like, and how each island's diving and approach are different. We have assumed that most divers reading this book will be diving off a dive boat or from shore with some direction from local divers. Most of the dive sites we've covered are in the known repertoire, but a couple of our personal favorites and a few that were shown to us under the condition that we not pinpoint their exact location, are either missing or only generally located on the maps. Divers know that half the fun is discovery, and knowing that an airplane exists somewhere off the north shore of Oahu or that a deep reef swarming with *ulua* is someplace off the south coast of Maui just adds to the challenge. This, of course, is part of why we dive in the first place, to explore, to learn and to experience something new about our world.

ACKNOWLEDGMENTS

We could not have done this book without the help of many divers who know their local islands and sites much better than we ever could. It has been our pleasure and delight to spend these months talking to divers who have had a lifetime of experiences on their particular islands: to be laughed at by Big Island divers when we told them of seeing our first Tinker's butterfly in five years, and to see disbelief in the faces of Oahu divers when we mention that we see longnose hawkfish almost every day off Molokini.

For help with the fieldwork on the Big Island we would like to thank Frank and Patrice Heller. They generously took us along the entire length of the Kona Coast, pointing out a bandit angel here, a hammerhead there, as well as provided Mike's favorite—avocado and apple sandwiches. Kendra Choquette recounted the story of the wreck of the bare naked lady and offered a wealth of other information from her vast experiences there. On the Hilo side, Mike Brandon talked for hours describing his favorite Hilo sites, and Del Dykes gave us descriptions of sites east of Hilo to Kumukahi point, sharing his years of Hilo experience. Paula Haight introduced us to the energetic Rebekah Keele who pin-pointed Kohala sites on maps and entertained us with unusually good diving poetry.

For areas of Maui that we had never dived, we relied heavily on the experiences of Chuck Thorne, Maui's shore diving legend. Drew Bradley, another absolutely fearless diver, shared some of his "youthful" (i.e., wild) experiences, which we were happy to be hearing of after the fact. Ryan McDonald and Andy Schwanke both recounted their Molokini dolphin encounters, which although experienced months apart, were remarkably similar. We are also pleased to be bringing Jennifer Anderson's manta story to print in this book. Though we have heard the story many times, it is just as amazing to us now as that first day when she returned from the charter, mass of fishing line in-hand, babbling with excitement.

Although Lanai is only a 30-minute boat ride away, we certainly haven't been there as often as Erik Stein, who knows it inside and out. He took time out from his busy schedule of lying in bed with a broken leg (from *paragliding*) to answer questions and lament about all the diving he was missing. Bo Lusher, our friend and crew member, shared his impassioned recollections of all that he had seen off both Lanai and Molokai over the years. Dan Saunders helped by drawing maps of dive sites for Lanai and Molokai, and passing along some interesting stories of diving with the black coral divers out of Lahaina. Our memorable sandbar shark dives were orchestrated by Dave Fleetham, and we thank him for that and his companionship and good cheer over so many years of diving.

Oahu was particularly challenging and required help from many, but Pete May put things in order right from the beginning, digging deep into his detailed dive logs and even bringing over videotapes. John Hoover, always just an E-mail away, answered question after question, offering an equal number of invitations to come over and see what he was talking about. John Earle told one amazing story after another, as only John can, from his decades of diving Oahu. Fritz Sandoz gave us details about some of his favorite dive sites, and Stephanie Kowalski, Bill Martin, Devon Merrifield, Ken Nichols, Dave Pence, and Richard Pyle also shared their Oahu dive experiences.

On Kauai our deep thanks go to powerhouse Linda Bail for providing a place to stay, some special diving off Kauai and Niihau, and a post-dive hot tub at a time when she had many more important things on her mind. She and others, including Max Anderson, Ken Bail, Kim Davenport, Dave Tanis, and the ever-friendly George Thompson gave us a good picture of what goes on way out there on Kauai.

Even further out, Kent Backman was our gracious and passionate host at Midway, and Keoki Stender, Midway dive operations manager emeritus, shared some of his experiences and thoughts.

In addition to help on the different islands there were many subjects that required the knowledge and expertise of specific people. George Balazs, Scott Castile, Tim Clark, Rod and Ruth Dyerly, MJ Harden, Skippy Hau, Brian Kanenaka, Keller and Wendy Laros, Cory Pittman, Jack Randall, and Rick Rogers all contributed with research, answers, and sometimes relevant trivia.

In a strange little coincidence Allen DeCoite, local airplane expert and a friend we hadn't seen in 15 years, appeared just as we were xeroxing the photo of the B-24. Allen's enthusiam for wrecked airplanes is contagious and led to a long conversation at Kinko's in which we learned of yet another F4U Corsair in the water off Mokuhooniki Rock—just another teaser for all of us in the years to come.

ABOUT THE AUTHORS

MIKE SEVERNS is an underwater photographer whose work has appeared in numerous books and magazines, including *Islands* and *Natural History*. With his wife, Pauline, he has produced two books of his underwater photography, *Molokini: Hawaii's Premier Marine Preserve* and *Sulawesi Seas: Indonesia's Magnificent Underwater Realm*. His most recent book, *Hawaiian Sea Shells*, is a comprehensive identification guide to the island's shells.

He is also a biologist who has undertaken a lifelong study of tree snails, from West

Megaptera novaeangliae Hawaii 1994

This book is dedicated to Dave Norquist,
good friend and mentor, whose elegant
and creative approach to diving in Hawaii
was unique and inspirational to anyone
who had the opportunity to dive with him.

Maui's rainforest to the remote Southwest
Maluku province of Indonesia. His research
in West Maui led to the discovery of living
tree snail populations that had been thought
to be extinct.

His explorations in Hawaii have also led
to the discovery, in subterranean lava tubes,
of the bones of birds that had gone extinct
before the arrival of Westerners to the islands.
As a result of these finds, 32 species (at last
count) of previously undescribed birds
have been named, one of them in his honor.

Underwater he has recorded several pre-
contact Hawaiian fishing grounds, the
longest underwater cave system in Hawaii,
and many new species of marine animals. At
240 feet off Molokini he discovered and photographed the wave bench left more than
10,000 years ago by the lower sea stand.

PAULINE FIENE-SEVERNS is a biologist
whose interest in nudibranchs is constantly
renewed by the discovery of new species and
the observation of nudibranch behavior. She
is currently completing a book, with Dr.
Terry Gosliner and Cory Pittman, cataloging
the Hawaiian opisthobranch fauna.

With more than 5,000 dives in Hawaiian
waters, Pauline has discovered many new
species of animals, including a sand octopus
and numerous species of nudibranchs, one
of which was recently named for her. Several years ago, after years of study, she pin-
pointed the precise time of annual spawning
of the coral *Pocillopora meandrina*. The results she published became the first record
of spawning for this species of coral.

Mike and Pauline are co-owners of Mike
Severns Diving, a dive charter business on
Maui that has been in operation for more
than twenty years.

Enchelycore pardalis   Makena 1990

Puhi kauila, the dragon moray, is perhaps the most beautiful of Hawaii's thirty-eight species of moray eels. The young ones, in particular, can be gorgeous. Although not the sweetest tempered moray, the long, sharp teeth and aggressively hooked jaw (in fact, the fish is unable to close its mouth fully) make the dragon moray seem even fiercer than it is.

THE FIRST CHANCE I got after arriving in Hawaii in the summer of 1968 I borrowed a car and drove straight to a scenic lookout at Koko Head. I parked at the lookout, climbed over the railing and stood on the dark lava cliffs watching as immense waves struck the rocks with such force they shook the ground beneath my feet and sent immense cascades of white water high into the air. Offshore the wind tore the crests off the waves and blew great plumes of mist across the blue ocean. It was beautiful. I was terrified.

Five years later I geared up on a 23-foot boat with five Hawaiian spearfishermen. We drifted on a windless sea with a massive lazy swell. The green, waterfall-streaked cliffs of North Kohala dropped vertically from charcoal clouds, and the thunder seemed to come from the cliffs themselves. Lightning snapped above us as we rolled into clear, black water and sank toward the lava sand and boulder bottom. It was beautiful, but I was no longer terrified—I was in love with Hawaii. Junior watched us get in. His job

Naso lituratus Molokini 1989

The orangespine unicornfish, called 'umauma-lei' in the islands, is an algae grazer and is common in pairs, small groups, and schools on Hawaii's rocky reefs.

was to follow us with the boat, and pick up the divers in the artificial twilight as they surfaced. But it was a strange day, all dark gray and wet forest green, and Junior was unhappy about it. Twenty minutes into the dive the rain came, and with it wind, and the lightning moved directly overhead. Even we could hear the rain hitting the water overhead,

drowning out all other sound except the thunder. Flashes of lightning lit the bottom.

If Junior had been nervous before we went in, he would be a basket case with the heavy rain, so I surfaced. The boat wasn't there. Junior had lost our bubbles in the squall and was circling for us, but he couldn't see land and without any reference in the driving rain he was using his wake and the direction of the swell to stay near. On the surface I heard the motor once but never saw him. He was waiting for the rain to back off and prayed the wind would not come up before he found us.

Back underwater I watched the surface, listening for the motor above the sound of the rain. The coast here was all cliffs, and without the boat there was no place to get out for miles. The others kept working while I watched—and waited.

When the earthquake passed through there was no warning or sound. I was hovering high listening for the boat and saw the entire bottom shift side to side, not once, but three times, as if I needed confirmation of what I thought I had just seen. I did. I was tired and the day was moody, but the third shock left no doubt. It was all visual. The bottom, with its car-sized boulders, leapt a couple of feet toward me, then fell back to its original position as if nothing had happened. Then again. It was over far too soon.

The rain, thankfully, subsided before the end of our dive and Junior was able to find our bubbles again. His impression of the earthquake came from looking at the waterfalls on the face of the cliffs—the entire island shifted from side to side a few times then stood still. Each of us had seen it, but no two impressions were the same. Junior had the real story to tell. How he had lost us and then, thanks to a cool head and an instinctive understanding of the sea, found us amid

DIVING HAWAII

rain, lightning, and earthquakes. He told us about the blinding rain and the pitch black sky and how the waterfalls had danced with the earthquake, but he told his story with modesty because he was only 12 years old and did not want to be disrespectful of the older men.

THE PIONEER DIVERS

Hawaiians have an enviably gentle manner when relaxing with family and friends, yet I have never known tougher men when challenged. That kind of determination was needed to explore the deep waters around Hawaii for the first time.

After the appearance of scuba diving in the middle of the last century, long before the invention of dive computers, Hawaiians were diving deep and long for black coral. Many found the U.S. Navy tables too conservative, so they abandoned them, trading higher risk for greater profit. Some dove until they got bent, then tried not to do that again.

Black coral divers were plummeting beyond 200 feet two or more times a day, followed by a shallow 100-foot last dive, then in the afternoon they would go play softball with their friends. Stories of men collapsing with the bends in center field are legend. Some drove home on the narrow roads from Lahaina to Kula every evening, to an elevation that would have given a diving doctor seizures.

Some got bent diving, some got bent playing softball, and some got bent just driving home, but it was a way of life and unless it was incapacitating, the rule was to keep it to yourself. A man afraid of the bends did shorter dives and thus contributed less at the end of the day. Everyone made less money since the take was divided into shares. This attitude was part of Hawaiian diving for many years.

One of the stories floating

around Lahaina Harbor in the 1970s, home of some of the more notorious and successful black coral divers in Hawaii, was the fact that though these guys were getting bent, for the most part they were not getting bent as often as they should have. Local divers didn't waste time getting to the bottom, which

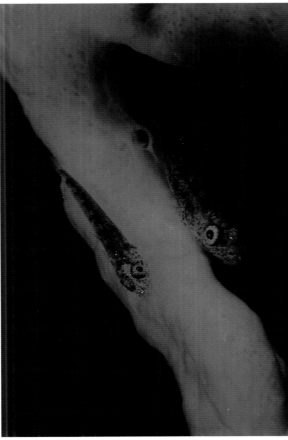

Bryaninops sp. Molokini 1991

was more than 200 feet down. They carried heavy hammers for breaking the black coral free, and in addition grabbed a large rock, and thus weighted would shoot to the bottom. Around certain deep sites 60-pound rocks still litter the bottom today.

Somehow, it was thought, this extraordinary technique was reducing

The little whip-coral gobies live on on gorgonians and antipatharian sea whips. In this case, the host has died, and become encrusted with a beautiful red sponge.

their chances of getting the bends. A theory developed that a rapid descent smashed the nuclear bubbles already in the blood, making them smaller and thus increasing the time it took for them to reach the threshold size needed to cause the bends. According to the theory, the divers could safely remain down longer, and on the second dive go deep again with reduced risk.

Unfortunately, the fast descent theory has no medical basis, and in the end it gave the men false hope—the bends still wreaked havoc among the divers. Something did seem to be working in their favor, but it was probably just a matter of individual tolerance to the bends. But, using a rock was a good trick, and it saved air and energy—if, that is, your ears cleared easily and you remembered to let go of the rock before hitting the bottom.

These same hard core deep and repetitive Hawaiian divers were often in the habit of drinking Primo beer during their short surface intervals and then pulling dive profiles that should have hospitalized them. Years ago, a young doctor on Maui told me that where he studied hyperbaric medicine they kept a small wooden box with a glass front on the wall next to the chamber. In the box was a can of Primo beer, and beside it on the wall was a brass rod hanging from a chain. The sign read: "If all else fails break glass."

Hawaiian diving was greatly influenced by these early divers. There are few places you can go today that they did not discover, and many of the sites they did find still have not been rediscovered. Armed with an innate understanding of the local waters and a working man's knowledge of the constraints of their equipment and boats, Hawaiian divers were venturing to the fringe of diveable depths in search of a living. Many were seriously injured, but those few who dove the same profiles and worked the same rough days without getting bent became local heroes.

Taking their lead from these pioneering black coral divers, more and more boats catering to recreational divers began to operate around Hawaii. Initially only experienced divers came, but as the sport grew, the clientele expanded to include beginners and less adept divers from all over the world.

At first these divers wanted to see big fish. In Hawaii, big fish mean deep dives, which were hard on operators and clients alike. It was much safer and more profitable to dive shallow, but Hawaiian reefs are not spectacular on a world scale, which frustrated many early dive leaders. The trend to go deep or hunt lasted a long time here, because this is where Hawaii's waters excelled.

Unlike many places on the mainland, until relatively recently in Hawaii you could still dive without taking a course. Homemade, three-prong spears and Hawaiian backpacks were sold at Longs drugstore, and you could get your tank filled without a certification card. Owning a tank meant you were serious enough about diving to get air. Lobsters, fish, and rare shells abounded in the beginning, and seemed to be there for the taking.

Slowly, however, an adjustment of thinking took place. This was not prompted by ecological concerns, but by financial concerns. Big fish hunters began having to venture further and further afield to find their quarry, and dive guides realized that a beautiful shell was worth more to them alive—where they could show it to clients, day after day—than cleaned and sold to a collector. Hawaii's reefs were becoming marketable like never before and needed protection.

Still, dive guides had reputations to maintain (or to build) and it was

Hemitaurichthys polylepis and Labroides phthirophagus Molokini 1997

the deep radical dives that bring fame and local recognition—which in its own mysterious way seemed to bring paying guests. The remarkable divers of the past had left a legacy that was hard to escape in those first stumbling days of the diving industry in Hawaii.

Over the last 15 years attitudes gradually changed, though to those of us diving for a living this change has seemed glacially slow. Marine conservation areas have been established, and spearfishing on scuba is now regarded with distaste. Hunting divers are now few except for those rare and hearty free divers hunting the blue water offshore with a mask and snorkel. Diving to over 100 feet on a breath of air or drifting for hours in blue water, these men still hunt the big fish.

I have dived with black coral divers, tropical fish collectors, and for a limited time with Hawaiian spearfishermen (the latter were by far the most exclusive bunch). What I learned from these men and what I saw diving with them has left no doubt in my mind of the incredible amount of local knowledge possessed by the Hawaiian divers.

Unfortunately, much of this knowledge was lost to the sport diving community in Hawaii because the two approaches—preservation and hunting—could not be reconciled. With the growing population of the islands, it was necessary to take preservation seriously, but it is also tragic that more of the knowledge of the hunters was not being passed on.

RIDING THE HOT SPOT

Although the volcanoes of the Big Island are among the most active on earth, Hawaii is not a young island chain. Nor is it as small as it appears on maps in comparison to the great Pacific Ocean. The Hawaiian chain is huge—with all of its submerged islands included, it is perhaps the longest island chain in the world. It is certainly the most isolated island group in the world.

Fins stiff and spread, faces blanched, these pyramid butterflyfish make it as easy as they can for the cleaners to do their job. Hawaii's endemic cleaner wrasse is without a doubt the most beautiful of the Labroides. Its unpronounceable species name, by the way, comes from the Greek for 'lice-eater,' which seems appropriate enough.

Sadleria sp. and Metrosideros polymorpha Maui 1994

A lush forest of ferns and ohia, above Ukumehame Valley in West Maui. The islands' unique native vegetation has been displaced by introduced species and weeds in all but the most remote areas.

A remarkable thing has occurred in Hawaii and continues to occur here daily. The islands are being formed as you read this, over a remarkably thin part of the earth's crust far beneath the surface of the sea. Called a "hot spot," it has not moved from its original coordinates since the first islands reached the surface millions of years ago. Instead the entire Pacific Plate, a huge piece of slightly convex rock thousands of miles across and cupped to conform to the curve of the earth, is slowly moving over this geographically stable point of formation with the islands riding on top.

It is here that lava is squeezed like toothpaste from deep beneath the earth's crust. So deep that Hawaii is one of the few places in

the world where pieces of the Earth's mantle can be found while simply strolling along the side of the road. This lava spring has created island mountains so large that when measured from their base to their summit are larger than any other mountains on earth. And these mountains have formed the most isolated and distant islands to be found on this planet, islands that are the substrate for a bizarre ecosystem, both unique and uniquely vulnerable because of their isolation.

As the Pacific Plate moves it drags Hawaii's islands from the time they begin to form at the hot spot until they erode away on a slow northwestern creep across the face of the planet. Each island will travel thousands of miles, from the tropical location now occupied by the island of Hawaii to the cold deep and dark waters of the northern Pacific, almost at Kamchatka. The Pacific Plate holds Hawaii's geological history for all to see.

The Emperor Seamounts are the submerged remnants of the oldest Hawaiian Islands. Beginning just a couple hundred miles west of Kure they dogleg north to almost connect with the easternmost Aleutian Islands, and almost double the length of the Hawaiian Islands. Now submerged deep in the abyssal black of the northern Pacific, they were once lush, green, and forest clad islands like those we now know in the southeastern chain. As these islands drifted north on the Pacific Plate they eventually eroded away and sank beneath the surface, where they have remained protected from the destructive erosion of the wind, rain and waves. Some lingered as atolls, capped by coral reef struggling to survive in the ever cooler waters as the islands' latitude increased, but in the end they submerged.

All stages of this process are still

evident today as some of the northwestern islands have yet to submerge and their reefs form the ghostly outlines of the islands that once rose into the clouds as lofty volcanoes.

The only accessible examples of Hawaiian islands in their final stage prior to submerging are the atolls of Midway and Kure. These are the oldest existing islands in the chain. These islands are on the very edge of extinction, standing only feet above sea level and destined to vanish shortly. Beyond them the islands have become sea mounts. One, near Midway, is not even 200 feet beneath the surface, and should the sea level drop once again as happened 18,000 years ago, it would once again be exposed above the surface. But for the others the struggle is over.

The Big Island is the youngest island in the chain. It is huge, about three times the size of Maui, which in turn is about three times the size of Lanai. Midway atoll, when it first formed about 14 mil-lion years ago, was probably no larger than Lanai is today. This tells us something of this process of formation and subsidence. It seems that the islands are now lingering over the hot spot longer, or for some geological reason more material than ever is able to rise to the surface, so that the younger islands are larger.

There is no evidence that any Hawaiian island has ever been larger than The Big Island is today. The Big Island's closest competitor is the island that preceded it, Maui Nui, now a complex of islands and connecting shallows recently submerged by rising sea levels and represented above water by Maui, Kahoolawe, Lanai, and Molokai. Even so, Maui Nui was less than half the size of the Big Island.

The Hawaiian islands, because of their location in the center of the vast Pacific, are exposed to constant, strong trade winds and heavy rain, and as soon as an island forms, regardless of it size or make-up, it begins to erode. Even the massive weight of each island bows the

A lava flow hits the water off the Big Island. This event took place in 1997, at Ka ili ili on the Puna Coast. Until Loihi reaches the surface, the Big Island is the youngest of the Hawaiian chain, and thus shows the most active vulcanism. Hawaii's basaltic lavas are famous enough to have contributed two Hawaiian words to vulcanology: 'pahoehoe,' a low-viscosity lava that forms smooth, ropey flows; and 'aa,' a stiff, sticky, lava that forms rough, clinkery flows.

The Big Island 1997

TINKERING WITH MOTHER NATURE
Fish Introductions

ONE OF THE MORE INTERESTING ASPECTS OF Hawaii's unique reef fish fauna is the relative lack of groupers and snappers here. Although these reef predators are common on reefs elsewhere in the Pacific, Hawaii has just two native groupers (both of which live very deep and are very rare in the main islands), and just two small native snappers. Forty-six years ago Vernon Brock, then the head of Hawaii's fish and game department, decided this was a problem.

Brock figured that if Hawaii lacked the commercially valuable snappers and

Ranina ranina Hawaii 1994

The angled pincers of the Raninidae led them to be called 'spanner crabs,' although it was obviously a Brit or Aussie who did so. The Kona crab, whether it suffers from taape predation or not, is a lot of work for a little meat, and not as tasty as the introduced mangrove crab, Scylla serrata.

groupers found off other islands, then he would just have to import them, and in the 1950s and early 1960s he introduced eleven non-native species. Most succumbed to Hawaii's unique ecological conditions, but three made it. The *toau* or blacktail snapper (*Lutjanus fulvus*) and the *roi* or peacock grouper (*Cephalopholis argus*) have become moderately successful in Hawaii; the *taape* or blueline snapper (*Lutjanus kasmira*), spectacularly so.

The roughly 3,000 *taape* from the Marquesas introduced off Oahu in 1955 spread and reproduced so rapidly that within ten years they were found off all the main Hawaiian Islands. Today, sweeping schools of these brightly colored fish are hallmarks of most Hawaiian reefs, and charm divers and underwater photographers.

Fishermen are not as happy. Over the years they have voiced several complaints about the explosion of *taape*, including that it has caused the decline of the Kona crab fishery, and that it has reduced catches of more valuable fishes such as goatfish, and particularly, *menpachi* or soldierfish. In response, a study of *taape* stomach contents was finally conducted in 1981. Unfortunately, the sample size was small and the results inconclusive. Fish, adult crabs, and mantis shrimps seem to be what *taape* like to eat, with large seasonal variations in percentages.

The crab carcasses were mostly decomposed beyond recognition, but appeared to be various species of swimming crabs, not Kona crabs. The fish were almost as hard to identify as the crabs, but the presence of some juvenile squirrelfish might support the fishermen's claims that *taape* were affecting *menpachi* populations. Squirrelfish are related to soldierfish, and *taape* and soldierfish have some of the same prey preferences.

Of course, at this point the horse has left the barn. Why not just eat *taape*? The species is tasty enough, but has a low market value because they are relatively small and have lots of bones. The state tried to promote *taape* consumption by distributing free recipes, but residents simply applied these to more favored species.

Nor has the peacock grouper worked out any better. Large specimens can carry ciguatera toxin, which when eaten causes a painful illness, and because of this even small specimens—which do not contain significant levels of the toxin—are avoided by fishermen. The result is that their population is slowly building, and their presence on Hawaii's reefs has become more noticeable.

Today, scientists and environmental policy makers frown on such manipulations (and at least one scientist tried to discourage Brock back then), and such experiments will certainly not be repeated.

Earth's crust beneath it, causing the island to slowly sink into the sea. Evidence of this subsidence is clear when you visit the place of Captain Cook's death in Kona. He died in a shallow tide pool in 1778, by one account knocked down and held senseless underwater until he drowned. Today that pool, recorded in history just over 220 years ago, is no longer tidal but has sunk beneath sea level. The Big Island is subsiding faster than the other islands because of its size. Scientists estimate that the island sinks 2.5–3 millimeters a year, or a little over two feet since Cook's death. Given an approximate colonization date for the Big Island of 2,000 years ago, this means the island would have sunk 180 feet since the Hawaiian people arrived.

But, as always, there is a new island forming, this one to the southeast of the Big Island. Loihi is rising from the Pacific floor and will first share with, then later inherit the hot spot from the Big Island. Though it is still 3,000 feet beneath the surface Loihi will eventually rise to form the next stepping stone in the Hawaiian chain. It is expected to break the surface within the next few thousand years, replacing Midway and Kure, which by that time will have vanished beneath the waves.

SPLENDID ISOLATION

The almost complete isolation of Hawaii in the middle of the world's largest ocean cannot be compared to any place else on earth, nor can its high rate of endemic flora and fauna, a result of that isolation, be equaled. You would literally have to travel to another planet to find a more isolated place with a higher rate of endemic species.

The isolation must have been practically insurmountable for the first terrestrial organisms that arrived on the barren rocks of the newly formed islands. The first ar-

rivals may not have survived at all, for there had to be an order to the arrival and if you were out of order you did not make it. The first terrestrial arrivals were no doubt littoral species such as sea snails and grapsid crabs which arrived with the unpredictable ocean currents and settled out on the rocky coast. Land crabs may also have been

Lutjanus kasmira Maui 1998

among those first arrivals spreading into the interior as the ever-expanding blanket of life permitted, but forever compelled to return to the sea to reproduce.

Long before the lava appeared and long before it cooled, animals and plants had literally been raining down on Hawaii from the jet stream far above and are still doing so today. Evidence of this mode of dis-

The bluestriped snapper is by far the most successful of the non-native fishes intentionally introduced to Hawaii. Now common everywhere in the island chain, all of Hawaii's taape are the descendents of 3,000 specimens from Tahiti released off Oahu in 1955.

Zebrasoma flavescens Molokini 1988

The yellow tang, lau-i-pala, is the most common species collected in Hawaii for the aquarium hobby. Statewide, the trade in 'marine ornamentals' is worth $800,000–$900,000 a year, and conflict between collectors and dive tour operators has been a recurring problem, especially on the Kohala and Kona Coasts of the Big Island, where most of the yellow tangs are collected. Conservation professionals generally consider net-based fish collection for aquariums not to have a major negative impact on the reef. But a 1998 study of Kona, where the collection can be very intensive, demonstrated significant species declines (e.g. 45 percent for the yellow tang), leading to the recommendation of a network of 'fish replenishment areas' where collection is prohibited.

persal is known from nets pulled behind airplanes at high altitude over the Pacific. Pioneering plants, especially ferns, which reproduce from microscopic wind-blown spores, were probably quick to take hold on the newly-formed islands, maybe within days or weeks of the cooling of the lava flows, as happens even now.

As plants became established, insect species formerly destined to fail could get a toe hold in the rapidly forming Hawaiian ecosystems. In the beginning there was no suitable habitat for most, and they simply perished when they arrived. Some of the insects may have arrived carrying eggs, but for others at least two individuals had to arrive, and within their short life spans had to locate each other and successfully mate. The odds were against these random immigrants from the moment they began the journey through the cold upper atmosphere, half frozen and tumbled wildly by the fierce wind of the jet stream.

For a developing island ecosys-

tem the formation of soil is the first step upon which all else will directly or indirectly depend. Although it is hard to image the time involved in the formation of soil from fresh lava, it is easy to see it happen quickly after terrestrial plants first became established. As the first plants died and decayed, more soil was formed and their habitat expanded. All the while arriving birds, insects and snails lucky enough to survive, accelerated the process of breaking down the detritus formed by the dying plants into even more soil. Once the pioneering plants had become established, things steadily progressed toward the formation of vast areas of suitable habitat for arriving organisms.

The first truly terrestrial animals, that is those not dependent on the ocean to feed, mate or reproduce, were probably insects adapted to life among the pioneering plants. Yet even these were at first dependent on the sea indirectly as nesting sea birds, uninhibited by predators except for other birds, contributed

Chelonia mydas Hawaii 1995

enormous amounts of nitrogen rich droppings to the developing ecosystems.

As the volcanic soils slowly formed, more and different species of plants were able to survive, and the complexity of the isolated Hawaiian ecosystem rapidly expanded to finally support forest and a terrestrial fauna. Terrestrial and forest birds had to wait a long time until enough soil had formed to support the kind of habitat they needed to survive. Once that habitat began to form, birds exploded into the evolving terrestrial ecosystem and into a myriad of untapped niches eventually radiating into one of the most spectacular avian fauna found anywhere.

Many of the newly arrived birds developed bills suited to feed from the blossoms of specific plants, leading to exotic looking new bird species, similar to, but distinct from the original pioneering species they evolved from. The plants co-evolved with the dependable pollen transporting birds, resulting in spe-cialized and exclusive relationships formed between some plant and bird species. Slowly Hawaii's ecosystems matured in complexity and eventually produced the forest we know now in which 98 percent of all the plant species are endemic, 100 percent of the forest birds and almost 100 percent of all the insects and snails. These are remarkable fig-ures.

Newcomers following these first successful arrivals now had to com-pete against well established bird species that had evolved specifical-ly in the Hawaiian habitats. Some Hawaiian birds evolved flightless-ness. The ability to fly consumes a great deal of energy, during the act of flying itself and in maintaining the muscles and skeletal structures needed to fly, especially for larger bird species.

How evolution could favor what appears to be (and indeed later proved to be) a suicidal trait for a bird is remarkably simple. In a predator-free environment walking and waddling were competitive

The green sea turtle received federal Endangered Species Act protection in 1978, and the Hawaii popu-lation has rebounded markedly since then. Honu, as they are called in Hawaiian, are now common around all of the islands, although the main breeding area is the French Frigate Shoals in the North-west Hawaiian Islands.

methods of getting around in the lush vegetation. Walking was more energy efficient than flying and so flightlessness was a successful trait for some species. Other advantages were that the birds could grow larger and produce larger eggs, which in turn produced larger and presumably better developed chicks. Though this fauna existed for hundreds of thousands of years, it was a fragile existence.

PEOPLE ARRIVE

Hawaii's isolation was so complete that no terrestrial reptiles, amphibians, or mammals, with the exception of two very small bat species that may have been almost indistinguishable from each other (one is believed extinct), have been recorded from Hawaii during its entire history. None of the smart and deadly ground-dwelling predators of those missing classes of vertebrates made it to Hawaii. Nor did the herbivores. This niche, usually occupied by mammals and occasionally by giant tortoises on other remote islands in the Pacific and Indian Oceans, was filled in Hawaii by large flightless ducks and geese. It must have been a remarkable sight to come across flocks of these plump, turkey-sized, flightless birds grazing their way through the fern understory unhampered by predators and supplied with a limitless source of plant material.

Imagine what it would have been like for the first people who arrived on Hawaii's shores 1,700–1,250 years ago. At that time the climate was warmer than today, and the dryland forest stretched farther up the sides of the mountains. These people may have come ashore onto beaches crowded with dozing monk seals and turtles, over reefs teeming with sharks and large fish. As they stepped onto land the seals most likely paid little attention to them. Large land crabs would have scurried through the underbrush and birds of all descriptions would have been common everywhere they looked.

These first human arrivals may

An old, dead, sponge-encrusted black coral bush on Molokini's reef has attracted at least six species of fish. These colorful landmarks are always worth a close look, and harbor gobies, frogfish, and interesting invertebrates.

Dascyllus albisella, Parupeneus multifasciatus, Chaetodon kleinii, etc. Molokini 1997

have encountered large flightless ibis and flightless rails just in from the shore where the vegetation began, and as they moved up the sides of the mountains they would have reached the cooler fringe forest where they would have begun finding the giant flightless ducks and geese. Like the moa of New Zealand and the dodo of Mauritius, these birds would probably not have run away. More likely they would have been curious, and innocently approached the first Hawaiians.

Molokini 1991

TROUBLE IN EDEN

For the first settlers of Hawaii the rich avifauna and abundant marine mammals and reptiles were a gold mine of free and easy food that must have seemed limitless. For the birds it was disaster. In fact none of the giant birds survived to be recorded by Europeans as anything other than decaying skeletons found deep in dry caves and buried in sand dunes. They were so long gone that not even legends or stories of their existence survived into modern times, though a brief look at a map often gives hints they were once here.

The word "moa" is not just used by New Zealand's Polynesians to describe large flightless birds, but also shows up in the Hawaiian language such as the hill on the island of Kahoolawe named Moa Ula which translates as "red moa." Maybe this implies a large red flightless bird was running around on Kahoolawe. The name Puu Nene which means "Nene Hill" implies there were once nene geese in the area where the Puu Nene sugar mill stands now. The nene had almost achieved flightlessness when the first people arrived, but it was lucky and could still fly, and apparently did, escaping extinction. The nene was a prized bird and accordingly, geographic locations have been named for it. It seems likely

Heterocentrotus mammillatus   Molokini 1988

then that geographic names using the name "moa" similarly honor the large flightless ducks, which laid huge eggs and had thick muscular legs.

Even easier prey were the sea birds that nested on the ground and in caves on the slopes of the mountains. To catch these birds the people simply discovered their nesting colonies, trapping hundreds of birds at one time. There are caves on Mauna Loa with the bones of literally thousands of sea birds, and the remains of campfires used to cook the birds or warm the hunters.

What happened in Hawaii is no different than what has happened on every island in the Pacific that has been settled by people (not to mention Australia, or even North America). The first human settlers

Tough clumps of Pocillopora meandrina and Porites sp. cover the rocky wave bench on Molokini's backside. At left you can see the beginning of this reef's profile: an almost sheer drop to more than 200 feet.

The beautiful slate pencil urchin is nowhere else as common as in Hawaii, nor is it elsewhere in the Indo-Pacific always such a deep red color. It has been observed to feed on encrusting pink calcarious algae, which doesn't seem like much of a meal, even by a sea urchin's standards. There's plenty of it around, however.

to become established on the island simply consumed the available resources of their new home, inevitably depopulating islands of much of their fauna. In the end they turned to those plants and animals that they have learned over thousands of years to carry with them: taro, sweet potatoes, yams, and more than a dozen other plants, and

Lentipes concolor Piinau Stream, Keanae, Maui 2000

These little gobies are able to work their way up swift, rocky streams and even climb waterfalls using their fused pelvic fins as a kind of suction cup. Like salmon they are anadromous, laying their eggs in freshwater and growing out in the sea.

dogs, pigs, and chickens (along with a few hitchhikers such as rats, geckos, flies, and head lice).

Once their domestic crops began to take hold, the first few generations in Hawaii would have lived in a virtual paradise. But as their population increased, the pressure was on to till more land to plant more taro, to cut trees for fires, houses, and canoes, and to clear the

land for ever-expanding villages. An imperceptibly slow degradation of the natural environment followed as Hawaii's population climbed. At the time of first contact by Europeans, 1,500 years after the arrival of the first settlers, the estimated population of the Hawaiian islands was more than one million.

At the time of European contact, agriculture had pressed far into the valleys and up the slopes of the mountains. Fish ponds had been built out onto the inshore reefs. Just the cooking fires alone, day after day, year after year, for one million people could push the forest well back from any settlements, if not denude the generally sparse lowland forest altogether. And with the loss of the lowland forest, soil began to wash into the sea, beginning to degrade the inshore reefs.

With the arrival of the Europeans the impact on Hawaii's unique ecosystem just got worse, particularly with the introduction of cattle and plantation agriculture. Over the years, introduced animals and plants have had perhaps the most damaging affect. In the first 1,500 years of Polynesian Hawaii, 30–40 alien species were introduced. Since then, the total has grown to 5,750, and increases every year. Largely because of this, Hawaii has 363 officially endangered species, fully 30 percent of the United States total.

While the terrestrial ecosystem of Hawaii was indelibly altered, offshore, life pretty much went on as usual. With the exception of the green and hawksbill turtles and the monk seal, no marine animals were seriously threatened by man in spite of almost constant fishing pressure. The value of the marine ecosystems were very well known to the Hawaiians and *kapu* were placed on some species to protect them from overfishing during certain times of the year—a practice that might have saved the passenger pigeon, great auk, and many other species had European people of the past few centuries imposed similar rules of behavior.

To comprehend what Hawaii's marine life must have been like prior to the disturbance caused by man one has only to get on a flight up to Midway Atoll and dive for a few days. Seasonally, Midway has millions of sea birds and hundreds of sharks and giant jacks to feed on them. Tiger sharks, thousands of reef sharks, giant jacks, snapper and a host of smaller game fish exist there in profusion, preying on an undisturbed reef fish population and, in the spring, hundreds of thousands of fledging sea birds. Going swimming at Midway while the albatross are fledging in the spring is something like walking naked across the Serengeti Plain at dusk. There is a complete food chain at both these places, and *Homo sapiens* is definitely not the apex predator. This is how Hawaii was when the first people arrived. It is certainly not like Hawaii is now, except in a few protected places.

A UNIQUE FISH FAUNA

The isolation that created such unusual land animals such as the flightless birds had much the same effect underwater. Hawaii has the highest rate of endemic inshore marine fish in the world (24 percent), and unlike the land fauna, nothing has gone extinct underwater—though the balance has shifted a bit here and there. From the yellow milletseed butterflyfish so prevalent on reefs and drop-offs, to the fast and aggressive saddleback wrasse that appears instantly to take advantage of any situation that may offer food, you are almost always in the presence of an endemic when diving Hawaii.

Endemic fish are the result of a long and unlikely process. It is ex-

tremely rare for fish larvae to survive the long ocean drift from other Pacific islands and to end up in Hawaii. But as an example, let's say an angelfish species reaches Hawaii and survives to adulthood, reproduces, and becomes an established breeding population. There are now two populations of this angelfish species—the small new

Centropyge interrupta Midway 1993

Hawaiian population and the larger well-established parent population somewhere else in the Pacific. Because of the extreme unlikelihood of additional larvae from the parent population reaching Hawaii, the two populations are unlikely to have any further contact with each other. Over time, the populations may become so different that if they were to come into contact with each other, they would no longer interbreed. The new Hawaiian species, being found no where else in the world, is now an endemic.

An example of this scenario has happened in Hawaii in just the last ten years. The Hawaiian sergeant, a pugnacious silver damselfish with thin vertical bars, is a species endemic to the islands. But then a decade ago divers began to observe another species, the Indo-Pacific sergeant, in Hawaiian waters for the first time in recorded history. It can be easily distinguished by its much thicker black bars and a beautiful

The Japanese angelfish is known from the Northwestern Hawaiian Islands, Taiwan, and as its common name suggests, Japan. The genus Centropyge, sometimes called the dwarf angelfish, includes a number of bright treasures, many of them found living quite deep.

Midway is an excellent place to see species that are either rare or absent from the southeastern end of the chain. Overall, the Hawaiian chain has a very high rate of endemicity—24.3 percent of the inshore fish species are found only here. In Midway and the Northwest Islands, the rate is even higher, approaching 50 percent.

splash of yellow on the upper back of the body. It is suspected that the Hawaiian sergeant had evolved from this Indo-Pacific species tens of thousands of years ago after an influx of that species. But the endemic species has changed so much that even though its parent species is again in Hawaii, they can no longer interbreed. They now live side-by-side as closely-related, but separate species.

Some of Hawaii's endemics have not changed much outwardly from their parent species in different parts of the Pacific, and may appear virtually the same to the untrained eye. Others have changed significantly, but their parent species can still be surmised. A third group has either changed so much from its ancestor species or the ancestor species has gone extinct, and therefore no obvious relative can be discerned. The bluestripe butterflyfish (*Chaetodon fremblii*) is a striking example of such a "relic" species.

One way that an ancestor species may become extinct is hint-ed at by the disjunct distribution of a fish called the morwong (*Cheilodacty-lus vittatus*). The mor-wong is found only at the edges of the tropics, both the cool wa-

Chaetodon fremblii
The bluestripe but-terflyfish is endemic to the Hawaiian islands, where it is common. This fish, with no obvious sur-viving parent species, is what ichthyologists call a relic.

ters of the more northwest Hawaiian islands and, thousands of miles to the south, at Lord Howe Island in the Tasman Sea. It is not found in the warm equatorial waters in between, nor is it found in temperate waters. It is apparently a relic from a time when the sea was cooler, per-haps during the last glaciation about 9,000 years ago when the morwong may have been found in a

continuous population from the South to the North Pacific. As the ocean warmed, the morwong pop-ulation was forced out of the tropics and into two distinct populations, one group to the north and anoth-er to the south. This is how the un-known parent species of some of the Hawaiian endemics might have dis-appeared—as conditions in their original region changed, they may not have been able to adapt.

When a fish has specialized to the point of endemicity it may be very hard for generalists to compete against. A fish that has evolved specifically in the Hawaiian envi-ronment will be very good at utiliz-ing that environment, and good at surviving endemic predators.

DISTINCTIVE REEFS

In addition to the presence of en-demic species, Hawaiian reefs have a characteristic look about them. The animals populating them are a unique assemblage, the result of chance arrivals of larvae and of the environmental pressures on those arrivals. Fish with longer larval stages, such as surgeonfish and moray eels, were better able to col-onize the islands and tend to be bet-ter represented. Species with short larval stages, such as clownfish and fusiliers, are missing completely. Na-tive snappers and groupers are few as well, and so Hawaiian reefs are heavily populated by moray eels which have filled the empty niches.

A slightly cooler water tempera-ture, the result of a cold current from the Bering Strait, has also shaped the Hawaiian reef community. Some common Indo-Pacific soft corals and hard corals are conspic-uously absent. On the other hand, some species have found conditions more hospitable in Hawaii than in other parts of their range and have proliferated. Yellow tangs and red pencil urchins are much more com-mon in Hawaii than anywhere else

Lybia edmondsoni with juvenile Triactis producta   Hawaii 1991

in their range, perhaps lacking a predator here or in some other way being better suited to the Hawaiian environment.

Hawaii's isolation, volcanic structure, warm but not torrid climate, varied and unique islands, and remarkably clean ocean waters have set the stage for an unusual and very rewarding dive experience here. Diving Hawaii allows people to see firsthand the evolution that has occurred in a reef system, and to visit a unique environment that until very recently was not well understood. With new species of marine life being discovered here all the time, it is also a place where a diver can do more than just look around and take pictures, but can actually contribute to the knowledge and understanding of an ecosystem.

Divers visiting Hawaii can find excellent underwater guide books covering all aspects of the reef from its invertebrates, whales, and turtles to the incredible fish life as well as guidebooks covering the birds and plants on shore. These books will point out the endemic species and give you a good understanding of Hawaii's reef system and forest inhabitants. It is relatively easy to educate yourself on what you are seeing, and if you can't find it in the books, especially underwater, then there is a strong possibility it is very rare or in some cases not even known yet.

Finally there are the people of Hawaii. Their legendary generosity and kindness have given the world a word that is recognized in almost any language anywhere in the world: "aloha." Hawaii is no longer just Polynesians, though these original inhabitants are certainly the heart and soul of Hawaii and Hawaiian culture. Today Hawaii is a mixture that is an example to the world of how different peoples can coexist, sometimes with conflict, but more often with humor. It is the center of the Pacific and a stage in which every player is an important part to every other player.

The boxing crab is not uncommon, but it is small and requires sharp eyes to spot in the rubbly environment it prefers. Some people call this the 'pom-pom' crab, but I cannot agree with this name—the tiny anemones it clasps possess potent nematocysts and are by no means harmless, at least on the scale at which they operate. Note that this little she-crab is gravid with eggs.

The lights from the Kona Surf Resort on the Big Island attracted swarms of mysids, which in turn attracted mantas. Until the mantas mysteriously left, in the late '90s, this was one of Hawaii's most famous dives.

Manta birostris   The Big Island 1994

Gnathophylloides mineri in Pseudoboletia indiana   Hawaii 1994

The Gnathophyllidae, or bumblebee shrimp family, includes some of the most colorful and interesting shrimps, including the
harlequin shrimp. This one is commensal on sea urchins. Note how he sticks his little paw straight up to mimic a spine.

The Big Island is Hawaii at its most primeval: lush green slopes, cliffs of lava, and the blue-black Pacific. The Kona Coast, with its whales, mantas, sharks, and dramatic lava flows, is the most famous area here, but Kohala, and the rough and tumble Hilo side, can be just as exciting.

The Big Island

LATE ONE NIGHT IN THE MID-1970S, I wandered out of the Village Inn, a long gone but once very good prime rib house in the cattle town of Kamuela. The Village Inn was on the shoulder of the Kohala Mountains and the parking lot looked out across the vast pastures of the Parker Ranch all the way to the distant silhouettes of Mauna Kea and Mauna Loa. The sky was black and there was no moon, but in the distance there was a reddish glow as if a cane field were burning. Looking again, I realized it was not a cane field burning, but the summit of Mauna Loa.

Mauna Loa is the largest mountain on earth, and this eruption was issuing from its huge summit caldera. Steam and fire and lakes of molten lava rising from the very depths of the earth. The billowing steam, rising thousands of feet above the mountain, had obliterat-ed the stars, and the red-orange glow I saw came from lakes of lava reflecting off the bottom of a huge gray cloud.

In Hilo, on the other side of the island at the foot of the erupting vol-cano, the heavy night rain com-pletely obscured the eruption. The people of Hilo wouldn't know Mauna Loa had erupted until they read their papers the following morning. This particular eruption was benign, but Mauna Loa lava is not always so well-behaved. A major eruption at night could easi-ly steal quickly and silently through the rain forest and reach Hilo well before the next morning's paper was delivered—a chilling thought.

Hilo is no stranger to natural cat-astrophe. In 1960 a tsunami devas-tated Hilo town, and yielding to the inevitable, the city built a large park-ing area where the buildings had once stood along the bay. Later, a

Big Island 1997

This lava flow took place in 1997 about fifteen miles south of Pohoiki on the Puna Coast. The Big Island is in a constant state of flux.

square miles it is more than four times bigger than the next biggest island, Maui). The Big Island's massive volcanoes, Mauna Kea (13,796 ft.) and Mauna Loa (13,679 ft.), have created the longest lee coast in the entire chain—the famous Kona Coast, one of the world's premier areas for diving and sport fishing.

Because of its size we have divided the most frequently dived areas of the Big Island into three regions: Hilo and Puna, Kona, and Kohala.

Kona is the most famous and popular dive area on the island. Because it is on the lee coast, sites can be reached from a variety of locations, primarily Honokohau Harbor. The Kohala sites are for the most part clustered near Kawaihae. Both Kona and Kohala are areas where traveling divers will find a broad range of accommodations, from relatively inexpensive to lavish resorts. This is the tourist side of the island, and you will find good restaurants and a variety of well-organized activities here.

The Hilo and Puna side is a bit different. This coast, though it offers some fine diving, is mostly a dive destination for locals and students at Hilo college. Access to both Hilo and Puna is from Hilo Harbor. Hilo, despite being the second-largest city in the state with its population of 40,000, has always had some small town attitude. Still, we were surprised at how little interest there was for promoting Hilo diving more widely, especially since the coast offers some spectacular diving, particularly toward Cape Kumukahi and Kapoho.

lava flow threatened to create another large parking lot in Hilo. Two years after the eruption described above, a flow from a flank eruption on Mauna Loa almost reached Hilo, but then turned east of town and stopped, just above a subdivision called Waiakea Uka. Waiakea Uka had been built to house the people who were driven from the coastal community of Waiakea by the 1960 tsunami. Nothing is permanent on the Big Island, and the gods, it would seem, even have a sense of humor.

BIG, AND STILL GROWING

The Big Island, unlike any other Hawaiian island, is still growing. It shakes, stretches, belches, and erodes. It is *alive*. It is also by far the largest island in the chain (at 4,028

HILO AND PUNA

This is a rugged and beautiful coast. It does not offer much shelter, and is not a place for those who get seasick easily. Tradewind-generated swell continuously pounds the cliffs, sending beautiful cascades of white spray high into the air to crash down on the black cliffs.

The bottom here is composed primarily of gray or black sand, and boulders with corals clinging to them that are tough enough to take the surge and breaking waves. The rough conditions of this coast seem to favor big fish, and sharks. Many reef fishes here reach impressive sizes in the rich shallows, and people familiar with these reef fish species are always impressed.

Since it is on the windward side of the island, the Hilo coast is wetter than the Kona side. The weather backs up against the tall mountains and frequently blankets the entire area in clouds and rain. Runoff from the heavy rains can reduce the visibility around Hilo and Puna, especially during the wet winters. But when the wind blows from the south, in what Hilo residents affectionately know as Kona weather, Hilo can be clear and sunny. At these times underwater visibility improves greatly. In Kona, of course, Kona weather has the opposite ef-fect—there it is not spoken of with affection. These infrequent rainy and windy conditions make the generally spoiled residents of Kona miserable. If you find yourself in Kona during nasty weather, consider driving to the Hilo side and diving there. It will more than likely be clear and sunny.

Although runoff makes the visibility poor right around Hilo, Puna, further south, is not as affected by runoff. On a calm day the rugged shore diving along the Puna coast is excellent, though things can get a little wild for an inexperienced diver. Boat diving is the best and safest way to dive this coast, but the diving industry in Hilo is not well developed. Sometimes the best way around this is to first find your guide, and then let them find a good boat.

KONA COAST

Kona rarely experiences the kind of poor visibility Hilo has or the strong winds, though seasonal Kona storms mentioned above can be as powerful as a hurricane. Nor-

The Moorish idol, despite its dated and orientalist name, is undisputably the most immediately recognizable tropical marine fish in the world. The family has but one species, and it can be found from the rocky Pacific coast of Mexico and Central America to the Red Sea.

Zanclus cornutus Hawaii 1993

Map 1.1 Hawaii (The Big Island) 1:700K

Hawaii (The Big Island) 1:700K

1 cm = 7 km
1 in = 7.66 st. mi.

40 kilometers
30
20
10
10   5   0
20 statute miles
10   5   0
10

155°
30'
156°
20°

Hilo
Hilo Bay
Keaau
Kaloli Pt.
Leleiwi Pt.
Pepeekeo Pt.
Pepeekeo
Honomu

HILO
FOREST RESERVE
UPPER WAIKEA
FOREST RESERVE

Kaula Gulch
Kalopa Gulch

Puu Makanaka + 12414
MAUNA KEA
Mauna Kea + 13796
FOREST RESERVE
Ahumoa + 7024

Waikii

Nohonaohae 8249+

Waimea (Kamuela)

Honokaa
Kukuihaele
Waipio Bay
WAIMALAHOA DR.

KOHALA FOREST RESERVE
Kaunu o Kaleoohie + 5505

Waimanu Bay
Akoakoa Point

Kapaau
Makapala
Hawi
Mahukona
Lahikiola 3383
Malae Pt.
Upolu Pt.

Kawaihae
Kawaihae Bay
Puako

Waawaa Pt.
Anaehoomalu Bay
Kiholo Bay

Honokohau
Kailua-Kona
Kailua Bay
Keahole Pt.

HAWAII

Map 1.4 Kohala 1:250K
Map 1.3 Kona Coast 1:250K

2882 2870 2590
2950 2730 2682 1690 1705
1664 1375 1301 1220 1210 209 206 120 80 179 189 180 123 22 36
1340 1287 1201 1139 953 916 739 9 50
490 461 421 236 206 200
772 577 172 150 100 75 81 28 25 60 77 173
210 216 88 72 69 29 270 250 270 3383
307 428 533 538 515 361 286 232 224 78
226 215 225 192 193 100 38 48 22 57 43 21 60 53 68 69 174
629

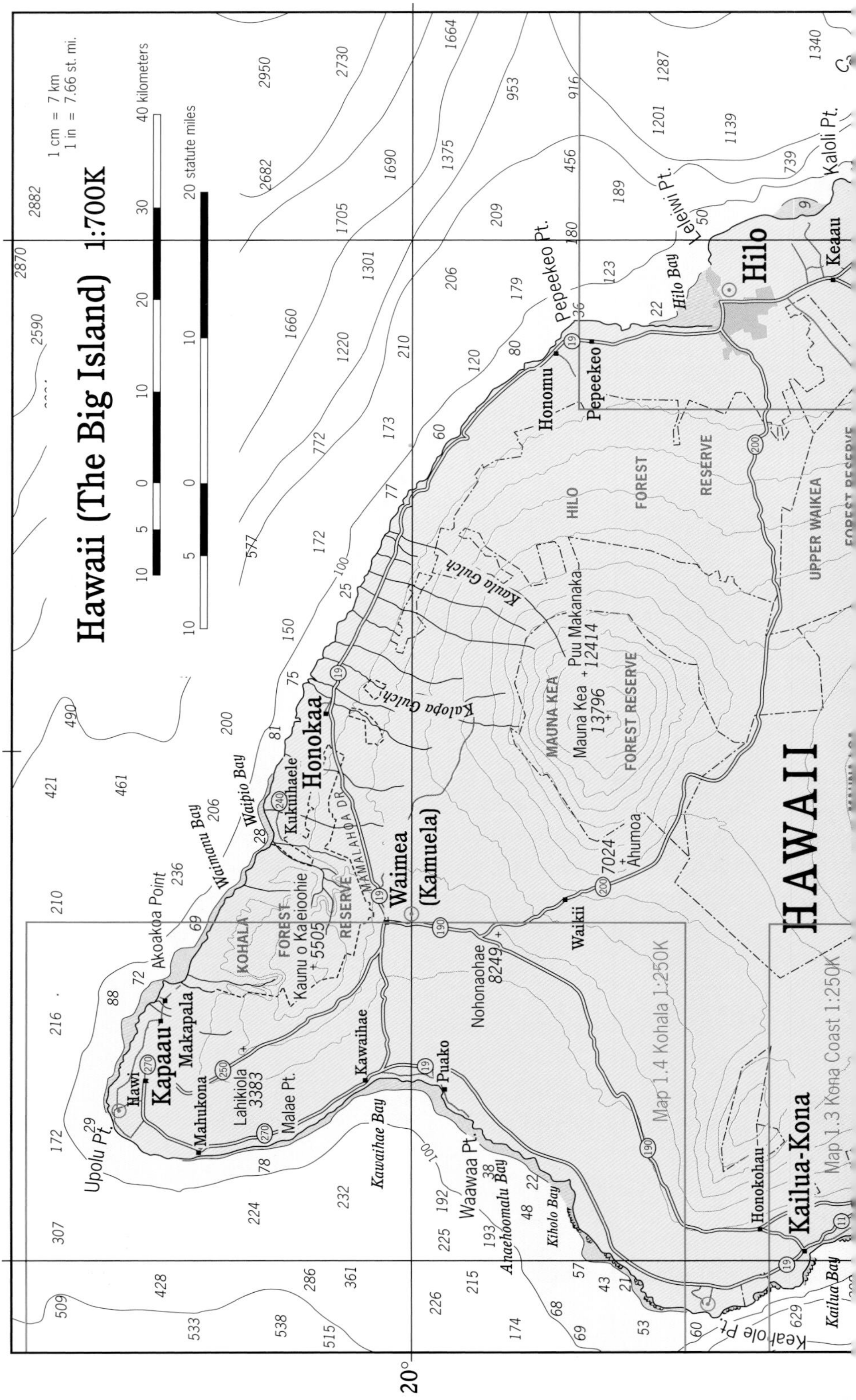

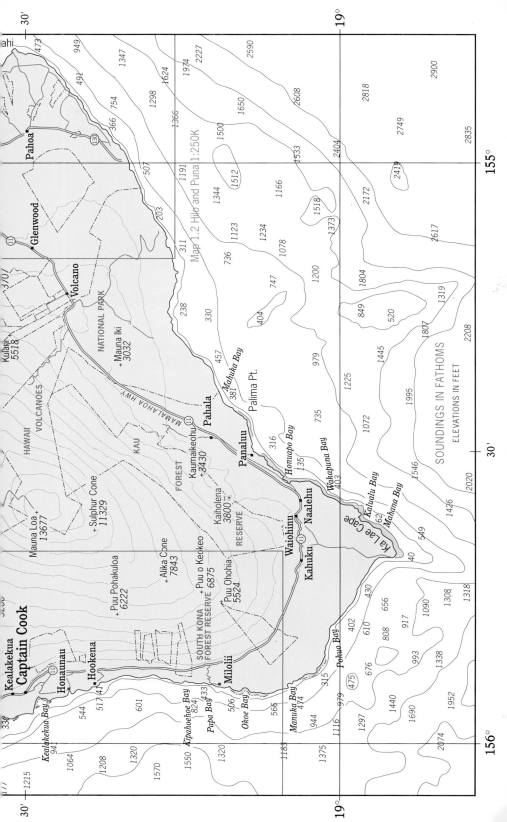

mally Kona is warm, sunny, and calm, with excellent underwater visibility, and miles of coast to dive. The Kona Coast, extending from north of Keahole Airport to South Point, is the longest stretch of calm water and perhaps the most inviting coast for divers in all of Hawaii.

If you base yourself in Kailua you will find ample facilities for divers

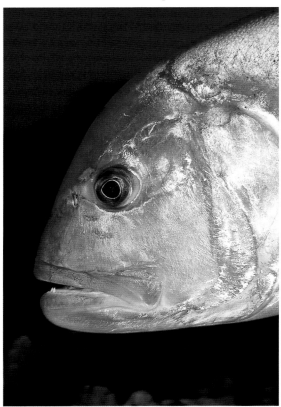

Caranx melampygus   Hawaii 1996

The bluefin jack, called 'omilu' in the islands, is the most common of the big jacks in Hawaii. The bluefin is thought to reach a meter in length, and is second only to the ulua or giant jack (Caranx ignobilis) in size and weight.

including numerous dive shops. Competition is fierce (but friendly) so the shop standards tend to be high. Good boat operations are easy to find, with everything available from elite little six-passenger whalers to a luxurious live-aboard. At sea on a calm day, the rugged beauty of the sunny Kona Coast is intoxicating. The distant volcanoes and forested slopes are a rare back-

drop for such an excellent diving area, and the view during the surface interval is one of the unparalleled enjoyments of diving the Big Island.

Since the sites are scattered along a very long coastline, it is best to dive Kona by boat, although shore diving here is decidedly safer than at Hilo and Puna. If you do shore dive, however, remember the Hawaiian proverb: never turn your back on the ocean. It is a good rule, and is in every guidebook including this one. Personally, I don't even look away for long.

KOHALA

North of Kona, at the other end of the Queens Highway and at the foot of the Kohala Mountains, are the districts of Kohala and the Port of Kawaihae. From Kawaihae up the coast there is excellent diving all the way to Mahukona and a little beyond. This coast is protected from the swell most of the year, but can be very windy almost any given day when trades are blowing. If you are going to dive this coast from shore the wind is not much of a problem, but by boat it can be a hazard to be reckoned with.

The Kohala Mountains are the oldest part of the Big Island, so the bottom here is much more like Maui than it is like Kona. Kohala is the beginning of the older bottom types found throughout Maui Nui. Since the water is generally very clear and the swell is modest, even the shallow diving along this coast is good. The deep diving, especially up near Mahukona, can be superb.

Just up the hill from Kawaihae is Kamuela and the Parker Ranch. This picturesque cattle town has an interesting history, and a couple of excellent restaurants that make a nice destination on a non-diving day. Kamuela (and Hilo) are perhaps the most truly Hawaiian towns in all the islands, and are worth a visit for this reason alone.

Hilo and Puna

Where to Go when the Kona Winds Blow

From Hilo, the Big Island's largest town, it is not unusual to look out at the night sky and see a red glow from the Puu Oo vent on Kiluaea to the southwest. This eruption started in 1982 and is still thundering along, daily adding a little more land to the island, and a little more bottom offshore. In Puna, south of Hilo and directly downslope from Kiluaea, the lava completely obliterated the town of Kalapana between 1986 and 1992. Today the site is a black field of rock, with just a few bits of twisted steel to mark where the town once stood. Not far away, in 1960, a vent opened up practically in the middle of Kapoho, burying the little town in ash. Needless to say, land is cheaper in Puna than anywhere else on the island.

In parts of Puna the volcanic activity warms the ground. There are small caves along the road from Pahoa to Kaimu that for years have been used as natural steam baths. At Pohoiki Bay, just south of Cape Kumukahi, there is a small pool of volcanically heated water just a little out of sight of the parking lot. There is nothing really special about this pool, until you come out of the water half frozen on a rainy, windswept day. Then it is a gift.

Rainy, windswept days are not rare in Hilo and Puna. Although Puna gets less rain than Hilo, it is by no means as dry as Kona, which sits in the rain shadow of the state's highest peaks. On the other hand, when the Kona winds come—*kona* means leeward in Hawaiian—and Kailua is being slammed by high winds and rain from the south, pack your gear and head over to the Hilo and Puna side.

Bill De Rooy, owner of Nautilus Dive Center in Hilo, says that many people express surprise when they see his dive shop, and ask him if there really is diving in Hilo. He reminds them that the water goes around the whole island, and explains that there is, in fact, some excellent diving on this coast. We agree—particularly for those who like to dive areas off the beaten path.

NORTH OF HILO

The Hamakua Coast is lush and green, and if possible, even more relaxed than Kona. Many people in Hilo consider a trip to

This is a rough, wet, windswept coast where lava pours into the sea and the black rock is brand new. It also has some remarkable diving, particularly when the weather cooperates.

Kona the way someone from a farm considers a trip to town. There are few entry points along the coast north of Hilo, but one that is almost always accessible is **Laupahoehoe**, a bit over 20 miles away on Route 19 (See MAP 1.1, pp. 40–41).

Here a small peninsula creates a lee on its south side which served as a landing for steam ships in the 19th and early 20th centuries. A small settlement sprang up on the hill above the landing, and a lovely school was built down on the peninsula along with cottages for the teachers. It was an idyllic setting until April 1, 1946. That morning a tsunami came ashore, destroying the school and killing 24 children and teachers.

This sad history notwithstanding, Laupahoehoe's pretty setting, isolation on the coast, and interesting bottom topography make the site a rewarding dive. Actually, there are two sites here, one south of the point, and one north.

South of the point, you get to the water by walking through massive concrete jacks that have been placed at the water's edge to protect the point from large waves. This area is protected, and the dive begins with with rock pinnacles down to 40 feet, followed by a ledge which drops to 90. At the bottom of the ledge there are large boulders and nice relief. Going left at the bottom of the ledge will bring you to two large mooring anchors. One dates from the 19th century, and the other is modern. From these you will find

a chain, which you can follow a bit before looping back to your starting point. The fish life here is good, including scorpionfish, schools of goat fish, soldierfish, some surge-adapted butterflyfish, and some wrasses including the brilliantly colored *awela* or Christmas wrasse (*Thalassoma trilobatum*).

Even more interesting is the dive from the windward side of the peninsula. Here the entry is across slick rounded boulders and can be painful. Mike Brandon at Aquatic Perceptions in Hilo suggests using kayaks to reach this area from the south, thus avoiding the boulder entry altogether. Mike says the bottom relief here is spectacular and anything can swim by, including giant *ulua* that come over the ridges surprising the divers. Soldierfish abound in the deep cracks and young jacks hunt in the shallows. Visibility along this entire coast depends on the weather, since the streams here flow through cane fields and may pick up a lot of silt in heavy rains. But you need a calm

These days it is rare to see a cave or ledge so chock full of lobsters. This species is the most common in most parts of the Indo-Pacific but is actually uncommon in Hawaii, where the endemic black-legged P. marginatus dominates.

Panulirus penicillatus Hawaii n.d.

day to enjoy Laupahoehoe anyway.

Much closer to Hilo, just five miles north of town along the Pepeekeo Scenic Drive, is **Onomea Bay**. This is basically a famine dive, and the main thing here is to get wet. The bottom in the bay is gray sand with a few boulders, and visibility is usually poor due to the streams that flow into the bay. Kayaks or scooters can get you out of the bay and around past **Fallen Arch**, where the visibility is usually much better, but the bottom is still nothing to write home about. Better to head to Lapahoehoe.

THE HILO AREA

Almost nobody dives Hilo Bay itself, although there is a World War II airplane lurking somewhere in the murky waters, and recently what appears to be a disintegrated railway car full of munitions was discovered near the harbor entrance.

East of the bay, where the breakwater comes ashore, there are two regularly dived sites. **Up Against the Wall** is probably the better of the two. This is a relatively shallow dive that follows the Hilo breakwater out and then loops back over a bed of coral, where you will find an assortment of reef fish and the occasional turtle. **Puhi Bay**, also a 60-foot dive, begins essentially in the same spot as Up Against the Wall, only heads off in the opposite direction. The bottom is a silty sand with some isolated coral formations. The sandy bottom is sheltered from current, and this is said to be a good invertebrate dive at night.

Richardson's, further out on the point, starts in a tidal pool and heads out into the ocean. It is far enough from the influence of the rivers to be clear, and there is reportly an F4U Corsair wreck nearby. Lots of jacks, particularly in the late afternoon, and surgeonfish and grazers in the surge among the boulders. This dive gets better and bet-

Lutjanus kasmira and Chaetodon miliaris Hawaii 2000

ter with each exploration.

Southeast of Leleiwi Point, there are several sites that can be reached from shore, including **Kings Landing (Papai)**, the odd entry from **Hawaiian Paradise Park**, and **Orr's Beach**, which is a black sand beach with a big archway and an easy entry. In general, however, access along this stretch is difficult and limited, and we recommend you dive here from a boat out of Hilo.

PUNA

As you near **Cape Kumukahi**, the island's easternmost tip, the diving gradually changes, becoming wilder and wilder. The area around the Kumukahi is all boat diving, and usually rough. Often the weather makes it undiveable. This is Hawaii's frontier. The bottom here

The blueline snapper is a common species found from the Red Sea to the Tuamotu Islands and, since its introduction in 1955, Hawaii, where it is called 'taape.' These fish form large schools during the day, and disperse at night to feed. In many parts of its range it is the mainstay of local fisheries.

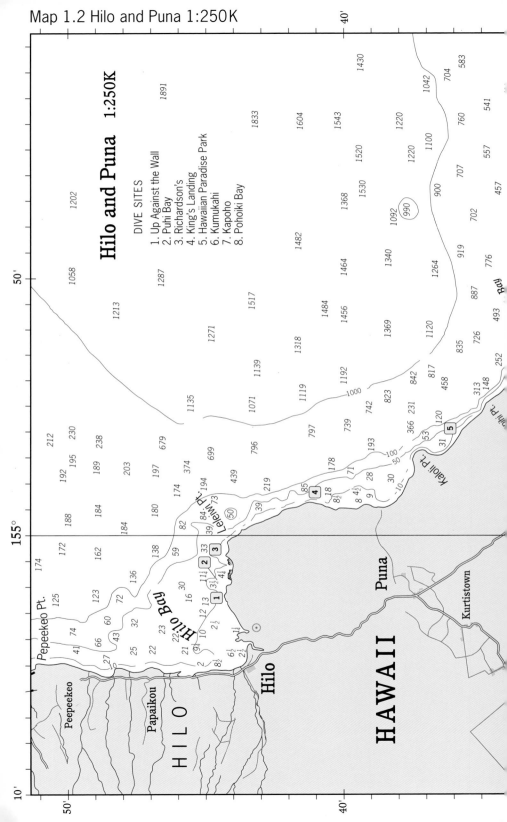

Map 1.2 Hilo and Puna 1:250K

Hilo and Puna 1:250K

DIVE SITES

1. Up Against the Wall
2. Puhi Bay
3. Richardson's
4. King's Landing
5. Hawaiian Paradise Park
6. Kumukahi
7. Kapoho
8. Pohoiki Bay

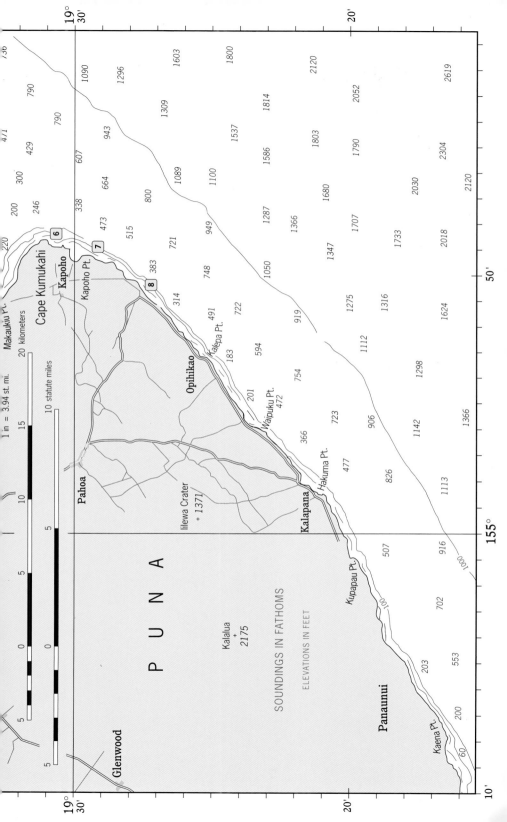

Antennarius commersonii   Maui 1993

Commerson's frog-fish is the largest member of its genus (reaching a foot or more in length) and the one most commonly seen by divers. Identification of these animals can be tricky, and usually involves minute details of the esca (the lure) and has little to do with color or pattern, which vary wildly. All frogfish are fascinating creatures, perching motionless or lumbering slowly about on their pectoral fins, which are like little hands. When prey is attracted to the lure, it is engulfed with an instantaneous snap of the jaw. This is considered to be one of the fastest motions in the animal kingdom—far too fast, for example, to see with the naked eye. There is a fish present, then there isn't, and the frogfish rocks slowly back into position.

consists of large boulders, caves, ledges, and a drop-off to impossible depths. There is a shallow shelf along the break, with boulders piled right up to it (and they occasionally wash up and over it). The site offers good deep diving as well. In fact, it seems to get better and better as you get deeper.

The current here can be very strong, and can run either way. The fish and sharks are aggressive—and big. It was here that one of us was surprised by the biggest jack he had ever seen. The huge fish burst out of a cave, looked at Mike, and went back in. We have only ever seen one other *ulua* in this size range (it was slightly smaller) and when landed it weighed more than 100 pounds.

Dives in this area are electric, and can bring the taste of adrenaline to your mouth. You never know what will happen next. This coast offers excellent shelter to an amazingly rich fish fauna, from the giant jacks to sharks and clouds of the smaller reef dwellers, including Tinker's butterflyfish, which is common

here. Also common here are viper morays (*Enchelynassa canina*), so watch where you put your hands.

From Cape Kumukahi south past **Kapoho** the bottom has a shallow ledge right on shore, then boulders down to about 90 feet and then the drop-off. The deep is in twilight even at midday. The water here is cooled by currents coming out of deep water, and the fish life is spectacular. Expect hammerhead sharks, barracuda, *ulua*, soldierfish, goatfish, snappers (*taape* and *toau*) and peacock groupers.

South of Kapoho is **Pohoiki Bay**, which has a small wall which drops about five or ten feet and forms a large amphitheater full of boulders. Here there are three anchors which once were used as moorings. You can explore parallel to the shore or go on down to some impressive depths. This is a fun dive with a relatively easy entry. In the late afternoon, large game fish, sharks, and even pelagic predators may show up, including *ono*, mahi-mahi, and barracuda.

WILD AND UNSPOILED

The Kona Coast
Wouldn't You Like to See 100 Hammerhead Sharks?

Have you heard about the wreck of the Bare Naked Lady? Our hostess, eyes flashing, was only too happy to tell us about Kailua Bay's only wreck dive. It seems a sailboat suddenly burst into flames one evening and then, still tied to its mooring, slowly sank 110 feet. About the same time that the boat touched bottom, a mysterious woman arrived on shore—with nowhere to go, and not a stitch of clothing on. It was an accident, she said.

Kailua is a small town with a lazy, tropical air, and rumors and gentle scandal flourish here—especially in the cool evening, with a background of Hawaiian music and the red glow of dusk.

Nestled in the lee of nearby Hualalai, Kailua serves as the base for most of the diving in Kona. From here you can find boats to take you to the north beyond the airport and to the south, if the season and weather are willing, as far as South Point. As a general rule, during the summer and fall months, June to November, South Kona diving is more reliable. During the rest of the year the areas north of town are better. But because the island curves around, and has so many points and bays, there is hardly a day you cannot dive somewhere.

Kona has taken an aggressive stand to protect its reefs and marine life by installing an extensive mooring system, which is maintained by the dive operations, and by limiting the areas the tropical fish collectors can work. A network of triangular signs posted along the coast indicates which areas are open for collecting and which are closed.

Compared to some other parts of Hawaii, Kona seems still wild and unspoiled. The sheer number and variety of sea birds one sees here during the boat rides is one indication. Since these birds nest on the ground and cliffs, their healthy populations show that, unlike on other islands, they are here undisturbed by human activity. Underwater, things are similar.

Kona, for example, is the best place in the islands to see Tinker's butterflyfish. They are everywhere, and curious and cute as can be.

The Kona sites give an impression of robust good health. Strong lava formations, sea mammals, excellent fish life, and hammerheads are the main attractions on the Big Island's signature diving coast.

Chaetodon tinkeri is the only butterflyfish that you can feel you have established a relationship with by the end of a dive. Then there are the large pelagic species. Close to a dozen whale species can be seen off Kona, including several dolphins, beaked whales, sperm whales, humpback whales, and even a blue whale or two. Oceanic whitetip sharks, silky sharks, and big-eyed thresher sharks can be found here as well.

And then there are the hammerheads. Whenever we asked anyone about the dive sites here, they always mentioned the hammerheads. Great schools of these sharks gather in October and November, when the weather is usually good for diving just about anywhere along the Kona Coast. Patrice Heller of Pacific Rim Divers told us of being suddenly surrounded by more than a hundred hammerhead sharks on a dive. Her client, in that state of paralysis common among prey animals, kept her camera clasped in one hand by her side. Thinking quickly, Patrice borrowed the camera and started snapping. We saw only one of the frames from that day, and there were at least thirty sharks in it. When someone says they saw a hundred hammerheads off Kona, few Kona divers doubt them.

The home port for most of the boats working this coast is Honokahau Harbor, just north of Kailua. This harbor itself is spectacular—it looks like a giant lava brownie with a chunk cut out of it. The walls are vertical and the water

lacks the usual silt of most harbors. You can see turtles grazing along the sheer lava walls even deep into the harbor. At the entrance, a massive school of *akule,* a small mackerel scad, changes shape like an amoeba with each passing boat. Just outside the harbor there seems always to be a pod of spinner dolphins, sometimes with spotted dolphins mixed in. By the time you reach open water you are already writing furiously in your logbook.

NORTH OF KAILUA

Just outside Honokahau Harbor is a large sloping gray sand area with some garden eels, and a little further along there is an area of shallow caves and arches cut into the shoreline where whitetip reef sharks can often be seen. This is **Suck 'Em Up.** (For this and the other North of Kailua sites, see MAP 1.4, pp. 66–67.) Here we found two large fine-scale triggerfish (*Balistes polylepis*), with their characteristically large waving fins. This fish, from the west coast of the Americ-

This bristle-toothed surgeonfish, called 'kole' in Hawaii, is found from the Red Sea to Hawaii, but only the Hawaiian populations have such a bright eye ring. The photograph clearly shows the eponymous bristles, which are a great aid in scraping filamentous algae from rocks, an activity that consumes the entirety of this animal's day.

Ctenochaetus strigosus Hawaii 1988

as, may be a rare stray in Hawaii. Around the point to the north is a site with the unfortunate name of **Golden Arches.** Here you can see mantas, dolphins, hammerheads, and a variety of spectacular rarities that swim or drift by in the deep water out from the moorings.

Further up the coast, and just off-shore from the airport is **Garden Eel Cove**, with sloping coral and boulders leading to a dark sand bottom full of silvery garden eels. The eels at this site are remarkably tame. Dolphins and manta rays are not uncommon here, and at night crocodile eels can be found in the sand. The lava shoreline is banded in colors—black on top, then gray, then green, then tan, and finally, in the splash zone, the pink of coralline algae. It is a subtle rainbow framed by the blue sea and the sky.

North of the runway, at a little-known spot called **Gunsight**, there is a real surprise for adventurous divers. Here the current requires careful planning and this dive is best done with a live boat. We dropped in slightly up current, and as the boat took up position down current we angled out into deeper water over sand filled with fields of garden eels as far as visibility allowed us to see. Then, staying well off the bottom, we followed a sloping boulder wall until we encountered a group of about 25 gray reef sharks (a number we all agreed on later on the boat) swirling in a ball below us. As we settled to watch, several broke off and came over to us, running low and fast. I love these sharks. While our attention was drawn to the shark display, we found we had been joined by two eagle rays silhouetted against the blue surface just above us.

On the way back upslope, at about 80 feet, we found forty-foot-high blocks of lava, with deep undercuts and in one place an arch 20 feet high. The lava chunks are divided by white sand channels.

Stylocheilus longicauda Molokini 1992

Large colonies of antler coral cover their flat tops. With the depth, the sharks, the lively current, and the majestic structure, you have to be careful not to get too excited to watch your gauges here.

Heading back south along the coast toward Kailua there is a series of basically similar sites, mostly shallow and with typical Big Island lava formations sheltering clouds of damsels and schools of butterflyfish and parrotfish. Most of these are best as a second dive, although one—called **Outhouse**—is good enough to seek out for its own sake.

Outhouse is a rocky shelf way out on the end of a lava flow. The lava flow that formed Kaiwi Point pushed well out to sea before it cooled, forming a shelf about 100 feet wide of alluvial material broken

The sea hares are a group of herbivorous opisthobranchs (a group of gastropod molluscs, the most famous of which are the nudibranchs). Most are green or drab, but this one is a dramatic exception.

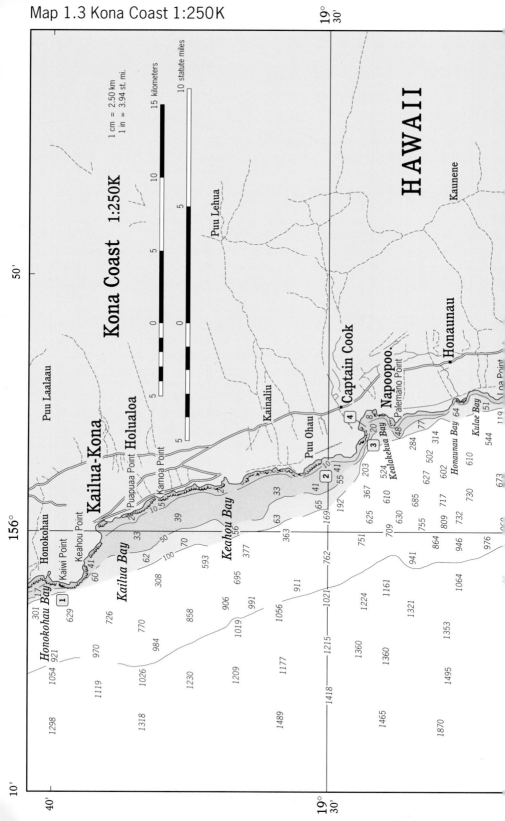

Map 1.3 Kona Coast 1:250K

Kona Coast 1:250K

1 cm = 2.50 km
1 in = 3.94 st. mi.

15 kilometers
10 statute miles

HAWAII

Puu Laalaau

Kailua-Kona

Holualoa

Puu Lehua

Kaunene

Honokohau

Kaiwi Point

Keahou Point

Honokohau Bay

Honaunau

Napoopoo

Captain Cook

Puapaa Point

Kamoa Point

Kainaliu

Puu Ohau

Palemano Point

Loa Point

Kailua Bay

Keahou Bay

Kealakekua Bay

Honaunau Bay

Kulae Bay

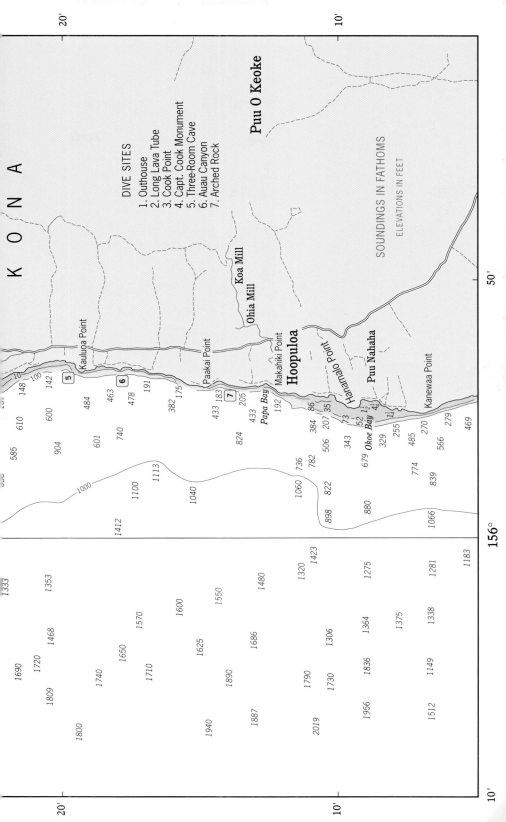

K O N A

Puu O Keoke

DIVE SITES
1. Outhouse
2. Long Lava Tube
3. Cook Point
4. Capt. Cook Monument
5. Three-Room Cave
6. Auau Canyon
7. Arched Rock

SOUNDINGS IN FATHOMS

ELEVATIONS IN FEET

Kauluoa Point

Paakai Point

Koa Mill

Ohia Mill

Makahiki Point

Hoopuloa

Papa Bay

Hanamalo Point

Puu Nahaha

Okoe Bay

Kanewaa Point

20'

10'

50'

156°

10'

20'

10'

Mulloidichthys vanicolensis Hawaii 1997

The yellowfin goatfish gathers into balls like this during the day as a kind of defensive maneuver (in this case, there really is safety in numbers). This is a strategy shared by a number of other species, such as barracuda and taape, to name just two, and these diurnal stationary schoolers are all night feeders. When the sun sets, the goatfish leave their comrades and forage individually.

from the flow. Floating over this relatively shallow shelf you face out into the inky deep, and can watch oceanic whitetip sharks, whales, hammerheads, dolphins and mantas cruise by from a safe platform. Along the narrow length of the lava flow are some spectacular coral formations, and the reef life that comes with such healthy habitat includes bandit angelfish, flame angelfish and the large spiny cowfish.

SOUTH KONA

About eight miles south of Kailua, a little past Red Hill, is **Long Lava Tube**. (For this and the other South Kona sites, see Map 1.3, pp. 52–53.) The site is in a bay created by a natural flying buttress of lava with two large sea caves carved beneath. This remarkable structure, about a hundred yards across, lies perpendicular to the shoreline, and with its two sea caves resembles an old stone bridge. It is a beautiful and very picturesque place, but in 2001 we saw the beginnings of development on the shore here, and it will no

doubt soon lose some of its charm.

Just south of the lava buttress, at a depth of about 50 feet, is the 70-foot-long lava tube which gives the site its name. The small tube runs straight offshore, and the shafts of blue light filtering through the darkness create a mysterious beauty. When you exit the tube look back—your bubbles, percolating up through the substrate, will leave a trail defining the path of the cave under the sea floor.

If you stop at Long Lava Tube early in the morning you may find black *ulua* hanging around in the cave and from the boat you can watch white-tailed tropic birds. These beautiful and graceful fliers nest in sea cliffs in May and June. Later in the summer you can see the chicks, which are almost the size of a hen, fledging from these cliffs.

Not far south of Long Lava Tube is **Kealakekua Bay**, the place where Captain Cook met his demise. Mistaken for the god Lono, Cook was treated accordingly at first, but when he returned with a

Gymnothorax meleagris Molokini 1991

damaged ship the local community began to question his identity. The point remains confusing, but perhaps the people most surprised by his murder were those involved on both sides on that fateful day in 1779. So respected was Cook by both the people he sailed with and the Hawaiians at Kealakekua that his mortal remains were divided between them. Some returned to England, and some were kept for ceremonial purposes by the villagers. It is thought that Cook's bones were used secretly in religious practices for a century after his death, and some say their location is still known.

Diving off **Cook Point** on the outside of Kealakekua Bay, according to reports, you may see hammerhead sharks and there is said to be a reasonable drop-off and good bottom contour. If you dive on the inside of the point, along that part of the bay beneath the **Captain Cook Monument**, you will find an incredible amount of very healthy coral and a good number of reef fish. Unfortunately, this solid field of coral can get monotonous, and there is very little else to see; we were restless after about ten minutes. Still, we recommend stopping by and at least snorkeling this historical site, just to say you did it.

FAR SOUTH KONA

South of Kealakekua Bay things begin gradually to get a little wilder and you can expect to see more giant *ulua* and more frequently encounter hammerheads. The shoreline is a spectacular series of lava flows. If you are interested, the date and point of origin for most of the lava flows you will see can be found on the Map of Hawaii by the University of Hawaii Press.

A highly recommended site about ten miles down the coast from Kealakekua Bay is **Three Room Cave.** This site, just north of Kauluoa Point, is difficult to find if you have never been there, but once you have you will remember it like it was your home. The site is inconspicuously close to shore and tucked into a corner by a ridge. The

It would be a very atypical dive in Hawaii if you did not see at least one whitemouth moray. This is a young specimen, and seems even more inquisitive and intelligent than most. Members of the genus Gymnothorax tend to have a rather sweet disposition, and in areas frequented by divers become quite tame. How these animals ever got their reputation for ferocity is a puzzle to me. I suppose, however, if you take the snake-like appearance, add to it the impressive teeth, add to these the gaping habit (the only way they can breathe), and finally throw in traditional diver machismo, you have your answer.

On the other hand, there is always Enchelynassa canina, which is just plain ornery. I always hope that people who like to bother morays find one of these to harass. Preferably a really big one.

A FEAST OF PLANKTON
Night Diving with Mantas

Mysids
(actual size)

THE MESSAGE WAS TOTALLY UNEXPECTED. *National Geographic* magazine was on the Big Island, photographing the manta rays feeding at night in front of the Kona Surf Resort. Could we come over and help? Particularly, the magazine wanted our help in finding out exactly what was in the clouds of plankton that the huge rays were eating.

The Kona Surf had been shining its lights into the ocean for more than twenty years, and the dive was gaining a reputation for its consistency. You would see the mantas you were promised. Then the local dive operators noticed something more than just the regularity of the feeding—the mantas attracted to the lights were the same individuals every night.

Upon arriving at the Kona Surf, we met Jim Watt, Joe Stancompiano, and *National Geographic*'s David Doubilet. David had come prepared: he had twelve cameras and housings, a technician (Joe), and a lighting and camera

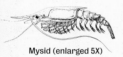

Mysid (enlarged 5X)

assistant, Nikki Constantino. They had also brought along a beautiful dissecting microscope, which looked distinctly out-of-place in the Kona Surf hotel's seventies decor. The microscope was to photograph the tiny animals that were attracting such a loyal following of mantas every night.

That first night with the mantas was unbelievable. Three hours and fifteen minutes of continuous bottom time flew by on the shallow, 30-foot dive. To keep the mantas in one area, the *National Geographic* crew had brought a powerful 6,000-watt light which they aimed straight down off the boat to focus the manta's food. The light fired an intense beam of pure white light all the way to the bottom, illuminating the rocks and coral—and attracting millions of planktonic animals.

The divers were enchanted as the planktonic animals began to form a swirling vortex all the way from the sea floor to the surface. This was manta heaven. One of the giant animals would open its mouth and soar upward

along this liquid pillar of life. The column quickly regrouped, and another manta would come in and feed.

The underwater dance continued over the next few nights unabated, as manta after manta barrel-rolled and looped in a gluttonous ballet, scooping huge mouthfuls of plankton. They never seemed to get their fill. After a couple days we began to recognize individuals. One had a scuff mark on its belly. Another a bent cephalic fin. One was literally crawling with tiny crustaceans. Only one was a male.

MYSID CHOWDER

Looking at the plankton chowder up close underwater, we saw tiny needlefish, larval octopus, larval crabs, two-inch larval lobsters as clear as crystal, and something else too small to make out. We took a bucketful of this briny broth back to the hotel.

The first time we put a sample under the microscope, we realized that our mystery animals were darting around way too fast to focus on and photograph. How to slow them down? Somebody suggested clove oil—the eugenol it contains has long been used as an anesthetizing agent. Clove oil is still sold as a toothache remedy, and David sped off to town to search the local pharmacies.

The next night, the exhausted divers stood around Joe as he put a drop of clove oil into a dish of tiny darting life and placed it under the microscope. Hundreds of clear crustaceans began to slow their jittering movements and for the first time we could see what they were—mysids. These are tiny, shrimp-like animals only five millimeters long.

AND THEN THERE WERE NONE

Our work with *National Geographic* took place in 1994, and for several years afterward, thousands of divers witnessed the nightly manta feeding just off the Kona Surf. And then the mantas stopped coming. Sightings gradually declined, and finally became so sporadic that it was embarrassing for the dive

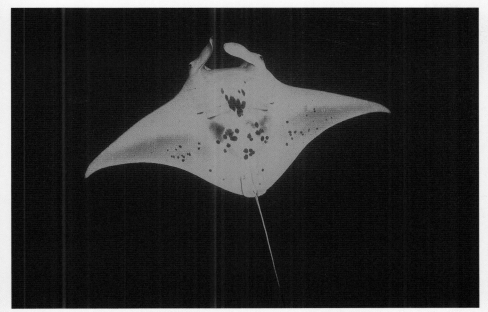

Manta birostris Hawaii n.d.

The pattern on a manta's belly is unique to each individual, and sixty members of the Kona population have been identified.

shops to offer the manta ray night dive anymore. The mantas had moved on. Facing financial problems, the Kona Surf closed in June 2000, and the lights were turned out.

During its heyday, the manta night dive was a boon for Kona operators. Nowhere else in the world did manta rays show such fidelity to a site at night. And nowhere else could divers see them at night, illuminated by and feeding in a diver's light. Keller Laros, now with Jack's Diving Locker, was so excited by his experience with the mantas that he left the mainland and moved to Kona.

Over the years Keller and his wife Wendy have photographed and observed the mantas on hundreds of dives. They have compiled these data as well as photographs and data from other Kona divers, and produced a catalog of more than 60 individual mantas, all identifiable by the unique pattern of spots and markings on their undersides.

According to the Laros's data, 15 percent of the Kona manta population consists of regulars, seen at least once in ten dives, while the other 85 percent are seen a few times then never again. It thus appears that a small percentage of the population is local, while the rest is nomadic or perhaps migratory.

Research by Tim Clark of Texas A&M, published this year in his master's thesis, also suggests that manta populations worldwide are essentially nomadic or migratory. Clark collected DNA from mantas in the east and west Pacific, the Gulf of Mexico, and South Africa, and found these scattered populations to be genetically similar enough to be considered the same species—thus genetic mixing between the groups must be ongoing.

A NEW FEEDING LOCATION

The void left by the exit of the mantas at the Kona Surf was deeply felt in Kona. Requests for the dive—which by the late '90s had been publicized in every guidebook and magazine—continued, and the dive operations began to look for new feeding grounds. One night a dive boat stumbled upon a few mantas feeding at a new location about 14 miles up the coast. They were able to keep the secret for about three nights before word got out. Some dive operators, who believe that it was the nightly visits by divers that chased the mantas away from the Kona Surf, don't even offer the dive. Others are trying to keep diver and manta contact to a minimum. How long they will stay this time, nobody knows.

cave opening is at 44 feet and it is low and not really very inviting at first. But once you are in out of the daylight and your eyes adjust to the cathedral lighting in the entrance you will feel more comfortable.

Immediately after entering the cave you will see a large pile of boulders directly in front of you. The spaces between the rocks make it appear as if the pile is loose, and you almost think if you so much as touched them the whole pile would come tumbling down and chase you out of the cave. You can relax, however—they are wedged firmly in place by friction and gravity. Beneath and between them is a multi-layered, very complex shelter for an unusual variety of lobsters.

It is not unusual to see Hawaii's two clawed reef lobsters (the rare *Enoplometopus holthuisi,* with a white "O" on each side, and the more common *E. occidentalis,* with scattered white spots), one of the islands' spiny lobsters (*Panulirus* spp.), the regal slipper lobster (*Arctides regalis*), and the mole lobster (*Palinurellus wieneckii*) on a single dive here. The most unusual of these is the strange mole lobster. These bright orange creatures are well-named. Like moles they have tiny eyes, a rounded head, and a small "face," and live all their lives in the dark. Their smooth carapace, relatively short legs and long, comparatively thin, body is well adapted for clambering about in tight places. They are rare in Hawaii.

The larger spiny lobsters can be seen hiding way up in the top of the cave, their long antennae protruding from the cracks. Also in this dark zone are a couple of large cardinal fish, cusk eels, and at least three species of soldierfish including a small, bright red species that is ordinarily very hard to find.

Just around the corner from the cave entrance there is a tunnel, hidden in the shadow of a large chamber in the surf zone. In the back of this tunnel, on the right, there is a crack big enough to swim through which opens into a 100-foot-long passage. Along this passage you will

The many-eyed snake eel (a literal translation of the species name) is very uncommonly encountered by divers. This one seems distinctly suspicious of our photographer. Hiding their bodies in the sand is standard operating procedure for snake eels, although some (including other members of this genus) do come out at night and slither about in search of something to eat.

Ophichthus polyophthalmus Maui 94

see many spiny lobsters, squirrelfish taking shelter for the day, and a very large pufferfish, who seems to have made this passageway his home. At the far end it is possible, after negotiating several boulders, to exit the passage without touching the walls (although when you come out it is a fair swim back to the cave entrance). Three Room Cave is an exceptional site.

A bit further north of Three Room Cave there is said to be another cave you can surface in, and even more enticing, it is said that somewhere along this coast is a legendary cave that has an opening underwater and then runs up on land. You can exit the water underground and go on exploring.

A couple of miles further down the coast from Three Room Cave, and well worth the extra effort, is **Auau Canyon**. This site has yet another species of lobster if you care to round off your day (*Justitia longimanus*). The long-handed spiny lobster is normally seen only in deep water but here it can be found relatively shallow. Unfortunately, we are sworn to secrecy as to their exact location. A small island of pahoehoe lava with a cable connecting it to the coast indicates that this is a good fishing area (since someone went to a lot of trouble to establish the crossing). Good fishing areas are almost always good diving areas.

Diving Auau Canyon is a unique experience. Starting at a modest 35 feet, we swam from the mooring over a series of smaller canyons running out from shore to reach the edge of the great canyon the site is known for. There we launched ourselves out and down into the canyon, gliding deeper and deeper down the smooth gray sand trough that forms the canyon floor. The water was clear enough to see the 150 feet across the canyon to the other side. The impression was of monumental depth and scale. It

Forcipiger longirostris Molokini 1991

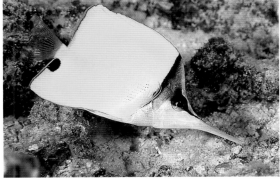

Forcipiger longirostris Hawaii 1997

was intoxicating to drift lazily down this huge chute and out to sea. At about 170 feet (and we were running about 40 feet over the bottom) the canyon was still falling away quickly, with no sign of stopping. We inflated our BCs and began moving toward the wall so that we could head slowly back up, looking for small animals along the way.

It immediately became apparent that there were almost no fish to be found in the canyon itself, only along the upper edges. The entire Auau Canyon appears to have been smoothed by rocks sliding down it and this featureless surface provides no shelter for reef fish. It is very reminiscent of a glacial valley scoured smooth by the abrasive ice.

As I rose up the wall I saw another member of our party hovering above me and then a hand signal.

The longnose butterfly fish, or more properly, the big longnose butterflyfish, has an unusual dark or melanistic phase, as seen in the top photo. This species is not as common as the similar, but shorter-snouted F. flavissimus, and the dark form is rarer still. The photographer, when pressed, guessed that the melanistic specimens were less frequent than one in ten, but more frequent than one in one-hundred. It is said that dark phase specimens can revert back to yellow.

He had seen a hammerhead shark. Where had I been? Deep. The shark had come right up to him, a rare occurrence, and then as he watched, glided over us as it crossed the canyon.

Four miles further south, at **Arched Rock**, named for a 100-foot-tall monolith rising from a 60-foot bottom, we found a series of

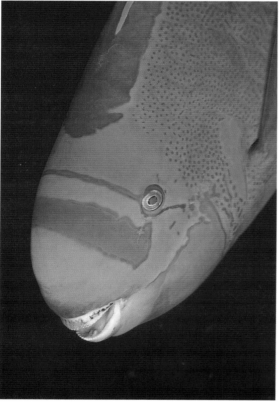

Chlorurus perspicillatus (male)   Hawaii 1997

similar chutes. These told a clearer story than Auau Canyon. Here each smooth canyon was clogged with large boulders at the shallow end like a soapbox derby ready for the gun to fire. The amount of energy stored in those rocks is almost incalculable. Below these thousands and thousands of tons of wedged boulders, these chutes were as smooth as Auau. Instinct

tells you that you don't want to be anywhere near here when the next earthquake hits.

Arched Rock was an interesting place to dive, with lots of Tinker's butterflies, the giant lined butterflyfish, schools of goatfish, hundreds of black triggerfish, and the other current-indicating species, the smooth-head unicornfish or *opelu kala*. Toward the end of the dive Pauline picked up the head and half the body of a freshly killed yellow anthias (she is good at finding dead fish), with the unmistakable teeth marks of a small shark. This told us that the beautiful endemic *Holanthias fuscipinnis* was in the area, but we didn't see them.

Arched Rock is another area noted for its hammerhead sharks, though we did not see any of these either. On the day we dove the current was running south, contrary to its usual direction, and we think this may have played a role in frustrating our shark watching.

KAUNA POINT

About 14 miles south from Arched Rock, we rounded a point and stopped. From here, off in the distance, we could see Ka Lae Cape or South Point, the southern tip of the Big Island and as far south as you can go in the United States. Where we stopped was **Kauna Point**, our final destination on the Kona Coast. (See CHART on pg. 62.) Kauna Point is not an easily diveable site. It can be calm one minute and be blown by 40-knot winds a few minutes later. This point helps define the southernmost end of the Big Island and currents can scream around it with overwhelming force. When it is calm and free of current, Kauna Point offers some superb diving. But most of the time conditions—and its own ornery reputation—keep divers away.

We rolled off onto a bottom with robust lobe coral formations grow-

A TALE OF RECOVERY
Hawaii's Green Sea Turtles

THEY HAUL OUT TO BASK ON THE HEAT OF THE black sand beach at Punaluu on the Big Island. They clamor at the water's edge to feed on seaweed (sometimes also tossed in by tourists) at a North Shore beach on Oahu. They are admired by thrilled snorkelers all along the leeward coast of Maui. Green sea turtles are everywhere in Hawaii.

This was not always the case. As recently as 1974 local sea turtle steak was offered at Hawaii's restaurants, and the turtles, rarely seen by divers and snorkelers anyway, would bolt upon being approached. But once Hawaii's green sea turtle was listed as a threatened species under the U.S. Endangered Species Act in 1978, the population began to rebound. Today Hawaii is one of the best places in the world to see these animals, which in most areas no longer seem afraid of people.

A TURTLE'S BEST FRIEND

This impressive recovery is in part due to George Balazs, who has been studying and fighting for protection of Hawaii's green sea turtles since 1973. That summer he visited their nesting grounds at French Frigate Shoals to count the females who were actually nesting. The number was discouraging—only 67 turtles came ashore. Since then George has returned almost every year, and in recent years he has counted as many as 500 turtles.

After hatching, a green sea turtle spends the next five years of its life drifting on the ocean surface feeding on jellyfish, fish, and invertebrates. Once the animals reach about a foot and a half in length, they settle down into their adult habitat, which for the Hawaii population is a coastal band, roughly down to 70 feet, surrounding the islands. At this point in their lives they become vegetarians, grazing on a variety of seaweeds, and grow slowly, reaching sexual maturity in 25 years or so.

In Hawaii, mating takes place in the French Frigate Shoals, and copulating pairs are rarely seen in the main islands. Every year in April, breeding males and females make the 600-mile trip to the shoals, where 98 percent of the population nests. After mating and laying, both females and males return to the foraging area they left a few months earlier.

Green turtles seem to be somewhat gregarious, and are often found in the company of other turtles. Occasionally they graze on

Chelonia mydas Hawaii 1995

Eretmochelys imbricata North Kihei, Maui 1998

The green turtle (above) has made an impressive recovery in Hawaii. The hawksbill (below) is still in danger, and here hatchlings are being aided by volunteers on Maui near Kihei.

algae at the water's edge or in deeper water. Every 20 minutes to 2½ hours they head for the surface to breathe. It is here that they are most vulnerable to their only predator, the tiger shark. Green turtles, by the way, are not sitting ducks for sharks—if necessary, they can reach an astonishing 30 knots!

Although their numbers have increased, Hawaii's green sea turtles are still protected, and it is illegal to ride them, or harm or harass them in any other way.

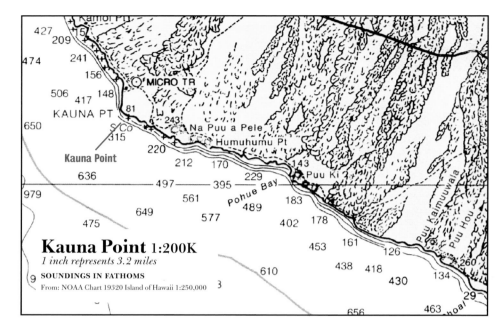

Kauna Point 1:200K
1 inch represents 3.2 miles
SOUNDINGS IN FATHOMS
From: NOAA Chart 19320 Island of Hawaii 1:250,000

ing around rocks the size of houses. Every few feet a very large peacock grouper would stick its head out and look at us. When fish stay near cover, this means something in the neighborhood feeds on them. A sobering thought when you consider that a very large peacock grouper is two feet long. At 60 feet, as we approached the edge of the narrow shelf, the bottom rolled over and started down. Just at that moment a large *ulua,* in the 60 pound range, shot by and continued on down the slope. As we went deeper the fish life became more scattered, but still plentiful. We saw a blueline triggerfish, a school of rainbow runners circled overhead, and another large jack went sailing past into deep water. A few *mu* (bigeye emperors) were hovering in the distance and a large school of *opelu kala* lingered along the edge of the shelf above me. This was a wild place. These fish were wary, but there were great numbers of them. This means they were not being hunted by man but a more natural predatory balance was in play.

Following the underwater contour around to the south we encountered a large and unusual formation. It looked like a natural stone pier jutting out into the deep. The top level was maybe fifteen feet wide, and it had vertical sides that dropped to the sloping bottom. This pier went straight out into the blue, then dog-legged toward South Point. It was magnificent.

Hovering above it we estimated its depth on top to be about 170 feet and the bottom on either side, sloping steeply down into dark blue, well below 200 feet. Growing on top were hundreds of wire corals, a current-loving species that were a warning not to stay here long. The current must be fierce as it sweeps along that steep slope and then leaps over this imposing obstruction. It seems clear that the current that came up one side would likely go down the other side just as forcibly. Getting caught here on the wrong day would be a good way to become a legend on the streets of Kona.

Kohala Area

Great Shore Diving, and a Little Taste of Maui

On the northern tip of the Big Island at Hawi, near the ruins of the house where Kamehameha I was born, there is a place on the shoreline where every year people once gathered to watch tiger sharks come and feed. A steer carcass was donated to attract the sharks and the crowd stood on top of a bluff to watch. The people usually had to wait a couple hours, but eventually the sharks began to arrive. It was fascinating to watch a big tiger shark first take its measure of the carcass, and then lunge in with full force, leaving a bite mark the diameter of a five gallon bucket.

And this sport was decidedly tame compared to the old days, when shark fishing was taken very seriously in North Kohala. According to one early 20th century source:

"The use of human flesh as bait was in great vogue among Hawaiian chiefs. It was cheaper than pig, was equally acceptable to the shark, and gave the chief an opportunity to kill anyone whom he disliked. The victim was cut up and left in a receptacle to decompose for two or three days. Kamehameha I was a great shark hunter and kept his victims penned up near the great heiau (temple) of Mookini near Kawaihae, Hawaii."—*Bulletin of the United States Fish Commission* Vol. XXIII, part II, 1903.

Fortunately, neither of these practices is likely to come back into fashion any time soon. Shark-baiting in Hawi stopped years ago, and the National Park Service has taken over the Mookini Heiau. No doubt one of their many regulations pro-hibits rounding up human beings to use as shark bait.

The sleepy port of Kawaihae has recently begun to bustle. The nearby hotels supply clients for the dive shops and there is even a small shopping center. Up the road toward Mahukona, where the hillsides were once covered in dead grass and thorny *kiawe* trees, upscale houses are being built, some of them right on the water. If you can afford it, these places have excellent views of

This photogenic coast offers healthy coral and fish life, nice lava walls, and even that great rarity on the Big Island—a shallow slope reef with white sand. A little windy, but calm seas make the shore diving easy.

this magnificent coast as well as of distant Maui and Kahoolawe.

Kawaihae Harbor is where you'll pick up your dive boat. Though the wind comes up around mid-morning on the northern dive sites, especially during the trade wind months of March through August, the southern areas down around Anaehoomalu Bay and Puako Reef remain calm most of the day.

ANAEHOOMALU BAY

The diving at Anaehoomalu Bay, about ten miles south of Kawaihae Harbor, developed not so much because it is an excellent site,

Acanthurus triostegus var. sandvicensis   Hawaii 1992

The convict surgeon-fish is a common species, especially in Hawaii. These animals are not as well defended as the other surgeons, having but a small caudal spine, nor are they as feisty. The more aggressive Acanthurids can bully them and keep them from the best grazing areas. Their response is to gather in big schools like this one, sweeping into an area and keeping out the competition by sheer force of numbers. The Hawaiian population is slightly different from those in the rest of the Indo-Pacific, and has been given the quaint subspecies designation sandvicensis.

but because of the resort hotels that sprang up here in the '70s and '80s. The diving here is good, but not great. It is very convenient to the hotels, but you won't see dive boats arriving at these sites from Kailua or Kawaihae. From Anaehoomalu Bay north almost all the dives have moorings.

The first site is **Pentagon**, located just outside Anaehoomalu Bay (See MAP 1.4, pp. 66–67). It offers lava caverns and good coral formations in very shallow water. Its shallow depth and abundant reef fish also make it popular with snorkelers. Another conveniently located dive, directly in front of a large hotel, is **Fingers**. Fingers boasts lots of coral, a few turtles and very shallow diving among fingers of lava that extend out from the inshore reef giving the area its name. There is excellent shelter here for reef species including a number of butterflyfish species. Turtles are also common. The site **Turtles**, a few hundred feet north of Fingers, is a little more interesting. This site has several lava caves with good invertebrate life, including cup corals, sponges, nudibranchs, cowries, and lobsters. Swimming north a bit from the mooring there is a turtle cleaning station, where several species of reef fish will pick parasites and graze algae from green turtles.

The next three sites to the north

are along an ancient lava flow that forms the Puako Reef. This reef offers excellent underwater topography, including a small wall that drops on average 20 feet all along its length. This wall is carved into small bays and passages creating a very interesting series of dives. The top of the lava flow is practically flat for a mile out from shore, reaching a depth of only about six feet at the outer edge, where it suddenly drops off abruptly to form the wall. This expanse of calm, shallow water has created something like a giant tide pool, where coral thrives and many species of fish, shells, urchins, starfish, and sea cucumbers can be found protected from many of their larger predators. Hundreds of pale-nose parrotfish live along the edge of the reef and can sometimes be seen courting and spawning just after sunrise.

THE PUAKO REEF SITES

Virtually the entire Puako reef has a small wall with rubble at its base and an apron of finger coral starting in 30 feet and bottoming out on sand at 60 to 130 feet. At the either end of Puako the lava flow becomes rounded and ends as fragments and boulders trailing off into sand and coral. If you walk along the southern shore at Puako you will find a number of ancient *konane* boards carved into the rocks of the shoreline just above the clear water tide pools. These boards are something like checker boards, and judging by the way they are grouped together and their location—overlooking the water with a perfect view of the sunset—it is easy to imagine this game having been a very enjoyable late afternoon or evening pastime.

All of the Puako sites can theoretically be reached from shore, but because of the beach cottages and private homes, access to the coast is limited to a few small lanes that reach the sea between house lots. Parking is almost impossible. The result is that unless you dive directly in front of one of these access roads or rent a house on the beach, you are in for a long swim along the outer edge of the reef to reach some of the destinations listed below. Otherwise go by boat. The interesting contour, the generally clear water, and the usually light current makes Puako a delightful area to dive.

The southernmost tip of the reef is known as **Paniau**. It has two moorings, but this one is also easy to reach from shore. The bottom here has a little more personality than most areas along the Puako flow, having some loose boulders and lava formations scattered out among the finger coral beds beyond the end of the reef. Barracuda, jacks, and turtles are occasional visitors, plus there is a wide assortment of resident reef fish—including large parrotfish, butterflyfish, damsels, and scorpionfishes.

North of Paniau, near the middle of the reef, is **Itels**, perhaps the de-finitive Puako Reef site. Here there is a shallow wall, rocks, ledges and finger coral interspersed with sand patches to 130 feet, then open sand. This site also makes an excellent early morning or late night dive, where you can spend your time watching animals leave or return to the shelter of the deep cracks and crevices along the shallow wall.

At the northern end of Puako, is **Eel Garden**. Here there is a massive colony of endemic Hawaiian garden eels (*Gorgasia hawaiiensis*). The eels are on sand at 70 feet, just far enough from the finger coral beds that an approaching predator would have to break cover to reach them. But there is more to this site than the eels. Eel Garden has a very healthy sand fauna including lots of sea cucumbers, sand-dwelling urchins, several sand-dwelling wrasses, and on a night dive you would no doubt find crocodile eels. Also, from time to time rare deep-dwelling animals, especially invertebrates, follow the sand up into shallow water (such as the blue-

Although it at first appears so, these orangeband surgeon-fish are not really eating sand. It is the film of algae, diatoms, and other organic debris that they are after. This seems a bit fussier than scraping algae from rock or coral, but I guess it's easy enough to spit out the grains.

Acanthurus olivaceus   Molokini 1986

Map 1.4 Kohala 1:250K

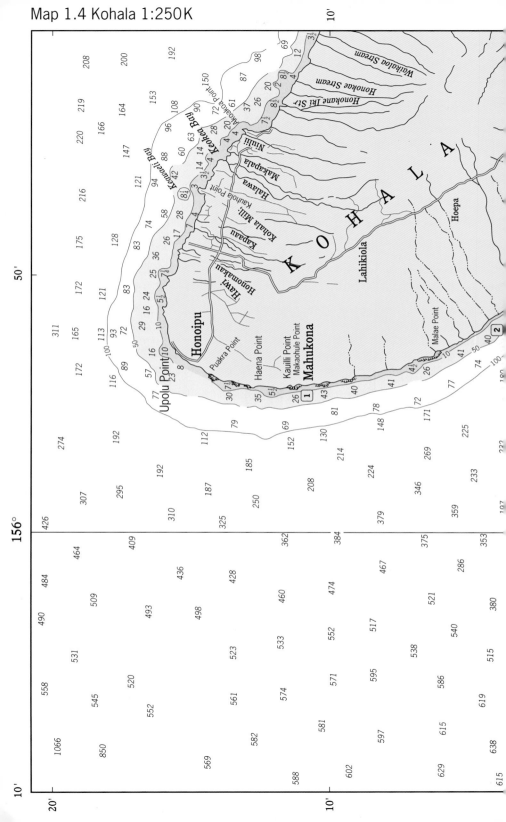

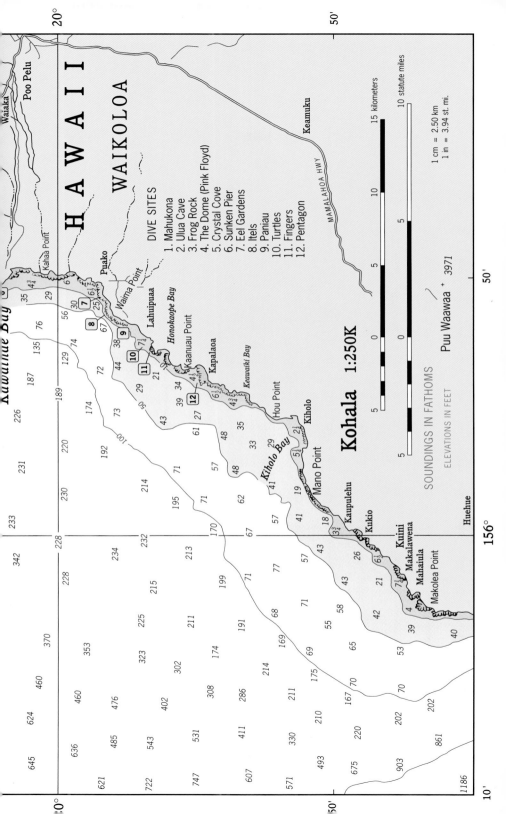

20°

Waiaka

Poo Pelu

Kawaihae Bay

H A W A I I

WAIKOLOA

Kahaa Point

Puako

Waina Point

Lahuipuaa

Honokaope Bay

Kaanuau Point

Kapalaoa

Keawaiki Bay

DIVE SITES

1. Mahukona
2. Ulua Cave
3. Frog Rock
4. The Dome (Pink Floyd)
5. Crystal Cove
6. Sunken Pier
7. Eel Gardens
8. Itels
9. Paniau
10. Turtles
11. Fingers
12. Pentagon

Hou Point

Kiholo

Kiholo Bay

Mano Point

Kaupulehu

Kukio

Kuini

Makalawena

Mahainla

Makolea Point

Keamuku

MAMALAHOA HWY

Kohala 1:250K

SOUNDINGS IN FATHOMS

ELEVATIONS IN FEET

Puu Waawaa + 3971

Huehue

50'

156°

50'

10'

50°

15 kilometers

10 statute miles

1 cm = 2.50 km
1 in = 3.94 st. mi.

35 43 29 6

30 **7** 25 6¼

8 67 74

9

38 74

10 7¼

11 21

29 34

39 34 4¼

12 6¼ 4¼

61 27

43 35 29

48 33 21 21

41 19

57 18

43 3¾

57 41 26 6¼

42 21 6¼

53 4

39

40

56 74 129 135

76 187 226

231 233

342

228 230 220 189 174

232 234

228

72 44

29

90 100

48 57 62

41 19

57 77

43

58 71

55

42 65

53 202 903

39 202 675

40 861 1186

71 174

195 214 192

199

213

211 215

170 67

68 69 71

57 169

175

167 70

70 220 330 571

210 211

214 286 411 607

191 308

174 302 402 543 722

211 225 323 476 460 636 645

215 353

370 460 624

231 621 485

747 531

621

spotted urchin, found by Rebekah Keele). If you look up you may see a resident school of Heller's barracuda lazily circling high in the water column above. Their large eyes give away the fact they are night feeders and come evening this school will disperse into deep water to feed on small fish. There are also many green turtles in this

Centropyge potteri Hawaii 1996

Potter's angelfish is a common species in Hawaii, and its attractive patterning has made it a staple of the aquarium trade. The animal pictured here is unusually beautiful, with more orange than the norm.

area and the occasional turtle cleaning station.

North of Puako the bottom flattens out, and stays like this all the way north to Kawaihae. Starting in front of Hapuna Beach this area includes large areas of white sand, with spectacular coral colonies and extensive rubble beds, and almost no lava rock. While not spectacular for general diving, these are excellent places to look for small creatures and some rare fish such as flame wrasses. This is the only place on the Big Island with this bottom.

NORTH OF KAWAIHAE

From Kawaihae north the coast is subjected to strong afternoon trade winds almost all year. But some of the more experienced captains and fishermen can predict the coming winds by looking at the clouds on the Kohala Mountains. It takes practice, but by noting how low the clouds are on the mountain, and how they angle across it, it is possible to predict the approximate time the wind will come inshore, and offer a fair estimate of its strength. These local skills allow this coast to be dived more often than it otherwise would.

All along North Kohala the bottom slopes gently off. Since the Kohala Mountains are heavily eroded, there is not as much ground up lava in the sand to darken it, and it is whiter than areas off new lava flows. In this regard it is a lot like Maui. Again because the area is geologically older than the rest of the Big Island, the sand is deeper, and only the peaks of the old lava flows stand exposed, especially in deeper water where the sand has accumulated from the shallows. Like coral bommies, these isolated rocky outcrops are magnets for fish.

There are three 19th-century wrecks along this coast of note. The first is the *Empire,* which burned and sank carrying a cargo of coal on July 26, 1901. This wreck lies on sand at 140 feet just south of Mahukona. The wreck was discovered in the 1970s by Dave Norquist while tropical fish collecting, when he came across the smoke stack standing in a pile of coal. Now the stack has fallen and just the coal and some debris are left to mark the wreck. At Mahukona there is another wreck, in shallow water

FISHING HAWAIIAN STYLE

Diving With the Locals

By Mike Severns

WE WERE STANDING AT THE DEMA TRADE SHOW a few years back when an old friend came up to talk. By way of introduction, he began telling us about the time I had climbed onto his boat in full gear, and without saying a word, fell over unconscious on the deck. I hadn't thought about that dive in many years. Actually I've never been able to put the whole story of that dive together and still can't. The middle is missing. I remember being at about 140 feet, on an open sand bottom, and generally snooping under every rock I could find, looking for interesting animals.

At that point in my diving career I wore blue jeans and a wetsuit top, and instead of a BC I used a homemade "Hawaiian backpack"—an aluminum plate with a tank band and a belt bolted to it, and two aluminum bars bent over the shoulders. I didn't have a high pressure gauge on my regulator, so I used my watch and timed the dives by feel. The lack of a pressure gauge keeps you unusually alert at depth. A subtle change in the draw from your regulator indicates you are getting low on air, and suggests an immediate change of dive plan.

On the dive my friend remembered, the last thing I recall was turning over a rock and feeling something sting my wrist—then having trouble breathing. I remember the attention I got when I regained consciousness on the boat. But I have no idea how I got from a 140-foot bottom to the boat.

I still carry a small scar on the inside of my wrist from that dive and think about it every now and then. It is a series of small brown dots in a slight curve. I have compared this scar to every animal I know that could have stung me, and for many years I couldn't decide what it was that administered the near fatal wound. Unfortunately, over the years I have had the opportunity to see and feel the results of many stings, and have now determined that the animal that left the scar on my wrist was not one of the sea's legendary vil-

lains, like a lionfish or a scorpionfish or a stingray.

No, I am rather embarrassed to admit, my near-deadly foe could only have been one

Makena Bay, Maui n.d.

The Maui fishing gang setting their net for taape in Makena Bay. These men, the author says, are the fastest and most skilled net fishermen he has ever known. Note the modified equipment, to reduce the chance of snags. The chopsticks are used to stitch sections of the net together underwater.

thing—a worm. Imagine if I had not made it back to the boat. My parents would have had to erect a white marble headstone with the epitaph: "SLAIN IN HIS PRIME BY A WORM."

HAWAII'S SCRAWNIEST SPEARFISHERMAN

Those days of diving are now gone, but a wetsuit jacket and a pair of jeans had its own elegance, and the Hawaiian backpack was a cheap and very practical solution to carrying a tank underwater. (The lack of a high pressure gauge, however, is not something I would recommend.) Another advantage was that the rig worked as its own dive bag. Flying inter-island I just wedged my fins and wetsuit into the tank band of my backpack with my mask and booties stuffed into my fins. I would check it in, and when I arrived it was always intact—in fact, I suspect it had received special handling.

My first real job as a diver came when I was living on the Big Island and became a spearfisherman on a crew of almost all

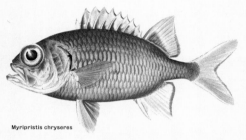

Myripristis chryseres

The uu or soldierfish is a very esteemed table fish among the Japanese community in Hawaii, and fetches a high price in Oahu. Various species in the genus Myripristis were the bread-and-butter quarry in the author's spearfishing days (although probably not the yellowfin soldierfish shown here, which lives deep). The Japanese call soldierfish menpachi, and this name is now used throughout the islands.

Hawaiians. I was the smallest and least experienced person on the boat, but I could shoot fish, which is why I was there. Onshore, however, I was somewhat of a liability, being barely half the size of most Hawaiian teenagers. But the respect of my crew helped prepare the local community for my presence and suddenly I found myself in a very different world than the Hawaii I had been living in up till then.

Once I came in, tired and cold, and found a Hawaiian guy big enough to be a navigation hazard sitting on my car. He started complaining about my working with the crew, when one of the guys cut him off. "Look, he is here every morning, he doesn't complain"—this was a lie—"and he can kill fish. If you want to replace him show up tomorrow morning at five." This was an effective argument because the man who was reshaping the hood of my car (and eliminating that annoying gloss from my paint with his sandy bathing suit) had been relaxing there for most

of the day. We, on the other hand, had been working since 5:00 a.m., and at the time of our discussion it was 7:30 p.m. From that day on I never had another problem, and my car was safer parked down at the boat ramp than anywhere else on the island.

Every morning I would arrive at the ramp early, and sometimes the wives of the older members of the crew would come down with pots of rice and stew. We would eat until we were so content we all wanted to go back to bed again. Then we would load the boat with tanks and coolers full of ice until there was barely room for us and head out.

The boat ride was usually long, sometimes unbearably long, and we went in a straight line regardless of the seas. The boat was fiberglass but we stuck a few two-by-fours up under the gunwales to keep it from breaking in half. The manufacturer guaranteed us this could not happen, but we all knew it would, since even with the two-by-fours it was already cracked almost all the way through. The spray coming off the bow was often so dense we wore our masks, which was literally the only way to see.

After running for close to an hour, which was about the maximum we could take, we would slow down and begin hunting for a bottom that might have small caves and dark ledges where we could find schools of soldierfish. These fish were very popular among the Japanese community, and were valuable enough to justify flying them fresh to Honolulu every day. We would lie in front of a cave and make a sound with our fingers that imitated the sound the fish made, and out they would come, one at a time, as if choreographed.

At the end of the day the catch was weighed and shipped. We split our profits evenly, with an additional share going for boat upkeep. If the condition of the boat was any indication of the profitability of this venture, we should all have found other jobs. But this life offered a kind of freedom we couldn't resist, and unless we were incapacitated—which happened from time to time, and usually from the bends—we were there every morning, ready to dive.

Our day involved three or four dives (sometimes as many as six) and since we were working hard and going through air quickly, and the dives were generally short, none of us paid too much attention to the tables. Generally we would dive in teams and when the first team returned, the second team went down, trading off like this all day long. When someone got the bends he flew to Honolulu for "repairs," and after the chamber treatment was usually back at work within a few days, contrary to his doctor's advice. One of our crew members had been bent so frequently that he complained of having read all the magazines in the chamber.

THE MAUI GANG

Years later I hung out with and occasionally dived with another "gang" on the island of Maui. These men ran a net-fishing operation. This sounds simple, but setting nets underwater requires a great deal of experience so nobody gets tangled up. The men kept their equipment to the bare minimum, modifying anything that might possibly snag on their net. They wore slip-over wetsuit tops without zippers, used regulators with the quick release, spring-loaded yokes found on high pressure gauges, and wore Hawaiian backpacks with just one shoulder bar and Velcro rather than a buckle. Even the loose ends of their fin and mask straps and their buckles were duct-taped down so they wouldn't snag. Weights, if needed, were put on the backpack belt and again often smoothed with tape.

Some of the guys carried three-pronged spears, which they used to protect the net from any large fish that might get tangled up, and to discourage sharks from participating in the event.

The net-fishermen targeted several schooling species, particularly the introduced *taape* (blueline snapper, *Lutjanus kasmira*), and the native *aholehole* (Hawaiian flagtail, *Kuhlia sanvicensis*) and *manini* (convict surgeonfish, *Acanthurus triostegus*). Schools of these species tend to flow along the reef in a set run. When they reach the end of their run, they bunch up, turn around, and head back the other way. Left undisturbed they will linger in a resting pack, generally facing into the current and staying close to the bottom to make it difficult for a charging predator.

The technique was to gently drive the school to the end of its normal run and hold it there while the net was set up. This involved using chopsticks to stitch the net together into two "fences" along either side of the run, with a bag at the end. The school was then allowed to return along its run, with an escort of divers, until it neared the bag. At this point the divers gently tried to persuade the fish into the bag, and as soon as they were successful the bag was stitched shut. If done carefully, this is a very effective way to catch fish. If done wrong, the school will panic, and any little hole in the trap end of the net would become an exit for a stream of fish. You could lose half a bag of fish in just a few seconds this way. Since I was not a regular part of the crew, I simply stayed

Makena Landing, Maui n.d.

The Maui gang landing their fish. At left is Mike Stoner, who later died from DCS-related complications. Mike, a good friend of the author, was a courageous and gifted diver, a fine writer, and remarkable personality. He is sorely missed.

out of the way until the fish were in the bag and then helped where I could.

Generally not more than half of the school was taken, and it was left to recover its numbers for a couple of months before the gang returned. In this way the schools could be fished sustainably for years. Unfortunately these fishing gangs are disappearing rapidly, and an entire way of life and knowledge of the behavior of their catch is vanishing with them.

Antennatus tuberosus Hawaii 1990

These little darlings are members of one of the smaller frogfish species, reaching just a couple inches in length. The animal in front wears a mask that resembles coralline algae, while his partner tries his luck as a yellow sponge.

across from the pier. This is the steamer *Kauai*, which ran on the rocks December 24, 1913, at the beginning of a Kona storm. You can still see the engine block and an old boiler that was part of the cargo. And at Honoipu Landing, not far from the quaint town of Hawi, there is one final surprise. The wreck of the *Like Like* lies here, on the rocks where it went aground and could not be recovered April 23, 1897. Bits of wreckage can still be seen in between the rocks at the water line.

Cattle, sugar, and passengers were the main cargoes of these old steamers and the landing at Kawaihae was a primary destination. Today there are the remains of an old concrete pier jutting out to sea where the ships used to moor. In the deep sand around this site, espe-

cially after a good storm, rare old bottles still can be found as well as anything else deemed of no value that was tossed off the ships and pier. This site is called **The Sunken Pier** and it is accessible from shore or by boat. The dive is shallow, but has lots of rubble where octopus can be found along with other small and interesting invertebrates. Whitetip sharks are also said to be common sights here. A little further up the coast are **Crystal Cove Inside** and **Outside Crystal Cove.** This is a single site that is done as a shallow dive and a deep dive. It has dark sand and you can see eagle rays, peacock flounders, and a host of sand dwellers as well as the occasional dolphin or manta going by in the deeper areas. It has good coral. The deeper areas of this site definitely offer the more interesting diving.

The **Dome** and **Pink Floyd** are dived off the same mooring and again it is just a question of dividing one site into two. Here there is a spectacular dome of plate coral, a swim through, the ubiquitous finger coral beds ending on sand, and a school of *taape.* You might see any number of large animals here, but these are just passing through on their way to somewhere else. With a good guide, however, this area can make a very nice second dive.

More interesting to me is a dive once known as The Wrecked Car, and now as **Frog Rock.** This site lies right on the boundary between North and South Kohala, and features a shallow cave with occasional spiny and slipper lobsters, and a long ridge running into deep water in which *mu* (bigeye emperors) and *uku* (jobfish; called gray snapper in Hawaii) can be found hanging around. As the ridge slopes down it opens onto sand littered with boulders. One of my best memories of this area is the acoustics it offered during whale season. The rocks in

Stenella longirostris   Hawaii 1995

this small bay really resonated when the whales sang.

Only a quarter mile away is **Ulua Cave** which features lava ridges, a large cave under the mooring that sometimes plays host to *ulua* in the early morning, and walls and ledges to poke around on and look for various nudibranchs. The best part of this dive though is you can get some depth on the ledges and may see some big animals, while at the same time enjoying just a touch of nitrogen narcosis. Manta rays, eagle rays, Galapagos sharks, a monk seal, and humpback whales have all been seen here and it is a great site for a night dive.

Though there is diving further north, **Mahukona** is about the last practical diving area on this coast. Any further and you are exposed to the rough and tumble winds and seas of the infamous Alenuihaha Channel. At Mahukona there is excellent deep diving with giant *ulua*, black coral, deep ledges with good overhangs, small lava caves—and some strong currents. This is also a good place to find antique bottles, some of which can be quite rare.

Years back, while diving at Mahukona, my dive buddy (I use the term loosely since I rarely saw him once we left the boat), picked up a beautiful round-bottomed Hollister bottle. These soda bottles, made in Honolulu, could not stand up on their own and had to be placed in a holder. They were popular on boats, which is probably how one ended up on the bottom at Mahukona. The bottle was worth about $100 at the time, which was a windfall for my buddy. The only problem with this find was that a very rare Rashleigh's cowrie had made the bottle its home. The cowrie had grown too large to escape, and was trapped inside. At the time, the cowrie shell was also worth $100. My buddy had made a $200 find, but with a major hitch—nobody wanted both the bottle and the shell. To sell the bottle he had to destroy the shell, or to sell the shell he had to destroy the bottle. Life is not always kind.

Spinner dolphins are common around Hawaii, but this is the way you will usually see them—from the boat.

rlequin shrimp, though only about the size of a finger joint, is a stunning creature. They live in pairs, and this species is the very few invertebrates able to recognize its partner as an individual. The starfish arm upon which it is perched is its —using their little nippers, harlequin shrimp tear at and devour the tube feet and flesh of sea stars, often Linckia.

cera picta on Linckia multifora Molokini 1995

This is the heartland of Hawaii diving, not least because more than two million people visit Maui every year. World-famous Molokini is the star of this area, but coastal Maui, Lanai, and Molokai offer some very fine diving of their own.

Maui Nui
Maui, Molokini, Kahoolawe, Lanai, and Molokai

TWENTY-ONE THOUSAND YEARS AGO, at the peak of the last ice age, Maui and Lanai were united into a single island. Molokai and the Penguin Bank lay exposed just a few hundred yards away. Go back several hundred thousand years more, and all these islands, together with Kahoolawe, stood together as one great island: Maui Nui. This ancient island was never seen by human beings, but even the first Hawaiians intuitively understood that these islands were closely related.

THE VALLEY ISLE

Today, Maui, Kahoolawe, Lanai, and Molokai make up Maui County. Maui is by far the largest and most populated of these islands, and except for west and southwest Molokai, all the diving in the area is from Maui-based operators.

Maui, covering 727 square miles, is the second largest island in the state. With a map and a bit of imagination the island looks like the head and shoulders of a woman. This elegant and complex shape is formed by two separate volcanoes: the West Maui Mountains, and towering Haleakala. The flat valley that joins these two mountains is usually stated as the source of the island's nickname, "The Valley Isle," although alternate etymologies have also been suggested.

Maui's central valley cuts from the windward to the leeward sides of the island, thus allowing the trade winds to funnel through. The winds affect the coastal town of Kihei on most days, and affect the diving practically everyday. The chop from the trades usually reaches the dive sites around mid-day, so to get two dives in and get back before the sea picks up, you'll want to get an early start when diving Maui's south shore.

Maui has a population of almost 100,000. There are four main centers of population: Wailuku–Kahului, the county seat and the location of the main airport and only deep water harbor; Kihei–Wailea, which has grown in just two decades from a few dusty houses on a seven-mile stretch of beautiful beaches to a

West Maui 1996

Eke Crater, atop West Maui, looking northwest toward Molokai. Relatively wet, very isolated, and high (4,480 feet), Eke is a biologically unique environment.

booming Gold Coast of tourism; Lahaina–Kaanapali–Kapalua, where tourism has built a magnificent array of hotels, shops, restaurants, and condos along the entire west coast of West Maui; and finally, lovely Hana, where life goes on simply, quietly, and delightfully, and where there is some of the most radically different diving in the entire state.

Maui has been the fastest growing part of Hawaii for two decades, and except for Hana, all the main population centers are experiencing difficulties with their infrastructure, as roads and water supplies scramble to catch up with growth.

A FAVORITE VACATION SPOT

Some 2.3 million people a year visit Maui, and since each visitor stays an average of about a week, at any given time almost one out of every three people on the island is a tourist. The formerly sleepy towns of Kaanapali and Kihei have become some of the most popular vacation destinations in the world, with hundreds of choices of hotels and restaurants, and of course a well-developed diving industry.

Maui's many hotels are spread out along the leeward coast. The less expensive ones can be found in the older parts of Lahaina and Kihei, with prices rising as you head outward towards either end of the island. Kapalua, at the far north on West Maui, and Wailea, at the far south, have the toniest resorts. Kaanapali, on the western tip of the island just north of Lahaina, has the best weather and the longest and nicest resort beach.

If you want to take a day off from diving, Maui also has the famous and spectacularly beautiful Hana Highway, which wraps along the rugged north coast. Here you will get a bird's eye view of the rough windward shoreline, and will have 54 bridges to count if you have children along. At many of these bridges, just upstream from the crossing, you will find waterfalls.

Then there is the majestic and exotic Haleakala crater. The best time to view the 3,000-foot-deep crater is in the early morning, when the crater floor is flooded with the early sun and the hiking trails and cinder cones glow. Haleakala offers excellent hiking, but be careful coordinating your hiking and diving schedules. The elevation gain at Haleakala (to 10,023 ft.) is significant enough to bring on decompression sickness if scaled too soon after diving. Approach ascending Haleakala like you would flying.

DIVING MAUI NUI

Maui is the center of Hawaii's dive industry, with more than 50 dive and snorkel operators (The Big Island is second, with 31, followed by Oahu, with 22). For choice of operators, and variety of sites, Maui— including sites on Molokini, Lanai, and eastern Molokai, which are reached by boat from Maui—is the best the state has to offer.

For practical purposes, we have divided this rich area into six sections: South Shore Maui, covering coastal sites from Maalaea to Kanaio; West End Maui, covering Olowalu north and around to Kahakuloa; Windward Maui, rarely dived shore sites stretching from Paia Bay east to Hana and on around to Manawainui; Molokini, a jewel reached by boat from the South Shore; Kahoolawe, wild and interesting, although currently off-limits; Lanai, reached by boat from Lahaina; and Molokai, reached by boat from Maui or, for the westernmost sites, by local operators.

SOUTH SHORE MAUI

The South Shore sites are reached by boats based in Maalaea Harbor or from the Kihei Boat ramp. A few boats make the run down from Lahaina, but this is becoming less frequent because of the distance. The number of divers vacationing on the South Shore means that the dive business here is thriving, and there are top-rate operations servicing this area. The crews and guides here are among the best in the world, being well-trained and giving exceptionally detailed dive briefings.

The weather on the South Shore is fairly predictable, and you can generally find a lee coast to dive. It is not everywhere the same, however, and you can set out from the Kihei ramp in 40-knot winds only to wind up at Kanaio, say, where it is sunny, and flat calm. Of course on many days you set out in calm water, and dive in

Maui 2000

calm water, only to get beaten senseless on your way home, because the trades came up early.

This is an area of nicely structured rocky points and rich bays. The fish and invertebrate life here is very good, and in many areas the animals can be almost tame. World War II training exercises have blessed this coast with several mil-

The tail gun of a PBY bomber that lies on a 190-foot bottom off The Pali of West Maui. The plane, which lies upside down, is mostly intact.

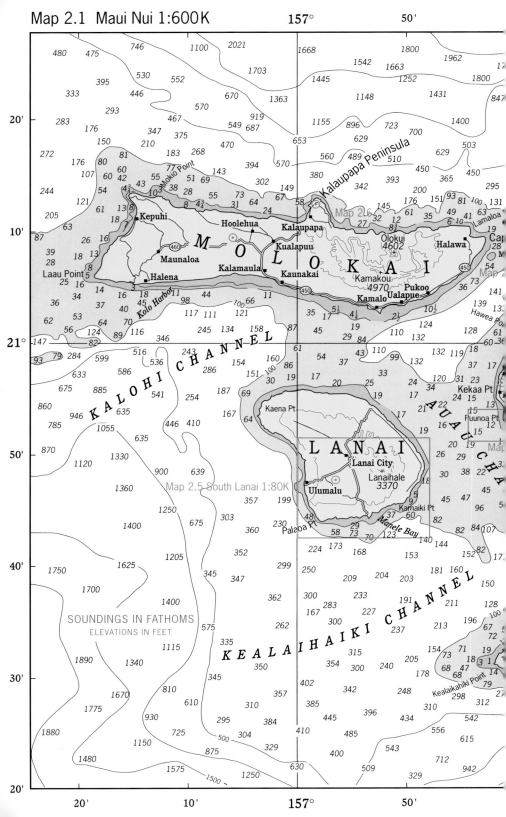

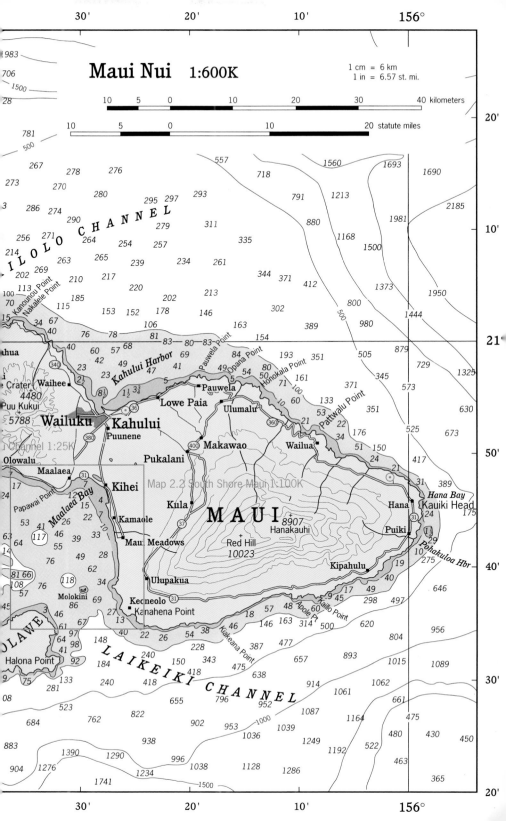

itary artifacts, including vehicles and at least three airplanes.

WEST END MAUI

All of the West End sites are located on the shoreline of West Maui, starting with the rich coral beds of Olowalu and going to the north, through Lahaina, and around Kapalua Point to the underwater monolith called Hidden Pinnacle off Kahakuloa on the north side of the island. These sites are all dived from boats operating out of either Mala Ramp or Lahaina Harbor. Though Hidden Pinnacle rightfully belongs to the windward side of the island, we have included it in this section because on the rare times it is diveable, it is always done from a Lahaina-based boat. Many of the West End dive sites can be done from shore (though not all of them), and even when shore diving these areas it is safer and more fun to hire a guide.

In the middle of the Auau Channel off Lahaina there is some very special deep diving on ledges and caves cut deep into the fossil coral bed. Although magical, the current here can be ferocious, and many of the sites are at tech diving depths—this is not a place for a beginner.

WINDWARD MAUI

After seeing this coast from land, most divers would not consider getting into the water, but for the hearty and experienced it can offer some fine diving. You certainly won't find any crowds. The weather is the determining factor on this coast. From Paia to Hana and around to Nuu the waves are generally big and the wind is strong. You need to pick a calm day, and patience is essential. A headstrong diver will get hurt here.

The rock and sand of this shoreline is darker than that of the lee shores, a product of the constant, heavy waves. These areas are dived almost exclusively by locals.

MOLOKINI ISLAND

This tiny crescent, just three miles off Maui, has become one of

The snowflake eel is commonly seen by divers, and unlike other morays, is often found crawling around in the open, as shown here. Instead of the typical moray canines, this fish has short, stout, molar-like teeth, which help it crack open its favorite food—fresh crab.

Echidna nebulosa Molokini 1988

the world's most famous dive destinations. Set in deep blue water, and with a beautiful clear bay, Molokini is about as good as it gets—whether you are just learning to dive or are practicing your tech diving skills at 300 feet down on the outer wall.

Molokini is a conservation district, so the fish you see there have for the most part learned that divers are non-threatening. These tame subjects offer a unique opportunity for photographers and fish watchers to get close to their subjects.

KAHOOLAWE

Kahoolawe, which is a piece of Haleakala's southwest rift, lies less than seven miles from Maui. In 1993 the island was transferred to native Hawaiian control, and it is now off-limits to divers other than researchers and those helping to survey its resources. This dry island, long abused by the military for target practice, is now being cleaned up of unexploded ordinance. An effort is also underway to restore the native vegetation, and eventually Kahoolawe will be a place where Hawaiians can practice their religion and customs in peace.

There are still many divers around who remember Kahoolawe's famously untamed diving, and especially, its many large sharks. Though it may forever remain restricted to commercial sport diving, we have decided to include a brief mention of the island's dives to aid those lucky few legally permitted to dive this unusual island.

LANAI

Across the channel from Lahaina is the privately owned island of Lanai. One small plantation town, Lanai City, sits high in the center of the island. Since the whole island has a population less than 3,000, calling this settlement a city seems a bit of a stretch, but it has a great lo-

Chlorurus sordidus (male) Hawaii 1996

cation, in the caldera of an old volcano. It is a quaint town, and the last time we visited, a Lanai City resident proudly pointed out that there were now four elevators on the island.

The jail in Lanai City is to be avoided at all cost. It is outdoors, and small enough to cause problems for those with claustrophobia. In fact it is seldom used, since it is easier and cheaper to let minor criminals sleep at home. Any really bad guys can be sent to Maui, if there is such a thing as a bad guy on Lanai. We never met any.

The people of Lanai are a colorful and friendly bunch. You won't see any "No Trespassing" signs here, and it is a great place to rent a jeep and drive around. There are now two upscale resorts here, one at Koele near Lanai City, and another

Parrotfish have strong, fused, beaks with which they scrape algae from rock and dead coral. In the process, they swallow bits of the coral limestone which, when ground by their pharyngeal teeth, becomes sand. In some areas, parrotfish are one of the major producers of coral sand. This specimen is a terminal phase male bullethead parrotfish.

Hawaii's Humpback Whales

OUT ON THE BOAT OFF MAUI'S LEEWARD COAST on a calm winter morning, we hear a sudden, crashing boom, and everyone's head snaps around just in time to see a huge geyser of white water two hundred yards off to starboard. A humpback! We cut the engine and watch. This time we see it: without warning, a forty-foot, forty-ton animal launches itself out of the water, twists in mid-air, and lands on its back with a tremendous crash. Because of the distance, the sound reaches the boat a fraction of a second late, and is almost drowned out by the involuntary ooohs and aahhs coming from our passengers.

A breaching humpback is one of the sea's most spectacular sights. Although several theories have been advanced to explain why a whale might expend so much energy in a breach, one of the most likely is also one of the most obvious: to see what is above the water.

A WHALE NURSERY

Hawaii is the annual winter destination for a migratory population of about 5,000 humpback whales. These whales spend the summer months in the northern Pacific, where herring and smelt are plentiful, and come to Hawaii in the winter to give birth. Swimming to Hawaii takes the whales one to two months, and there is nothing here for them to eat, but Hawaii's waters are warm and free of predators. If the humpbacks gave birth at their feeding grounds, cold water and killer whales would claim many calves.

Because mating and calving take place in Hawaii, the whales spend alot of time on the surface here. Calves need to breathe more often than adults—every three to five minutes—and so they and their mothers are often at the top. During the season in Hawaii, it is not necessary even to go out on a boat to see them—you can watch them from hotel balconies, restaurants, the beach, and even from the side of the road.

Some of the most exciting behavior is produced by males competing for access to a female. While jockeying for the position next to a female (to increase the likelihood of a mating opportunity), the males create a lot of white water and exposed fins and flukes. The female may join in, by rebuffing males with slaps of her flukes and body, or by leading a high-speed chase—either to ditch her suitors, or to test the males for fitness as a partner. Once a male has successfully positioned himself next to a female, she may get frisky, slapping him with her long pectoral fins in courtship.

WHALE SONGS

Male humpbacks in Hawaii produce a distinctive "song," which at thirty minutes, may be the longest call produced by any animal. Since the males sing primarily during the breeding season, it is thought that the songs are a form of male competition.

Divers and even snorkelers sometimes hear these songs underwater. When the whale is within a hundred yards, the sound can be so loud that it vibrates within your chest cavity, but more often the song is coming from far away. Then it sounds eerie and musical, varying from something like moaning, or a lowing cow, to a kind of chuckling.

A few incredibly lucky divers each year find themselves in the presence of whales underwater. Hawaii's humpbacks are protected by law, and swimmers, snorkelers, kayakers, and boat captains are required to stay at least 100 yards away. Thus any underwater encounter is by the whale's choice. Usually there is a calf involved, as juveniles seem to be more curious than adult whales about divers. Nothing compares to the thrill of being approached by a whale underwater.

A NEW THREAT

The Northern Pacific humpback population once numbered 15,000, but by the time commercial hunting of these whales was banned, in 1966, less than a thousand were left. Since then, and since the world moratorium on whaling went into effect in 1986, the group has crept back to about 9,000. But PCBs, ozone depletion, and dredging, blast-

Megaptera novaeangliae Hawaii 1995

During the U.S. Navy's month-long LFA sonar test in Hawaii, in March 1998, humpbacks left the area in droves, 80 percent of the males stopped singing, and perhaps most disturbingly, one humpback and two toothed whales abandoned their calves.

ing, drilling, and boat noise remain threats.

For decades after World War II, U.S. Navy pilots in Hawaii used humpback whales for target practice in war games. This disgusting practice has ended, but the Navy has a new toy that may prove even more damaging: low-frequency active (LFA) sonar. Designed to detect a new generation of silent submarines, this system transmits very high energy sound pulses—up to 235 decibels—that can travel hundreds, or even thousands, of miles.

letting the
and simi-
systems.
and test-
of all ap-
nly when
that puz-
nade the
nar tests.
e been as-
nounced
e Canary
aii, 1999
ahamas.
I massive
s.

In response to the protests that resulted, in 1997 and 1998 the Navy finally conducted a study of the system's impact on whales. They tested at very low power (1/5,000 th intensity, 1/70th sound pressure) and on just four species—blues, fins, grays, and humpbacks—and concluded the sonar's impact is insignificant. This seems rather puzzling given that the Navy's own data shows a 30–80 percent decrease in calling, and that the grays detoured from their migration route.

Even the Navy seems to know their conclusion is specious, since they have applied to the National Marine Fisheries Service for a marine mammal "small take permit." Hearings were held in April and May 2001, but since environmental organizations, members of Congress, and the media are now aware of the threat presented by LFA sonar, the Navy is facing formidable opposition.

Perhaps the Navy should apply for a take permit for scuba divers as well. In 1994 a diver accidentally exposed to an LFA sonar test complained of disorienting chest cavity vibration. This may seem mild, until you realize that the sonar was not at full power, and the ship transmitting it was 100 miles away.

on Manele Bay. There are two harbors on Lanai: Kamalapau Harbor, dredged for commercial shipping, and Manele Harbor, a modified natural harbor used exclusively for small boats.

Much of the bottom around Lanai is a dull sandy slope, but in areas along the south and southwestern sides—wherever there are cliffs on shore—the diving can be spectacular. The south shore in particular is very popular with Lahaina-based operators. Here you can find dramatic arches, cathedral-like caves, pinnacles of rock towering off the bottom, and a few fish, such as lined butterflies, only uncommonly seen off Maui. For those who want to try something a little more exotic, the island casts a wind shadow far out to sea, and on a good day you can do some excellent blue water diving and see pelagic sharks and big game fish.

MOLOKAI

North of Lanai and west of Maui is Molokai, the "Friendly Isle." A glance at a map of Molokai shows something odd: half the island is missing. The entire north shore of Molokai slid off into the sea following an immense earthquake sometime after this island formed 1.9 million years ago. Later, as if to heal the wound, the Kalaupapa Peninsula formed when a small shield volcano erupted at the base of the cliffs on the north shore. This site, isolated by cliffs on one side and water on the other, was chosen for the island's famous leper colony in 1865.

Most Molokai diving is off the south and west shores using the island's land-based operators. Sites on the north shore from Kalaupapa to Mokuhooniki Rock are generally reached by Lahaina-based boats, with Mokuhooniki Rock being the closest and thus the more frequently dived.

Off the western end of Molokai the Penguin Bank extends to the southwest for forty miles or more. This expanse of relatively shallow water is a remnant of the ancient Maui Nui island.

The Hawaiian longfin anthias is one of the most beautiful of the islands' fairy basslets. At first, ichthyologist John E. Randall considered this fish to be merely a larger and more brightly colored subspecies of P. ventralis, but he has recently determined that it is different enough to warrant its own species designation.

Pseudanthias hawaiiensis Molokini 1997

EASY, VARIED, AND RICH

South Shore Maui
An Area with Something for Everyone

Maui's South Shore is a large, sandy basin, formed over hundreds of thousands of years as sand blowing across the island's isthmus has collected on the relatively shallow, flat bottom connecting the islands of Maui Nui. This is a very different habitat from the Big Island's raw lava cliffs and outcrops. On the South Shore you will find sandy bays, extensive reefs of finger coral, and a very healthy population of fish and invertebrates.

This habitat suits a different set of animals from the Big Island or other rough and rocky coasts. For example, here is one of the best places in Hawaii to find frogfish, the beautiful and otherwise rare dragon moray (*Enchelycore pardalis*), and a number of interesting sand-dwelling species. Lest you begin to think this coast is all one big "critter dive," note that the South Shore is also a preferred calving site for humpback whales, and that it has one of the largest resident green turtle populations in the islands.

The habitat along this coast—shallow sandy bays, flat expanses of coral, and rocky outcrops—nicely complements Molokini's steep walls and slopes, and a few days or a week of diving both makes for a nice mix of underwater experiences. (For locations of the sites below, see Map 2.2, pp. 88–89.)

MAALAEA BAY

This interesting dive site is, well, a huge, flat, featureless expanse of gray, silty sand. Tired of coral, clear water, and brightly colored reef fish? Then this is the place for you.

The **Maalaea Mud Flats** is a tough sell without explanation, but for the more curious or experienced diver this dive comes with a guarantee you won't get at most sites—here you are sure to see something you've never seen before, and usually it's something bizarre.

A mostly flat mix of sand, coral, and rock, at least until you get to the southern points, this coast is easy and convenient to dive, and a great place to find interesting animals.

For example, this eerie expanse of silt is home to thousands of long-eyed swimming crabs (*Podophthalmus* sp.). An occasional individual lets you get close enough to see it, half-tucked into its burrow (sideways), with one incredibly long eyestalk raised up like a periscope. Eventually you get too close, and the eyestalk snaps down into its carapace and the crab scoots deep into its burrow.

It is at this point that you realize that this wasteland is not really featureless. Little trails radiate out from each crab burrow, connecting one to another in an endless network. In fact, tracks are everywhere, because living on and just beneath this surface is a host of animals—small fish, crabs and foraging shrimps, mollusks, sea urchins, brittle stars and sea stars, and anemones.

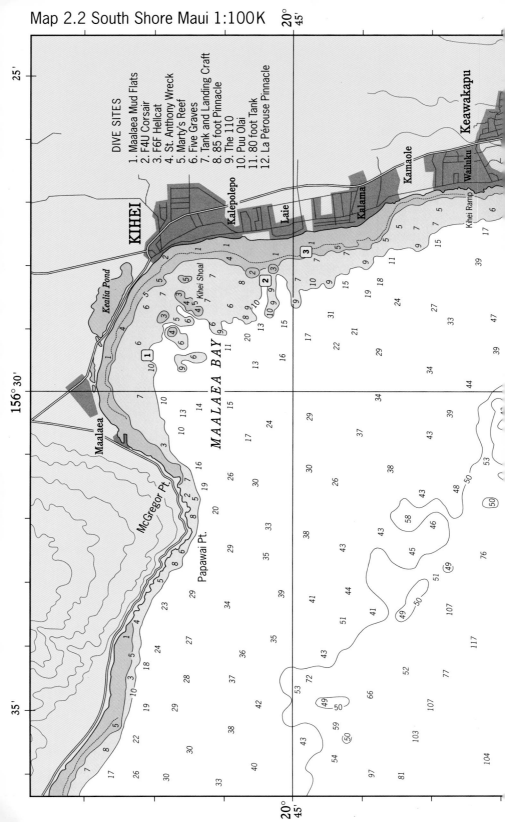

Map 2.2 South Shore Maui 1:100K

DIVE SITES
1. Maalaea Mud Flats
2. F4U Corsair
3. F6F Hellcat
4. St. Anthony Wreck
5. Marty's Reef
6. Five Graves
7. Tank and Landing Craft
8. 85 foot Pinnacle
9. The 110
10. Puu Olai
11. 80 foot Tank
12. La Pérouse Pinnacle

KIHEI

Kealia Pond

Kalepolepo

Laie

Kihei Shoal

Kalama

Kamaole

Wailuku

Keawakapu

Kihei Ramp

MAALAEA BAY

Maalaea

McGregor Pt.

Papawai Pt.

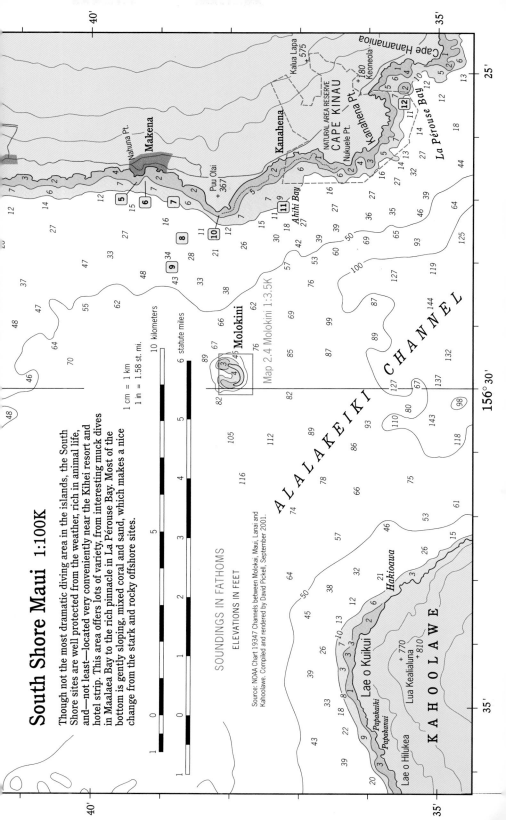

South Shore Maui 1:100K

Though not the most dramatic diving area in the islands, the South Shore sites are well protected from the weather, rich in animal life, and—not least—located very conveniently near the Kihei resort and hotel strip. This area offers lots of variety, from interesting muck dives in Maalaea Bay to the rich pinnacle in La Pérouse Bay. Most of the bottom is gently sloping, mixed coral and sand, which makes a nice change from the stark and rocky offshore sites.

SOUNDINGS IN FATHOMS

ELEVATIONS IN FEET

Source: NOAA Chart 19347 Channels between Molokai, Maui, Lanai and Kahoolawe. Compiled and rendered by David Pickell, September 2001.

1 cm = 1 km
1 in = 1.58 st. mi.

10 kilometers

6 statute miles

Makena

Nahuna Pt.

Puu Olai
+ 367

Kanahena

Kalua Lapa
+ 575

Keoneola
+ 180

Kanahena Pt.

Nukele Pt.

NATURAL AREA RESERVE
CAPE KINAU

Cape Hanamanioa

La Pérouse Bay

Ahihi Bay

Map 2.4 Molokini 1:3.5K

Molokini

ALALAKEIKI CHANNEL

KAHOOLAWE

Lae o Kuikui

Lua Kealialuna
+ 770
+ 810

Papakaiki
Papakanui

Lae o Hilukea

Hakioawa

Maui 1984

Puu olai, on the western side of Maui's southernmost tip, points westward toward Molokini. This was a popular fishing spot for the ancient Hawaiians, and two sets of pinnacles, just northwest of the tip, offer some excellent diving.

Thousands of shrimp gobies and their snapping shrimp partners can also be found living on the soft bottom of the bay. Digging and maintaining the burrow is the shrimp's work, while the goby perches just outside the hole watching for danger. If you are stealthy enough to get close without disturbing the goby, you can see the shrimp, claws full of sand, shovel out the burrow like a tiny bulldozer. It then backs into the burrow for another load. When the goby feels threatened, it turns and dives head-first into the hole (with apparent disregard for the shrimp's location at that instant).

At the southern end of the bay is one of Hawaii's many World War II–era casualties, a badly damaged **F6F Hellcat** which crashed just off Lipoa Street. The wreck was further modified in a 1980 storm. The airplane sits upside-down, and hosts a fish community that includes a little Hawaiian damselfish—also damaged (in his dorsal fin)—which has lived there for eight years.

About a mile north of the Hellcat is the tantalizing debris trail of an **F4U Corsair**, the engine of which has never been found.

KIHEI

Piloting the wreck of the *St. Anthony* through its first few years on the bottom off Kihei was a pair of Commerson's frogfish. These turned each dive into a game of hide and seek as they found more and more places to perch. The 65-foot longliner seemed to be big enough for the two of them, as long as they gave each other space. Several times a year, however, the male could be found pressing against the female with his pectoral fin as she swelled with eggs. After spawning, they returned to their separate lives on different parts of the boat.

The *St. Anthony* was sunk in October 1997 on the site of a desig-

Not everything here is small, either. You approach a mound of silt, with two eyes showing, and suddenly a great patch of the bottom quivers and levitates, as a six-foot stingray lifts off the bottom and undulates into flight.

One of the clownfish host anemones is found in Hawaii, and Maalaea is where it can be seen. Clark's anemonefish, which lives in this anemone (*Heteractis malu*) elsewhere in the Indo-Pacific region, has not yet colonized Hawaii, nor have any other clownfish species (they have a very short larval stage, only about a week). But juvenile Hawaiian damselfish hover near the stinging tentacles of the pancake-sized anemones, and small crabs live just under the edge of the crown of tentacles.

nated artificial reef area off Wailea. This reef was started 45 years ago when 150 automobiles were dropped to the bottom. The cars have now dissolved away, but the *St. Anthony* rests among hundreds of tires embedded in concrete blocks. It was interesting to watch the wreck "season," as it were. It was first colonized by algae, then coralline algae, and finally, after the second year, hard coral colonies began to grow on the ship.

The turtle population off the Kihei coast took advantage of the wreck, with several taking up residence immediately, finding the hold a perfect shelter. More turtles rest among the tires, where they are as well-camouflaged as in any natural reef area. The artificial reef also shelters fish, lobsters, nudibranchs, and many other species of animals.

MAKENA

Five Graves (Nahuna Point) off Makena used to be one of Maui's best shore dives, but runoff and dive and snorkel boat pressure have degraded this site. One by one, large antler corals were brought down by carelessly placed anchors and chains—not storm surf, as some like to claim—and runoff from development onshore has choked the young coral colonies. Some picturesque caverns, arches and lava formations, covered with multi-colored sponges and orange cup coral, are still interesting, and frequently house turtles and whitetip reef sharks. The site of a well-used turtle cleaning station is obvious even when the turtles are not present, since the coral is ground down by their frequent rubbing to scour colonizing organisms from their shells. Starting your dive further out, from a boat, means better visibility and more turtle sightings.

Because of its protected location, Makena Landing (the entry point for the shore dive) was busy during

the 1800s. Here cotton, sugar, poultry, and pineapples and other produce were loaded onto steamers for transport to the other islands. Cattle were driven by cowboys on horseback to swim out to waiting boats, from which they were transferred to the steamships. To this day, coal from the many steamships that stopped here can still be found

Chelonia mydas Hawaii 1995

rolling around on the sea bottom.

Just out from Five Graves is a boat dive site called **Marty's Reef**. The site is named after Marty Oschner, a long-time Maui diver who retired from diving in 1999 at the age of 86. For many years this living room–sized reef was his favorite dive. It is the only shelter in the middle of an area of open sand, and is thus packed with fish. The fish,

Adult green sea turtles are for the most part vegetarians. Here one chomps algae from a coral knob.

Belly-up at 190 Feet

Tail turret with twin
50-caliber machine guns

This aircraft, a late version Consolidated PB4Y-1 Liberator bomber (a Navy version of the B-24), lies on a 190-foot sand bottom a couple miles off The Pali in South Maui. The fuselage and main wings are upside down; the tail section is upright. Much of the fuselage is crumpled and buried under the port wing. The four Pratt & Whitney engines show varying degrees of damage. The cockpit is crushed and almost unrecognizable. The bomb bay doors are open. The wreck sits out in the open, and is always swarming with taape and big ulua. It is a beautiful, pristine wreck, if a little on the deep side.

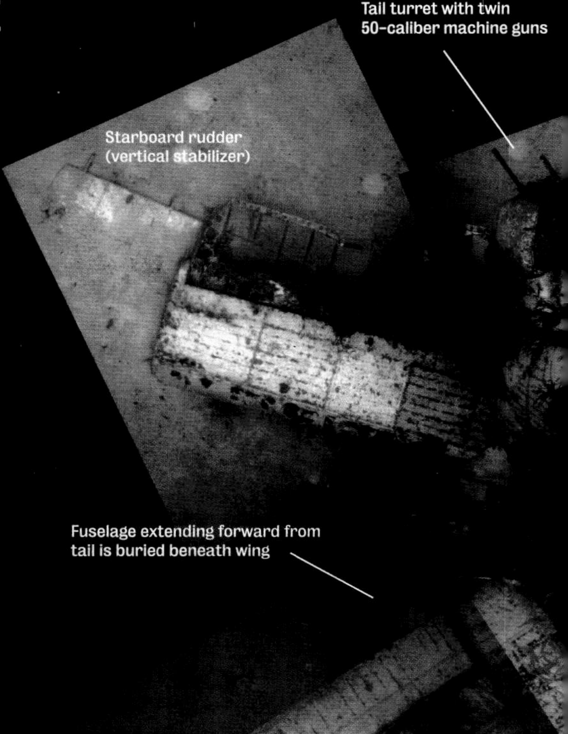

Starboard rudder
(vertical stabilizer)

Fuselage extending forward from
tail is buried beneath wing

Hard coral growth

Heavily damaged engine

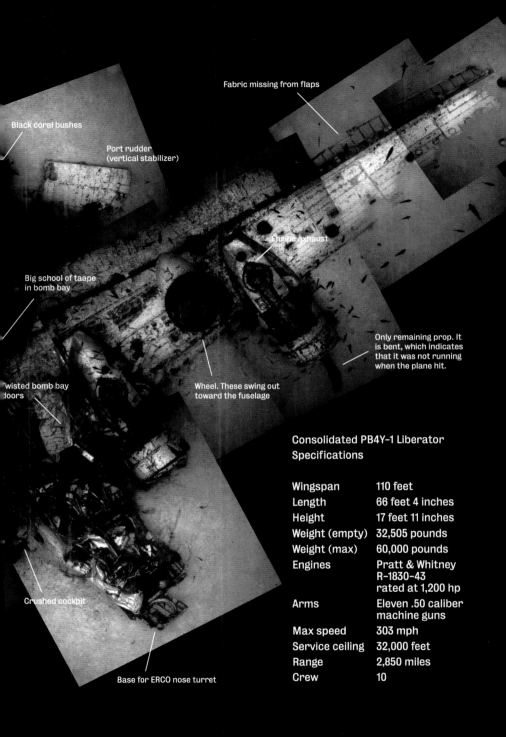

Fabric missing from flaps

Black coral bushes

Port rudder
(vertical stabilizer)

Engine exhaust

Big school of taape
in bomb bay

Only remaining prop. It
is bent, which indicates
that it was not running
when the plane hit.

wisted bomb bay
doors

Wheel. These swing out
toward the fuselage

Crushed cockpit

Base for ERCO nose turret

Consolidated PB4Y-1 Liberator
Specifications

Wingspan	110 feet
Length	66 feet 4 inches
Height	17 feet 11 inches
Weight (empty)	32,505 pounds
Weight (max)	60,000 pounds
Engines	Pratt & Whitney R-1830-43 rated at 1,200 hp
Arms	Eleven .50 caliber machine guns
Max speed	303 mph
Service ceiling	32,000 feet
Range	2,850 miles
Crew	10

Monachus schauinslandi and Homo sapiens   Molokini 1997

This young male monk seal appeared irregularly at Molokini for about seven months in 1997. He seemed to crave companionship, and would swim among the snorkelers for hours. He could also get rather horny, and would grab snorkelers from behind, wrap his flippers around them, and bite their backs. Pauline, in the photograph above, suggests wearing a wetsuit was a very good idea during that period. The seal, identifiable by a scar above his right eye, still appears in the area once in a while, and was seen as recently as September 2001.

Remember that it is against the law to approach monk seals. The individual in the photo above did the approaching, and his was an unusual case. Beyond the question of legality, it is very unlikely that a monk seal will appreciate your attentions.

mainly *taape* and goatfish, hover here during the day, and disperse over the sand at night to hunt mollusks, worms and shrimp.

This is a small, but wonderful spot, particularly if you are accompanied by a good guide. Male Hawaiian damselfish can be seen courting females or guarding nests of eggs, lobsters collect in large holes, octopus guard their eggs in a den, trumpetfish stalk smaller fish, devil scorpionfish lay in wait, leaf scorpionfish mimic debris, and occasionally frogfish take up residence.

South of Marty's Reef, in 60 feet of water, are the remains of two World War II amphibious vehicles, usually called AMTRACS (from amphibious tractor) or officially called LVTs (Landing Vehicle Tracked). **The Tank**, an LVT(A)-4, has a collapsed turret with its 75 mm Howitzer clearly visible. The other vehicle, about 75 yards downcurrent, is an LVT-4 locally referred to as the **Landing Craft**.

These vehicles were lost during the war with their full complement

of guns, ammunition, and their crews' personal gear. Unfortunately, amphibious work meant they were only lightly armored, and they have degraded rapidly underwater. The special treads, designed for pushing through water, are still intact, and Howitzer rounds can still be seen around the tank and in the tubes below the turret.

As Hawaii's green turtle population has rebounded, they have begun to occupy deeper areas such as these vehicles. Sometimes as many as seven can be seen in and around the Landing Craft—one or two taking up the positions of the driver and assistant driver.

PUU OLAI

At the **85-foot Pinnacle**, off the Puu olai cinder cone, two large lava pinnacles and several smaller rocks protrude up through fossil coral covered by a thin layer of sand. These pinnacles are the only landmarks in an often current-swept area, and each supports a school of *taape,* which form a dense forma-

Synodus variegatus Hawaii 1995

tion on the up-current side of the pinnacles. The fish pack tightly together, facing into the current.

The ancient Hawaiians used to fish this area by lowering a package of chum to the bottom using a smooth beach stone. Once it hit bottom they jerked the line to open the package. The stone fell to the bottom and the chum was carried downcurrent, where it attracted fish to their baited hooks. Each time the line was lowered, a new stone was used, and today divers can see thousands of these stones on the bottom. Rarer, though still occasionally found on the site, are carved stone sinkers. These were used as part of octopus lures, and to hold fishing line and hooks in place when the current was strong.

Further out, a series of lava pinnacles emerges from the sand to form a rock cluster covering several acres known as **The 110** because of their depth. Because of the depth, and therefore reduced competition from light-requiring competitors, the rocks here are densely covered with a brilliant red sponge. Without a light it appears almost black. Frogfish in this area frequently assume the red color of the sponge and are beautiful (but challenging to find). Although black coral was harvested from these pinnacles years ago, there is still good growth of two species, with longnose hawkfish perched among the branches.

Puu olai is a nearshore site just off the tip of the cinder cone. Because there is often current here, this is usually done as a boat drift dive. Most of the dive is between 35 and 45 feet with 20-foot-high lava ridges running perpendicular to shore alternating with sand channels and reefs of finger coral.

Divers are usually dropped in well before the point, where many different species of eels can be seen, including an infrequent dragon eel. In spring, young manta rays, their cavernous mouths open, scoop up copepods hovering here along the edges of rocks.

There is a picturesque cavern right on the point. The black lava

Lizardfish might look vaguely reptilian, but they are much less skittish than their namesake. This pair seems perfectly calm. Note the teeth, however. These are estimable predators, and can take a fish that weighs almost half what they do.

silhouetted against blue makes a beautiful backdrop for any turtle or shark that happens to enter or exit. Lizardfish and scorpionfish take advantage of the dappled light and lay in wait. In the surge above the cavern, young turtles feed on long filamentous algae.

AHIHI BAY AND LA PÉROUSE BAY

Maui's most recent lava flow poured into the sea 500 years ago between Puu olai and Cape Hanamanoia, creating Ahihi Bay and La Pérouse Bay. Waters within about 2,500 feet of shore around this point (roughly the 70-foot contour) are part of a Natural Area Reserve. Motorized vessels may not enter, and fishing and taking anything is, of course, prohibited.

Plunked in a huge expanse of sand in Ahihi Bay sits another LVT(A)-4 AMTRAC, called the **80-foot Tank** because of its depth. Its isolated location has made it a popular shelter for fish that feed at night in the featureless sand around it. It is such good shelter that it is often

difficult to distinguish the tank through the nebula of fish hovering around it. Octopus nest in the safety of its crevices year after year, and lobsters emerge at night to feed. Only about 30 feet long, this wreck is apparently big enough for only one frogfish—typically that post is held by a small Commerson's or Hawaiian freckled frogfish (*Antennarius drombus*).

If you aren't one hundred percent sure where this isolated island of life lies, you must at least entertain the possibility of doing the entire dive in open sand. If this happens, fortunately there are holes in the flat fossil coral bottom where you can find moray eels, cleaner shrimp and triggerfish. Razor wrasses and tilefish find some refuge in the open, and mantis shrimp thrive here.

Encircled by lava flows, La Pérouse Bay (Keoneoio) is somewhat protected from the easterly winds and surf that pound the shoreline coming out of the Alenuihaha Channel, and as a result the bay is the daytime shelter for a pod

Reef flounders are among the absolute masters of camouflage. This talent, combined with the fish's low profile, serves it well as cover while it sneaks up on its prey. Members of the genus Bothus are called lefteye flounders, because during development the right eye migrates to the animal's port side.

Bothus mancus Molokini 1996

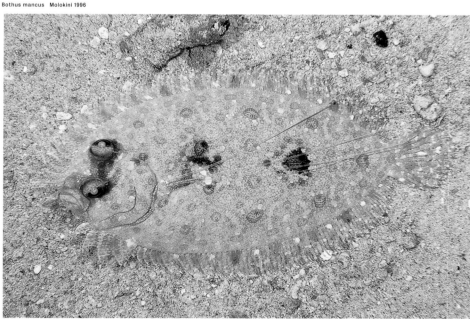

of Hawaiian spinner dolphins. In the deeper water, near the center of this otherwise monotonously flat bay, rises a miraculous lava ridge called the **La Pérouse Bay Pinnacle**. The ridge juts up from about 70 feet and rises to just a few feet below the surface. With all of its small cracks and arches it supports a large number of plankton-feeders. Long used by ships, the old mooring chain can still be seen at the base of the ridge's highest point.

Cauliflower coral thrives in shallow water on the ridge providing food for a few crown-of-thorns sea stars. Around the periphery, at about 50 feet where finger coral reef begins, are languid schools of nocturnal goatfish and soldierfish waiting out the day. Where the finger coral meets sand, at around 70 feet, helmet shells feed and lay their egg cases. Although covering a relatively small area, this pinnacle is home to a remarkable variety of fish, including rarely seen species such as flame and bandit angelfish, the bird wrasse, and the stocky hawkfish.

The bay gets its name from the French navigator Jean de Galaup, Comte de la Pérouse, the first documented European to land on Maui, who came ashore for a few hours in May of 1786 at Keoneoio (which Vancouver later renamed La Pérouse Bay). Although honored for this discovery, La Pérouse's captain thought that the Hawaiians had encountered Westerners before, probably Spaniards, since they immediately wanted to barter their pigs and vegetables for iron.

KANAIO

The distinct earthy smell of wet lichen coming off the mountain just before reaching La Pérouse Bay is the first hint of Kanaio's undeveloped, rugged slopes ahead. As the boat rounds the southernmost point of Maui (Cape Hanamanioa) a stunning view of vast ranch land,

Hypselodoris paulinae   Molokini 1991

untouchable lava flows, and abandoned Hawaiian villages provides a sharp contrast to the perfectly laid-out golf courses and planned resort communities left behind a half-hour before. The surf here is relentless, and the beaches consist of chunks of white coral coughed up by the sea. Massive logs and tree trunks, some of them having washed here from as far away as Southeast Asia and the Pacific Northwest lie bleaching in the sun.

The coastline just west of **Kamanamana Point** is marked by a dramatic formation of columnar basalt. It is as if the cliffs were built up of great, six-sided pilings of black rock. Seeing this geological feature from the boat while gearing up is interesting enough, but diving along it is even better.

This beautiful nudibranch was discovered by the co-author at about 150 feet on the backside of Molokini. It seems to be very rare, and since its discovery, only three others have been found, all off Oahu. With all the scientists who have been in the water in Hawaii, most new species are drab little things trawled out of the sand at 500 feet. Finding this one was not bad going at all. Good work, Pauline.

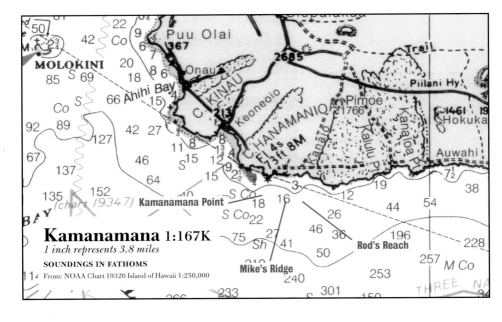

Kamanamana 1:167K
1 inch represents 3.8 miles
SOUNDINGS IN FATHOMS
From: NOAA Chart 19320 Island of Hawaii 1:250,000

Underwater, the face of the formation at Kamanamana stands 30 feet high. The columns are perfectly smooth, and so massive that they escape notice at first. This pattern forms when a basaltic magma cools slowly, on the inside of the flow. When the sea level was lower, surf carved arches into the edge of this flow, and now that it has again risen, these arches, covered with orange cup coral and sponges, provide beautiful relief.

The top of the formation has a completely different feel. Here the lava is a type called aa, rough and jagged, which cooled quickly and formed an insulating crust. Kamanamana is a beautiful site, and the animal life here is diverse.

Further along is **Mike's Ridge**, which rises 20 feet above the bottom. White sand borders it on one side, and a lava flow on the other. The ridge literally swarms with fish, including a huge school of *taape*. Frogfish, lobsters, and the vampire moray—more common on this side of the island—are easy to find here.

East of Mike's Ridge, on the other side of the lava flow, is a stunning expanse of black lava pinnacles and ridges called **Rod's Reach**. Antler coral trees grow here, and yellow tangs and red-and-white striped squirrelfish hide among their branches, instead of the Hawaiian damselfish seen almost everywhere else. On a good day, the stark formations on white sand bottom here offer one of the best underwater views on the island.

A wash rock just off a point called Pohaku eaea, or "The Rock that Smells of the Sea," marks a site called the **Kanaio Arches**. Underwater here three arches melt together. The formation houses a community of surge zone inhabitants such as surgeonfish and lobsters, and is blanketed on top by leathery gray mats of zoanthids, about the only invertebrate able to withstand the pounding surf at the exposed tip of the island. On the seaward side, the bottom drops off steeply, and schools of pyramid butterflyfish hover along the drop—a site more redolent of the Big Island than elsewhere on Maui.

West End Maui

Easy Shore Sites and a Wild Channel

MOST LAHAINA DIVE OPERATORS load up their clients in the morning and head out to dive the lava formations off Lanai. The coastal sites on Maui's West End, in comparison, seem tame. Still, there are some rich and interesting sites here, and since they are shallow and protected, these can be more suitable for less experienced divers. Interested in something more adventurous? Try the deep, current-swept ledges in the middle of the Auau Channel—we guarantee a memorable dive here.

Inshore along the West End the current is almost always light, and the West Maui mountains block the afternoon trade winds from Olowalu all the way up past Kaanapali, often leaving the water glass calm. Surf can be an issue, especially during the summer, but even that rarely interferes with the diving, though entering and leaving Lahaina Harbor can be interesting with a large swell.

MALA WHARF AND BLACK ROCK

If the water is clear, **Mala Wharf** can be one of your most memorable Maui shore dives (see chart page 106). In 1922 the Territory of Hawaii erected Mala Wharf as an alternative to the perilous Lahaina Harbor. But its exposure to strong currents and large swell was its downfall (literally), and today the 300-foot pier is the site of an excellent shallow dive.

The pilings are covered with sponges, hydroids, algae, and corals. Frogfish are common, as are camouflaged lizardfish and scorpionfish. This is consistently the best place to see some of Hawaii's larger nudibranchs. Look carefully on the yellow sponge for the yellow *Noumea* nudibranch, a screaming yellow dorid and its matching yellow egg mass.

Further out, massive fallen pillars and concrete slabs, viewed against a backdrop of crystal blue water, create an exotic, futuristic scene. Openings in the rubble provide shelter for a myriad of small reef fish,

This area, usually bypassed by divers anxious to get to Lanai, offers some nice calm sites for interesting small subjects, and a deep, current-swept channel.

as well as many of the larger reef species, including porcupine puffers, peacock groupers, sailfin tangs, the rare lined butterflyfish, turtles, and even whitetip reef sharks. Divers have been able to clean up most of the litter cast down here over the years when the wharf was standing, although you still find the occasional shopping cart.

As the sun sinks into the ocean at the end of every day, the Hawaiians bid farewell to the spirits of their deceased. Each island has a prominent western point where the spirits of the dead would leap out into the spirit world. Kekaa Point was

Map 2.3 Auau Channel 1:25K

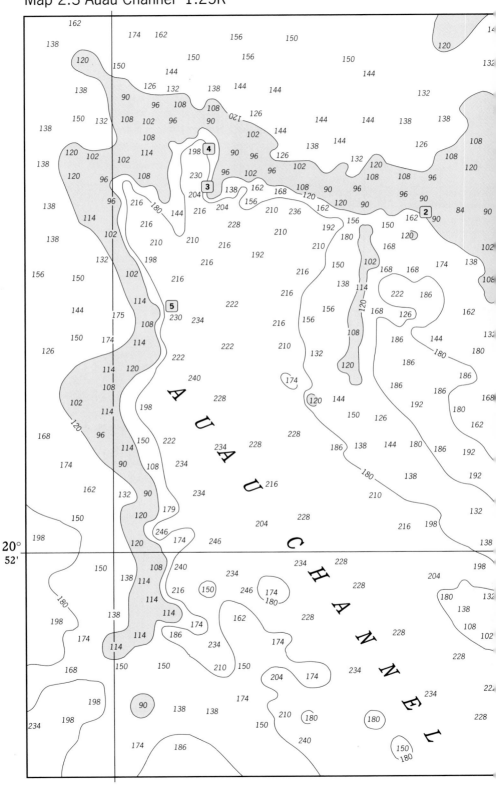

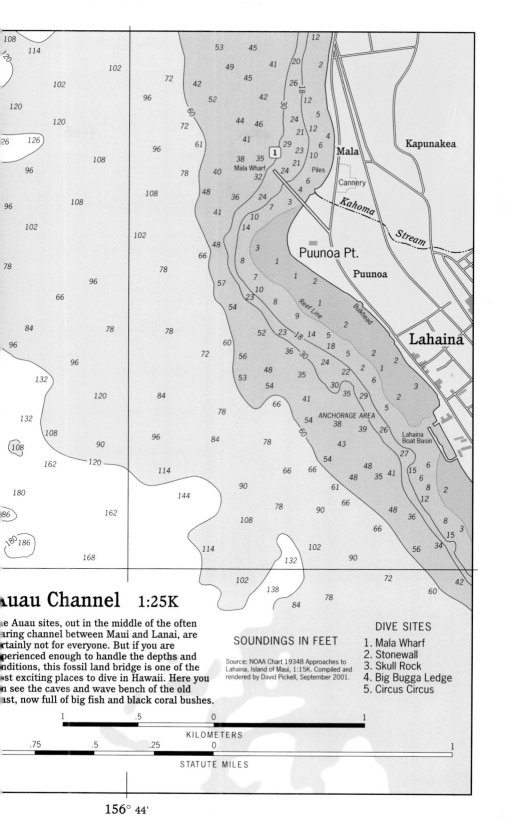

Auau Channel 1:25K

...e Auau sites, out in the middle of the often ...aring channel between Maui and Lanai, are ...rtainly not for everyone. But if you are ...perienced enough to handle the depths and ...nditions, this fossil land bridge is one of the ...st exciting places to dive in Hawaii. Here you ...n see the caves and wave bench of the old ...ast, now full of big fish and black coral bushes.

SOUNDINGS IN FEET

Source: NOAA Chart 19348 Approaches to Lahaina, Island of Maui, 1:15K. Compiled and rendered by David Pickell, September 2001.

DIVE SITES

1. Mala Wharf
2. Stonewall
3. Skull Rock
4. Big Bugga Ledge
5. Circus Circus

Mala

Kapunakea

Mala Wharf

Piles

Cannery

Kahoma

Stream

Puunoa Pt.

Puunoa

Reef Line

Bulkhead

Lahaina

Lahaina Boat Basin

ANCHORAGE AREA

KILOMETERS

STATUTE MILES

156° 44'

Maui's sacred leaping place, and may still be, though it is currently occupied by the Sheraton Hotel. Around this prominent point is one of the most dived sites in Kaanapali, **Black Rock**.

Black Rock is an eroded cinder cone that extends into the water, forming a wall, steeper on the north side, about 20 feet high. In addition

Carcharhinus amblyrhynchos   Off Kihei 1989

All requiem sharks must maintain forward movement in order to get water past their gills, so when this gray reef shark became snared in an old fishing net it suffocated.

to the many reef fish, which have grown bold from years of fish feeding, Black Rock has a large resident school of bigeye scad (*akule*), and eagle rays and turtles are common.

At night, fragile harlequin shrimp creep out of hiding to search for sea stars, and rare nocturnal nudibranchs emerge from the rocks. Conger eels are common here, and on a night dive it can be

alarming when they appear suddenly and suck up fish that have been blinded by your dive light.

MAUI'S NORTHERN TIP

Further north along the coast are a series of well protected bays which provide relatively easy shore diving, except during periods of northwest swell in winter. The first of these, **Kapalua Bay**, is a shallow, well-protected site that is highly recommended as a night dive. Most memorable are the numerous Borradaile's ghost shrimp. Without leaving the protection of their burrows, they constantly wave their large, bright-red claws in the water. All this work for bits of algae—their only food. Also found here on most night dives are squid, which come in from deeper water to feed.

A couple miles further north is picturesque **Honolua Bay**, literally "protected bay," a haven from both the trade winds and from fishing pressures. Honolua (and **Mokuleia Bay**, one-half mile to the south) has been part of a Marine Life Conservation District for 22 years, and it shows in the health of this reef. This is one of only two protected areas on the island (the other is in the south between Ahihi and La Pérouse Bays) and taking anything, alive or dead, is prohibited.

Along either side of Honolua Bay are collapsed lava tubes, small walls of lava, and piles of large boulders which provided shelter for many small animals. The hard coral in the bay is very well-developed. Some lobe coral colonies on the north side reach 20 feet in height, and you can also find the rare blue rice coral (*Montipora flabellata*) here, one of the few blue animals encountered while diving in the shallows. A pod of Hawaiian spinner dolphins moves into these protected waters for resting and socializing during the day.

Mokuleia is similar to Honolua,

and both are best done from a boat. On the northernmost tip of the island is **Nakalele Point**, which can be dived from shore only with difficulty—we recommend a boat, although it is usually a rough ride. The point is one of very few places on Maui that could be considered a wall dive. The dive is on a rock ridge, topped by a navigation light, that juts out perpendicular to the coast. The ridge runs down to 130 feet before hitting sand and rubble.

Around the point, five miles past Nakalele, you come to Kahakuloa and **Hidden Pinnacle**. Almost a half mile offshore, and just about in the middle of the bay formed by Kahakuloa Head and Hakuhee Point, this site is a pinnacle of rock that comes straight up off a 100-foot, dark sand bottom. On a rough day whitewater marks the top of the pinnacle, and it occasionally even breaks through the swell.

The pinnacle is covered with hydroids and sponges, and attracts and shelters a variety of plankton-feeding and bottom-feeding fish. It

From "Maui: How it came to be" by Will Kyselka and Ray Lanterman, University of Hawaii Press 1995. Used by permission of the author.

is not unusual to see gray sharks and *ulua* here, as well as lots of gray snappers coming in off the open sand. *Menpachi* crowd every nook, and a school of *taape* manages to stay one step ahead of net fishermen on the nearly round pinnacle. Scorpion fish are common, as are barracuda and a very large school of sleek unicornfish.

THE AUAU CHANNEL

Today, the Auau Channel between West Maui and Lanai is an

Black Rock, as it must have looked when the cinder cone was still active. Illustration by Ray Lanterman.

The whitetip reef shark is a common, quite harmless species. Despite its species moniker, it is also rather slender. It is a bottom-feeder on fish, crustaceans, and octopuses.

Triaenodon obesus; also Lutjanus kasmira, etc.   Hawaii 1990

Anampses chrysocephalus Hawaii 1992

Luidia magnifica Molokini 1989

The psychedelic wrasse sucks up worms, small crustaceans, and any other tasty morsels it can find from the bottom, and then blows the excess sand out its gills (as shown here). It is endemic to Hawaii.

A sun star buries itself in the sand. This is an interesting thing to watch, as it looks as if the animal is melting into the bottom.

area of fast-flowing and relatively shallow water, most of it 60 to 250 feet deep. But many thousands of years ago, when sea levels were lower, this channel was an expanse of rich, shallow reef. It must have been spectacularly beautiful, a sea of beiges, greens, and bright yellows, split by white sand channels, that stretched for miles. Most of this reef would have lain just a few feet below the surface, and in the lee of West Maui, the water would have been calm and the skies clear.

Eventually, the sea level rose and flooded this reef. On a good bathymetric map of the area, you can still see the bottom relief from the old bays and channels. And, although few people think of this, this fossil reef offers some exciting and very unusual diving.

We have listed just four sites, all

on the edge of just one of these old bays (see below and MAP 2.3, pp. 100–101). This is just a taste of the excellent diving in this area. If you had a boat and the time to spare, exploring the walls and ledges of the Auau Channel could easily turn into a lifetime hobby.

To anyone used to diving Hawaii's coastal sites, it is unnerving the first time you stop your boat and anchor this far offshore. These sites are more than three miles out, and from this distance the Lahaina and Kaanapali hotels look like toys. You won't get any jetskis or parasail boats this far out. Your only company is an occasional fishing boat working the deep ledges for *ulua*.

Though these sites border on deep water, they are not impossibly deep themselves. Most are within the recreational diving limits. Still, this is definitely not an area for inexperienced or tentative divers. The flow that moves through the channel gets trapped in underwater bays and funneled over coral ledges and walls, creating some formidable currents. Even if it is calm when you start, current can come up suddenly in the course of a dive, and you should always plan your diving here accordingly. Unless you want to experiment with new forms of inter-island travel, or to meet new people in bright orange overalls with "U.S. Coast Guard" stenciled on them, you should be very careful on these sites. An experienced dive guide and boat captain are essential.

DIVING THE FOSSIL REEF

Three miles off Lahaina, an 80-foot pinnacle of fossilized coral rises from a 200-foot bottom. On the top of this pinnacle is a rock formation that looks so much like a human skull it is unnerving. This is **Skull Rock**. It stares out into deep water like a sentinel. The first time you see it, slightly narc'ed from the depth, it will bring Indiana Jones to mind. The formation is large enough to accommodate several seldom-seen yellow anthias, which live in the eye sockets and a small cave behind the face. Cup corals and red sponges give the skull color.

A friend of mine once did a night dive here, just to see what might swim through his light. He anchored his boat at sunset and, well after dark, pulled himself down the anchor line, swam across the bottom and rose up the outside of the pinnacle to the skull. Then he sat down in the eye socket of a giant skull, 100 feet underwater, three miles offshore, alone, and in the dark— watching the beam of his light. Nothing much happened, so after about 20 minutes he went up. He is certain he gained something from the experience of that night, but other than a state of sustained adrenaline-enhanced consciousness, he is still not sure what.

Not far from Skull Rock is a legendary site called **Stonewall**. This is a wall, formed by the edge of the ancient reef, that runs perpendicular to the Auau Channel across the head of a large submerged bay. The floor of the bay is more than 200 feet deep, but the top of Stonewall is only 100 feet. Water, flowing through a 200-foot-deep channel, encounters Stonewall and is diverted upward like an underwater river.

This dive site can actually be seen from the surface. Around Stonewall, the surface is full of boils, smooth patches formed by the strong upcurrent. It is an upside-down waterfall of a sort, and to dive it you have to pull down an anchor line against the current (if you can—sometimes this current here is too strong even to pull against). Once you reach the top of the ledge, you haul yourself over the lip, where the current is always raging. But as soon as you are over the lip you reach quiet water. You can then sit on the 150-foot bottom in front

of an undercut, and watch your bubbles rise lazily until they are grabbed, shattered, and swept away by the current above your head.

When the sea level was lower, Stonewall was inside of a large bay, so it is remarkably constant in depth along its half-mile length. Along most of this length it is undercut, caused by wave action over

Heniochus diphreutes, Antennarius sp. Molokini 1990

the many years it was a shoreline. Living in this undercut are magnificent black coral trees with longnose hawkfish, and butterflyfish and other planktonic feeders shelter beneath the ledge, particularly when the current is strong. Other visitors to Stonewall are gray sharks, giant *ulua,* and the usually invisible tiger shark.

Across the submerged bay from

An old black coral tree, 220 feet deep off Molokini, provides shelter for a group of butterflyfish. The pinkish lump in the center of the sponge-encrusted bush is a frogfish.

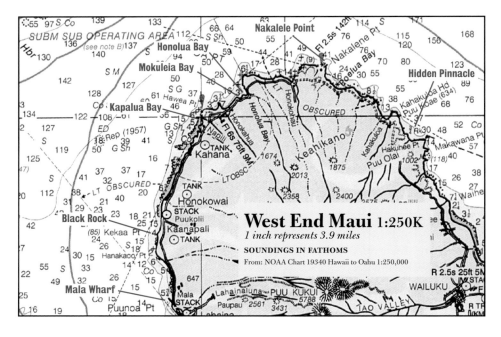

Skull Rock and Stonewall is **Circus Circus**. Like Stonewall, this site is a ledge, most of it undercut. Here a 60-foot portion of the ledge has split off and fallen away, and since the broken off section was undercut, it has formed a long cave, full of large *ulua*. Big jacks always know the location of good shelters like this. If you disturb or chase them, they will gather together and all depart in the same direction—to the next shelter imprinted on their mental map. Following these departing fish will lead you to another *ulua* hole.

Circus Circus is an old black coral and spearfishing site, and one that offered as much sport as profit to the divers. The men would use large stones, brought from shore, to hurtle to the bottom. You can still see these stones here, concentrated near the broken part of the ledge and along the bottom, near the cave.

Big Bugga Ledge consists of a large block of fossil coral the size of a cottage and several smaller blocks that have broken away from a nearby ledge. The larger rock rolled out away from the main ledge and acquired a position that is just about perfect for fish, providing shelter and ample water movement. The block is 150 feet deep at the base and 110 feet on top.

The ledge's namesake is a large tiger shark which has regularly been seen in the area. It seems to have become familiar with divers, an unnerving habit for a tiger shark. I never saw a tiger here, but I always wonder if the Big Bugga tiger was the same one we met repeatedly on a nearby site. This fish thought it was great fun to join us while we hung in blue water on our decompression stops. Once he found us, he never seemed to get bored or tired, and would fade in and out of visibility several times, a trick tigers do very well, for sometimes 20 minutes of decompression. We eventually got used to him, but the first time, after seeing this huge animal rise up ominously from beneath us, and then disappear, and then rise up again, we all got onboard amid a chorus of beeping dive computers.

Windward Maui

Diving with the Locals and Spearfishermen

You CAN LOOK ALL YOU WANT, BUT eventually you will have to get in, or your friends will leave you standing there on the rocks, in full dive gear. All your equipment is ready to go except for your brain, which is telling you that you are going to bleed if you get in that water.

The windward side is like this. Rough, rocky, and intimidating. You probably will bleed, too, either getting in over the rocks and coral, or getting out, so you might as well put it into your dive plan. I don't think I've ever dived the windward shore without at least needing one Band-Aid by the time I got back to the car.

This area is dived mostly by tough locals hunting fish. The *uku* (gray snapper) is one of the best. *Uku* eat crabs and shrimp which gives their meat a very nice taste. Unfortunately, they seem to know this, and are one of the most difficult fish to spear in Hawaii. The *uku*'s buck-toothed grin makes it look foolish or simple, but this fish has an uncanny ability to determine the range of a spear gun. If it is three feet, it stays four feet away. Lengthen the cord by two feet, and then it stays six feet away. If you manage to shoot an *uku,* you will want your picture taken with it.

Chuck Thorne, our guide to this side of the island, knows how to shoot an *uku.* But there are always bigger fish in the sea. One day, off Kipahulu, Chuck was getting ready to put an *uku* on his stringer when he felt a nudge from behind. He turned around and found himself staring into the eyes of a huge grouper. For two or three minutes, a very distracted Chuck tried to string his catch under the gaze of a fish more than twice his size—big enough, he estimates, to have swallowed him down to his booties.

We almost never see these giant fish along the lee shore, but you will encounter them on occasion off the windward coast. Big groupers are old. Jack Randall once estimated that a 500 pound grouper might be 70 years old, maybe much more. A fish the size of the one Chuck saw

Many of the sites on Maui's north coast are rough, with a shallow, gray sand bottom, but the far southwest offers the wildest and richest shore diving found anywhere on the island.

might have been spawned in the 1930s.

Most of the diving on the windward coast is from shore, if the surf isn't too rough, and if the wind isn't too strong you can also go by boat to some sites. Shore entries can be made at several places along the Hana Highway and on around to Manawainui Gulch past Kaupo. These are almost all difficult entries. You should pay attention not just to getting in, but getting out. Diving at slack high tide is always recommended, to minimize chances that the current will come up and sweep

*Available from Book-
linesHawaii.com,
Amazon.com, and
other sources, or
directly: Send check
or money order for
$10.95 ($8.95 + $2.00
S&H) to Diver's Guide
to Maui, PO Box 40,
Hana, HI, 96713, (808)
248-7308.

you away from the area you have picked out for a safe exit.

KAHULUI TO HANA

The north shore sites are all gulch or valley dives. Characteristically, the bottom is rather poor, generally gray sand until you swim out and around the points where you will get into some boulders and a lit-

Callechelys luteus   Hawaii 1990

This odd character is a freckled snake eel. This particular species is known only from Hawaii.

tle more relief. Typically, the boulders disappear to sand at about 60 feet. Because the bays are at the mouths of seasonal rivers, heavy rains can ruin the visibility here.

The fish species in these areas are a different mix than you will find on the lee shores, with more surge adapted species such as the larger tangs and surgeonfish, more goatfish and, when there is shelter, more sol-

dierfish. Most evident, however, is the greater number of large predator species like jacks.

The sites below are marked on the CHART on page 109. For more detailed descriptions and maps of these sites, we recommend Chuck Thorne's excellent *The Divers' Guide to Maui.**

Most divers at **Keanae** (Kawee Point) get in at the old landing at Nuaailua Bay and swim out along the reef on the west side of the peninsula. But the right side of the peninsula, which unfortunately is rarely diveable, is much wilder, and has better coral and fish, including *moana, uku,* snappers, and jacks. On both sides the reef runs out at about 60 feet.

Nahiku (Kaelua) usually has poor visibility, and has a reputation for sharks, although Chuck says he has never seen any here. The entry is at the end of a paved road at the old landing, and the dive proceeds out along a lava finger which runs seaward. There is excellent reef beginning at about 60 feet which thins out down to sand at about 80 feet. This is a good place to see the rarely encountered *awa* or milkfish (*Chanos chanos*), which was raised by the ancient Hawaiians in ponds.

Further up the coast, almost at Hana, is **Waianapanapa Park.** Here you can enter at the black sand beach inside Pailoa Bay and head out to explore the shallow points to the east. Or you can make a long swim north along the shoreline until you make it to the point past Keawaiki Bay, and descend. There you will find good bottom relief, including lava ridges coming off shore which extend down to 130 feet, with a couple of large arches at 60 feet. The further along you swim, the more big fish you will see, including the occasional gray reef shark. The swim is a tough one, and this is a good dive for a scooter. Strong currents develop on this site,

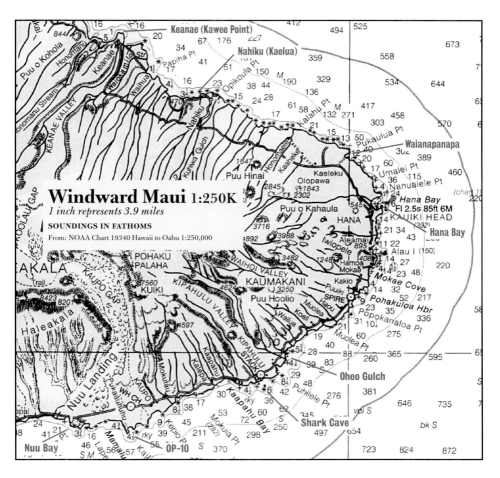

so always dive on high tide and when seas are very low.

Hana Bay is another dive that is better with a scooter. You enter the water at the point nearest the little islet of Puu kii and stay on the bay side as you head out. The depth is not impressive, but it is a good dive and there is a small cave at the base of Puu kii and a good boulder and low ledge bottom out beyond. You are in fairly protected water for the entire dive. The reef fish life is good here, and in late afternoon sharks, barracuda and *ulua* may come by.

OHEO GULCH AND BEYOND

One of the best dives on Maui is just east of **Oheo Gulch** (Seven Sa-cred Pools) where the stream enters the ocean. Enter at the end of a dirt road on the west side of Kuloa Point, swim out around the point on the surface, and descend. Here there is a drop-off, from 20 to 80 feet deep, that roughly parallels the shore. This is another dive that would best be done with a scooter or even from a boat.

About a third of the way along the drop-off you pass over the entrance to an *ulua* hole. At the top it is about 40 feet across, and it opens up underneath into a massive underwater chamber, 100 feet long and 50 feet wide, open at both ends and simply teeming with life. Leaving this cathedral, follow the reef edge and you will come to a huge, horseshoe-shaped canyon, which bottoms out at 75 feet.

Here you will find an explosion of fish life. *Uku* swim in circles, and *taape*, soldierfish, *mu*, large Bleeker's surgeonfishes, *nohu*, *uhu*, *nenue*, and *moana* are everywhere, with the *ulua* hanging out in a small cave at the shoreward end of the

Molokini 1991

Molokini's famous crescent shape is not the result of erosion. The eruptions that created the island took place underwater, and the trade winds blew the resulting ash to the south.

canyon. It is simply overwhelming.

Although difficult to reach, **The Shark Cave** is worth the effort. This cave is off a small wash rock called Ahole Rock, which can be seen from the cliffs near Charles Lindbergh's grave. The cave is on the shoreward side of the rock, near the western corner, at a depth of 60 feet. It is full of reef whitetips. Be cautious here: the sharks are so numerous that the risk of startling them and being rammed is very real.

OP-10 is, beyond a doubt, the most extreme dive location accessible from shore on the island of Maui. At the point you jump into the water it is already 50 feet deep and swirling with fish. Currents funnel past this point at up to three knots, which keeps things stirred up and rich (and dangerous, if you don't watch the tide). A short swim from the entry puts you onto the reef and immediately the wild feel of this site becomes apparent. *Ulua, uku, mu*, barracuda, *moana*, and soldierfish are here in droves. Gray sharks are not uncommon.

This reef has fantastic relief, with deep crevasses, a cave, and a large lava tunnel with an inner chamber that often hosts sleeping whitetips. At 90 feet, there is an *ulua* cave, with vast schools of big jacks.

Beyond the *ulua* cave, the reef continues out to an incredible bottom of 70-foot-high rolling hills on a 170-to 200-foot base. OP-10 is a large and complex area, and highly recommended for experienced divers interested in exploring.

The dive at **Nuu Bay** is off a lava flow that forms the east end of the bay. The flow stays shallow for a while, then drops off in a steep slope. At 120 feet the bottom levels out, and there are tree-sized black corals and hundreds of wire corals. The endemic bandit angelfish is always here, and we have seen many big animals at this site over the years, including *ulua*, *kahala*, barracuda, and several species of sharks. Nuu Bay is an hour-long boat ride from the Kihei Ramp, or even longer if you drive, but this dive is definitely worth the trip.

You could spend your time on Maui diving the clear, calm water of the lee coast. But if you want to see something new—and windward Maui certainly qualifies—you have to put some effort in. Give it a try.

HAWAII'S JEWEL
Molokini
One of the World's Top Dive Sites

ORDINARILY I WOULDN'T PICK UP A dead fish—flies or no flies. But when, on a dive, I found a male barred filefish lying dead on the bottom, I decided to pick it up and do some experimenting. I held it out to cleaner wrasses. They eagerly cleaned its leathery skin, even swimming between my fingers to get at it. I moved my fish near a damselfish's eggs. The male damsel, though one-tenth the filefish's size, did his job and chased and pecked at my fish. I held it near an octopus. It tentatively extended a tentacle to investigate.

Then, like Alice falling into the rabbit hole, I stepped into another world. As I swam along with the fish dangling by my side, looking for another creature with which to continue my experiment, several barred filefish approached me. When I realized they seemed to be challenging my fish, I decided to give it life, and moved it around as if it were alert and swimming. Immediately the other filefish got their hackles up, and began displaying. I decided to escalate things further, and made my fish bold and aggressive. A few challengers charged straight at it, and even attacked, slashing at the corpse with the spines near their tail!

This fish led me on a tour of his world that was unforgettable. I was now aware of the many invisible territorial boundaries on this reef. I became familiar with the filefish's character, and that of his neighbors. The fact that there was this human being attached to him didn't seem to matter at all. For the first and only time in my life, I was an actual member of the reef community (albeit not a particularly welcome one). I *was* a barred filefish; Pauline the diver did not exist.

A SANCTUARY

An event like this could only have happened at a place like Molokini, a Marine Life Conservation District visited by so many divers and snorkelers over the years that many of the fish are completely unaffected

Not every famous dive site deserves its reputation, but this one does. From its rich central reef to the stark drop-off of the back wall, Molokini has something for everyone.

by us. Rock-turning, feeding, territory defense, courtship, mating, nesting—at Molokini, all of these behaviors go on as if the diver swimming nearby didn't exist. It is an underwater photographer's dream.

This is only one reason Molokini is the state's premier dive site. Some others: Three quarters of the island consists of almost vertical walls, some starting at the surface and others beginning much deeper. The other quarter is a very healthy coral slope, surrounded by bright sand channels, that trails off into the deep blue distance. Since the island has no soil and lies three miles off-

Naso maculatus, Heniochus diphreutes, and Forcipiger longirostris   Molokini 1991

Molokini

This submerged half-crater, a short boat ride from Maui's South Shore, is the most popular dive site in Hawaii, and the photographers' favorite. Molokini is a kind of microcosm of all the southern Hawaiian island reefs, with habitats ranging from shallow sand bottoms to deep walls. Still clinging to the rock at more than two-hundred feet, a dead black coral bush, covered with sponges, attracts unicornfish and butterflyfish (left). In the southern Hawaiian chain, you will only find this unicornfish deep. In the shallows there are harlequin shrimp (right), although these improbably beautiful creatures are always rare. Tinker's butterflyfish (below), known only from Hawaii and the Marshall Islands, is almost always found at more than one-hundred feet, sometimes much deeper. This one was photographed on Molokini's back side at one-hundred and sixty feet.

Hymenocera picta on Linckia laevigata Molokini 1986

Chaetodon tinkeri Molokini 1989

Unidentified rhizostome jelly   Molokini 1990

Holanthias fuscipinnis   Molokini 1999

Brachysomophis crocodilinus   Molokini 1995

A drifting jelly (above left) floats near the surface just off the island. The yellow anthias (above) is a rare Hawaii endemic. It can be found hovering upside down in rock shelves in the deepest part of Molokini, well below suggested sport diving depths. The graceful whale shark (right) is a rare visitor to the island. The crocodile eel (below left) lies buried in the sand, ready to strike at any fish unlucky enough to pass nearby. It is a formidable predator, and its jaws extend even further back than is visible in this photograph.

Rhincodon typus Molokini 1996

shore, visibility is almost always a crystalline 150 feet or even more—even when it is raining.

The state made Molokini a marine sanctuary in 1977, and since then it has been illegal to fish here or collect anything, living or dead. The following year the island became a bird sanctuary as well.

Because of its location in the middle of the Alalakeiki Channel between Maui and Kahoolawe, humpback whales, bottlenose and spinner dolphins, monk seals, whale sharks, and game fish such as yellowfin tuna, mahi mahi and *ono* periodically visit Molokini. Mantas are almost always present.

These open ocean animals approach the crater, and some even enter it. Whale sharks have been seen with some frequency over the years, especially during coral spawning weeks, and humpback whales approach often enough that every season at least a few lucky divers happen to be in the right place at the right time.

Mantas regularly enter the crater bay to be cleaned. A host of reef fish, including cleaner wrasses, Klein's butterflyfish, saddle wrasses, and others pick parasites from the huge animals as they circle lazily. But the most remarkable cleaner species for mantas (and whale sharks) are jacks. We have seen 50 pound *ulua* rush up to the mantas and tear five- or ten-pound remoras from their backs with such force that chunks of flesh drift away in the wash. These are snapped up by gray reef sharks, which follow the jacks. This is cleaning on a titanic scale.

Molokini's exotic crescent shape is the result of a submarine volcanic eruption. When the vent opened up, and molten lava came into contact with the overlaying sea water, violent explosions atomized the lava, sending tiny ash particles hundreds of feet into the air. In this manner the cone built up, layer by layer.

This ash was light enough to be at the mercy of the breeze, and since the tradewinds are so consistent, a lopsided half cone formed, higher on the downwind side than the upwind side. Though it appears that half of the crater rim has fallen away, actually it never existed.

Molokini's shallow, protected cove, called Kahuluele, is filled with clear water and a mix of healthy coral and white sand channels. Diving is pleasant here for beginners. The outer wall is deep and challenging—ideal for advanced divers. In a relatively small area, there are coral flats, slopes, and walls, allowing excellent multi-level dives. Even tech divers will find something here to please them, since Molokini bottoms out at more than 300 feet in places. And there is a nice steep wall for the descent and for staging tanks.

THE WESTERN ARM

The tip of the crater's submerged western rim, called **Reef's End**, has been the site of so many special animal encounters over the years that a book could be written about it alone. (See MAP 2.3, pp. 118–119.) More people have seen their first shark here than anywhere else in Hawaii, endangered monk seals and hawksbill turtles have stopped by, and two mated pairs of large yellowmargin morays have lived in this area for more than 23 years. These eels used to be fed by divers, but even though this is no longer allowed, they continue to remain calm and tame, seemingly holding no grudge that their meal ticket has been revoked.

In the sand adjacent to the point, a colony of endemic Hawaiian garden eels occupy an area that begins at 70 feet and extends down slope to 240 feet. By day they extend their slender bodies two feet above the sand to feed, then withdraw for the night. Tiny juveniles

Cirrhilabrus jordani (male)   Molokini 1991

can sometimes be spotted among the adults in the spring. Because of the number of divers they have seen, they are somewhat more approachable than other populations of garden eels, although photographing them is still one of life's photographic challenges.

At least three times in the last few years divers have been entertained by bottlenose dolphins while lying on the sand watching the garden eels. All three times, a dolphin repeatedly powered down to the sand, picked up a black sea cucumber and shuttled it 70 feet up to the surface where it let go and watched it drop. On one occasion this game continued for twenty minutes. Each time, it appeared that the dolphin was trying to drop the sea cucumber on the divers.

While cleaner wrasses can be found throughout the crater, there is something about the cleaning stations at **Mid-Reef**, halfway back along the western arm, that manta rays seem to prefer, and they have been coming here for years. If not

approached too closely, the mantas will remain in a holding pattern over the cleaning station indefinitely. If divers crowd them, they usually head back out to sea.

Big surf from the west periodically crashes down on the rim of the crater, tumbling fragments of broken coral to the inside. Mounds of these tiny pieces are then occupied by small fish and octopus. Flame wrasses, which need only a small crevice to hide, hover above the rubble picking plankton and performing their harem duties. Octopus find lots of building materials in the rubble, building small walls and excavating holes from which to scan the reef for food.

If there is current, activity at Reef's End is cranked up a notch. Hundreds of planktivores position themselves in the water column to have first choice at whatever the current brings. Schools of pyramid butterflyfish and banded butterflyfish face into the current, or if there is none, hover at ease out in the blue. They never venture too far from the

The flame wrasse, endemic to Hawaii, is one of the real jewels of these waters. It is usually found rather deep (although less so at Molokini), and typically a group will consist of a male and a harem of females. This is a so-called flasher wrasse and, it must be said, a real nightmare to photograph. Our photographer deserves full points for capturing the display posture above.

Map 2.4 Molokini 1:3,500

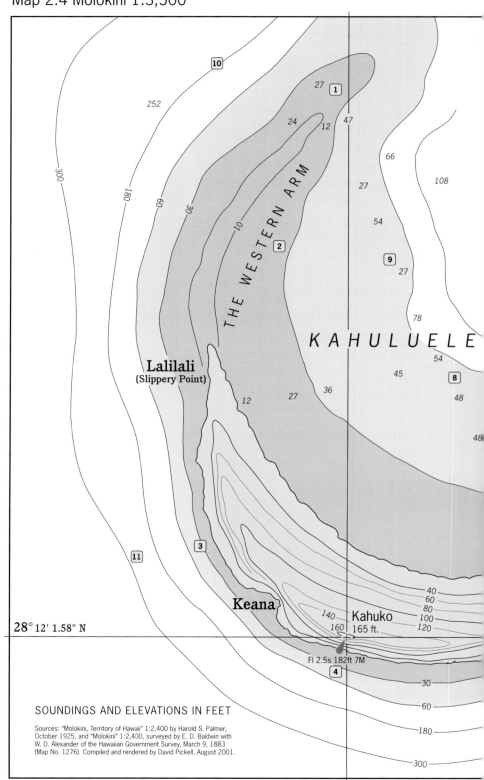

10

252

27 1

24 12 47

66

108

300

180 60 30 10

T H E   W E S T E R N   A R M

27

27

54

2

9

27

78

Lalilali
(Slippery Point)

K A H U L U E L E

54

45

8

48

12 27 36

48

11 3

Keana

140

160

Kahuko
165 ft.

40
60
80
100
120

28° 12' 1.58" N

Fl 2.5s 182ft 7M

4

30

60

SOUNDINGS AND ELEVATIONS IN FEET

180

Sources: "Molokini, Territory of Hawaii" 1:2,400 by Harold S. Palmer,
October 1925, and "Molokini" 1:2,400, surveyed by E. D. Baldwin with
W. D. Alexander of the Hawaiian Government Survey, March 9, 1883
(Map No. 1276). Compiled and rendered by David Pickell, August 2001.

300

156° 30' 0.24" W

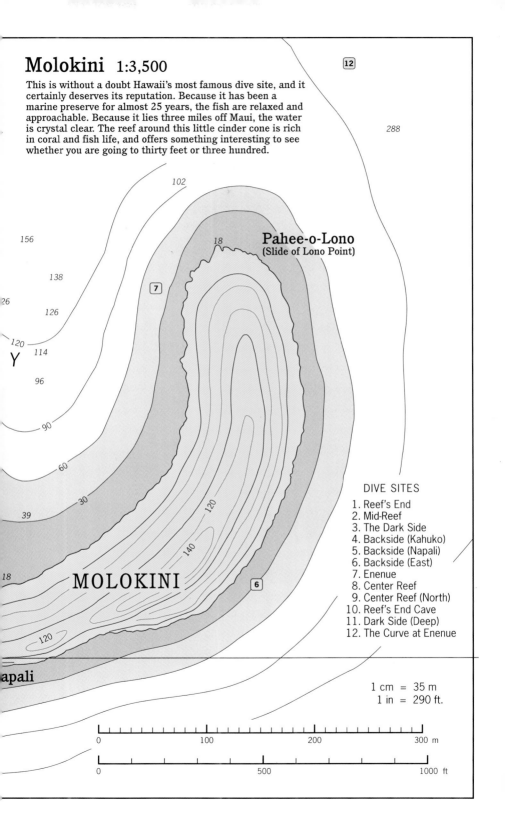

Molokini 1:3,500

This is without a doubt Hawaii's most famous dive site, and it certainly deserves its reputation. Because it has been a marine preserve for almost 25 years, the fish are relaxed and approachable. Because it lies three miles off Maui, the water is crystal clear. The reef around this little cinder cone is rich in coral and fish life, and offers something interesting to see whether you are going to thirty feet or three hundred.

Pahee-o-Lono
(Slide of Lono Point)

MOLOKINI

DIVE SITES
1. Reef's End
2. Mid-Reef
3. The Dark Side
4. Backside (Kahuko)
5. Backside (Napali)
6. Backside (East)
7. Enenue
8. Center Reef
9. Center Reef (North)
10. Reef's End Cave
11. Dark Side (Deep)
12. The Curve at Enenue

apali

1 cm = 35 m
1 in = 290 ft.

0   100   200   300 m

0   500   1000 ft

ledges and crevices on the slope, however, so they have a place to dart to if predators, such as jacks, appear.

THE BACKSIDE

Sometimes the current is just the right strength for a diver to drift from Reef's End along the western arm, passing over brilliant cauliflower and antler corals in the top 30

Aluterus scriptus Hawaii 2000

The scrawled filefish is an odd-looking beast that is found in tropical waters everywhere in the world. It must have a cast-iron stomach, as it is known to eat sponges, gorgonians, coelenterates, and other toxic and gristly items.

feet of water. High water exchange on the outside of the crater and intense sunlight available to feed the corals' symbiotic algae, make this one of Molokini's most spectacular views. The longer the drift the steeper the slope becomes until you reach the western tip of the crescent, where it becomes a vertical wall.

For the entire morning this area is shaded by the rim, and has be-

come know as **The Dark Side.** Here the wall plummets to nearly 300 feet and some areas are even undercut, creating permanent shaded areas, even in the afternoon when the sun comes around to the west. The undersides of these overhangs are covered with orange cup coral, a plankton-feeder that specializes in dark places. Orange mop-shaped nudibranchs and pillow-shaped sea stars feed on the orange coral tissue leaving stark white coral skeletons as evidence of their feasting. The nudibranchs feed at night and withdraw into an adjacent crack during the day (where they also lay their eggs), while the cushion stars feed during daylight hours.

Camouflaged frogfish tuck up under the bracket-shaped corals, aided in their disguise by the darkness. Whitetip reef sharks rest under shaded ledges. As the sun peeks over the rim, divers can look out from the shadows at crystal blue water penetrated by white beams of light. Huge schools of silver mackerel (*opelu*) shimmer past, with amberjacks and rainbow runners sometimes charging the school.

Cobalt blue clarity and the dramatic wall are what divers remember of **The Back Wall** of Molokini. Schools of planktivores such as pyramid and banded butterflyfish occur in distinct areas. The rare Thompson's butterflyfish sometimes enters the mix, but its solid gray body does little to draw attention and divers rarely notice it.

Huge black coral trees once grew here, but were heavily harvested in the 1950s. These are now just re-establishing themselves. Black coral trees are always good places to look for animals taking advantage of the confusion of branches for shelter—or stalking. When small fish swim near the tree, a stick-shaped trumpetfish might dart out and capture it. Longnose hawkfish perch among the branches, their

First Person: Helping a Manta

By Jennifer Anderson

THE MORNING BEGAN LIKE MANY OTHER MAUI mornings, with the sun rising over Haleakala as we greeted our divers for the day's charter. There was little evidence that this day would turn out to be unforgettable. At first, I wanted to forget it.

The last guests to arrive were two brothers. They were European, and spoke very little English. During the course of explaining the procedure for the dives, the brothers would every now and then stop us and ask us to repeat what was said. They would then discuss it between the two of them. We soon learned that when their heads began to nod up and down, we could continue the briefing.

The captain progressed slowly through the information until he came to the part where he told the group, "Jennifer will choose the dive site and brief you on what you will see." Here was when we knew we had a problem. Our European guests were obviously unhappy with the idea of diving with a woman divemaster. We tried to assure them that everything would turn out fine, but finally the captain had to say: "Look, if you want to dive today, you're diving with Jennifer."

The day had not begun smoothly, and to add to my worries, I noticed the wind line moving into Molokini. I hurried through the dive briefing and the gearing up. I was careful to do everything by the book, so the divers would feel confident in their leader. Then the group descended, some using the mooring line and others in a slow, effortless freefall.

Our dive went pretty much the way I said it would: the garden eels performed their beautiful underwater ballet, the parrotfish grazed on the coral, and the ever elusive male flame wrasses flared their fins in challenge to their competitors.

The divers and I were nearing the final level of our dive when the two couples signaled to me that they were beginning their ascent. As luck would have it, the two remaining divers were the brothers. They had ignored me the entire dive. Whenever I stopped the group to show them something unusual or that they may have missed, the brothers hung back, and acted indifferent to the whole experience. Now the three of us caught the current and were carried along the reef. We were enjoying the ride, and slowly ascending, since the brothers were nearing the end of their air.

THE MANTA

Then something far below caught my eye. I could just make out the white shoulder patches of a manta ray in about 120 feet of water. I was thrilled—my greatest love is the manta! I have been trying to learn more about mantas since my first encounter with them years before in Mexico. I was amazed to learn how little is known about these animals. One thing I did know was that each manta had a unique pattern on its underside. In 1992 I began to identify the animals we sighted at Molokini and surrounding waters. My goal was always to get beneath them to get a sketch of the pattern, and a photo if possible.

When I saw the manta below me, I knew I faced a dilemma—the manta or my boys. I was trying to be a respectable dive leader, and plunging to 120 feet at the end of the dive was not going to help this image. Even though I had plenty of air and lots of time on my computer, I reluctantly decided to stay with them and try to get the manta's attention.

I started calling through my regulator: "Come up and see me!" Audible calls sometimes work with dolphins and whales, so why not a manta? The looks my divers gave me said they were certain they never should have trusted the captain about diving with me. They, of course, had not seen the manta and had no idea what I was yelling about.

Another group of divers ahead of us on the drift heard me yelling and stopped their dive to see what all the commotion was. I was feeling a little foolish, until I saw the manta begin to roll from side to side, looking around with those big dark eyes on the side of her head.

Manta birostris with Remorina albescens Molokini 1995

Is it possible for a manta to understand the intentions of a human? Stranger things have happened.

That gave me hope, so I kept calling to her and waving my arms, repeating over and over, "Come up and see me!"

After a minute or two, the manta lifted off the reef and made a wide circular glide, until she was directly below me, but still deep. Then she lifted her great body and began to fly in a direct line to me. The divers were all smiles. They loved me now—*She calls mantas!* I was a little surprised, to say the least.

I did not recognize this manta. She was very large for the mantas we get in Hawaii, about fifteen feet from wing tip to wing tip. We usually see them at six or eight feet, with an occasional twelve footer. There was something different about her, however. I noticed that her tail area, instead of a smooth line, was jagged, and seemed to ruffle in the water as she came closer. Then I saw large V-shaped wounds in the same area.

The divers were intimidated by the manta's approach, and disappeared. I continued to study her. Something just wasn't right. I could see marks from her head, along her back, and to the tail area. I thought maybe she had been hit by a prop and cut. It wasn't until she was just ten feet below me that I finally could understand what was wrong.

She had two large fishing hooks embedded in her shoulder and eye area. From there, stainless steel leader and then fishing line wrapped around her from head to tail five times or more. She had most likely been hooked, and struggling to free herself, resorted to barrel rolls which had tied her up tight. She couldn't open her mouth to feed and the lines had torn into her body. The V-shaped wounds were five inches deep, and parasites swarmed in them.

I felt sick. I didn't know what to do. I have been around wild animals and know they are usually untrusting. Even though you may be trying to help, if you inflict pain, they bolt. But I had to try.

HORSE SENSE

I went down to her very, very slowly. I grew up with horses, and my horse sense kicked in. I started talking to her in a low soothing tone, asking for her trust. I touched her very lightly and was amazed when she quivered, just like a horse would. Then I put both of my hands on her, talking to her all the time. I took a long time with this, knowing that at any moment, with one flick of her great wing, she could be gone. When I felt the time was right, I took my knife and lifted one of the fishing lines. It was as tight as a guitar string. She shook, which told me to be very careful. Obviously the slightest pressure was painful.

As I cut through the first line, it pulled into her wounds. With a great beat of her wings she bolted. I assumed this would be the end of it. But, to my surprise, she came back, again hovering right below me. I then understood that she was allowing me to do this, and went to work. I cut through one line after another. When she had all she could take, the manta would glide away, only to return in a minute or two. I never chased her. I never grabbed her. I didn't have to.

When I had all of the lines cut on the top, I looked at her as she was circling me, and realized that she could leave now and they would all eventually fall off. But she came back again and this time I went underneath her. I hooked my hand on the front of her body and began to pull the lines through the wounds. As I did this, I felt a slight pressure on the hand that I was holding on with and realized I had my fingers in her mouth. When I pulled a line through the wound, she bit down on my hand, letting me know when it hurt.

When the lines were free, I pushed away and watched her circle me again, and then move back to her position. The lines were hanging off her head as I approached her, gathering them up in my left hand. All I had left to do was take the fishing hooks out.

One of them came right out, since the flesh around it was rotten. I tried the other one. It was buried to the end of the barb. I used my knife to try to pull it out. Again, she let me know it hurt by rocking back and forth, but never enough to knock me off. I finally worked it free and put all of it into my left hand and laid myself on her back. She was free.

REALITY INTERVENES

I was oblivious to how much air I had left, how deep I was, everything. All I knew was I felt such love for this great creature that I did not want our time to end. But reality has a way of breaking up the most beautiful moments, and I remembered something about a boat and . . . oh right, my divers! I came to my senses and pushed myself away.

At first, she stayed below me. And then, when she realized she was free, she came to life. I had assumed she was weak from her ordeal. I was wrong. With two beats of those powerful wings she was rocketing along the back wall of Molokini, and then directly out to sea. I lost sight of her, and reluctantly turned to look for my divers.

Remarkably, we hadn't traveled very far. My divers were right above my head and had witnessed the whole event (thankfully, since no one would ever have believed this one without witnesses). The other dive group had stayed with me and the dive leader threw up his hands as if to say, "What was that?"

I was trying to make sense of it myself. I wondered if it even really happened. But the evidence was in my hands: hooks and line, and the torn calluses from her rough skin. Yes, it had really happened.

I kicked in the direction of my now very excited divers (the bubbles and the big eyes gave them away) only to have them stop and signal me to turn around. Until this moment, the encounter had been amazing. Then it became magical.

I turned around and saw the manta slowly gliding towards me. With barely an effort, she approached and then paused, her wing just behind my head. I looked into her round, dark eye, and she looked deeply into mine. I felt a rush of something that so overwhelmed me, I have yet to find words to describe it. Perhaps, a manta thank you.

She stayed with me for a moment, or an hour, I don't really know. Then, as sweetly as she had come, she lifted her wing over my head and was gone. I drifted in midwater trying to collect myself before joining the others on the boat. It took time for my heart to beat again and to remember to breathe.

Sadly, I have not seen her since that day. I am looking! For the longest time, I wouldn't even wear my new wetsuit because I hoped she would recognize me by my old one.

I call to every manta I see, and they almost always acknowledge me in some way. One day it will be her. She'll hear me call and pause, remembering someone that relieved her pain. Then she'll come to me. At least that is how it happens in my dreams.

—Part of a work in progress entitled *A Mermaid's Tale—the Water Nations.*

plaid pattern blending perfectly with the branches. Winged oysters attach themselves to the trees, where they filter plankton.

A dive light adds considerably to this dive. A light will reveal pairs of brilliant red Baldwin's pipefish, the males carrying tiny pink or silver eggs on their underbelly, and Potter's angelfish darting into cracks.

THE EASTERN TIP AND THE BAY

Enenue, just inside the eastern tip, is the place to see big gray reef sharks during the mating months of summer. During the 2000 season, this site surprised us with the birth of more than 30 baby gray reef sharks. When first born, they packed tightly together and kept just inches from the bottom, gradually expanding their territory outward and upward as they grew. Many of them still live here, now swimming boldly in the midwater and facing the current.

This site was named for the *nenue* or sea chub (*Kyphosus* sp.), which are found here. There are several species of these fish, which are all drab and gray, and would normally escape notice completely. But they are easily tamed to feed from divers' hands, and apparently gained enough recognition from this for the site to bear their name.

The bottom is a mixture of coral and rubble, and slopes steeply toward the inside of the crater, hitting a sand bottom at about 100 feet. A large population of endemic flame wrasses resides here in several harems, the males displaying by turning on brighter colors and flaring enlarged fins to keep other males at a distance and to keep females nearby.

A ledge at 130 feet is the daytime resting place for several whitetip reef sharks. Long-fin anthias hang upside down underneath the ledge. These are beautiful when illuminated by a powerful light. Endemic

banded lobsters, often brooding orange eggs, retreat here for the day. Even deeper, black coral grows in abundance and deep water fish such as the sunset basslet, boarfish, Thompson's anthias, and blueline triggerfish can be seen.

The current can rip here, but like at Reef's End, sometimes it is just the right speed to drift from the inside to the outside. Just before gliding over the rim is the time to look out into the blue for gray reef sharks and rays. Once on the outside many species of triggerfish tuck into crevices upon a diver's approach, slipper lobsters can sometimes be seen, and old coral-covered bombs from Molokini's years as a practice target during World War II balance on ledges.

One of the most striking and beautiful features of Molokini is the extensive, climax coral reef growing throughout most of the central crater. This is the **Center Reef**. Because large surf is blocked by Maui and the crater rim, and because the water is deeper (40–120 feet), corals in the center are not periodically broken. New habitat is rarely opened up for other species of corals to get a foothold, and so over time the most competitive species, rice coral and spreading coral, have come to dominate. This, according to coral biologist Jim Maragos, is an unusual combination of co-dominant species for Hawaii.

Beautiful synchronized night spawning occurs over this reef in the summer, when the rice coral releases thousands of tiny pink bundles of eggs and sperm. Slowly released over a period of about 15 minutes, the bundles rise to the surface like a beaded curtain. Soldierfish and damselfish pluck what they can from the darkness, but the loss is low and when the bundles arrive at the surface they break apart and cross-fertilization begins.

So built-up is the reef that when

DAYTIME CORAL SPAWNING
Springtime at Molokini

CORALS SPAWN IN MASS, SYNCHRONIZED events, to increase the chance that eggs and sperm will meet, and particularly, to encourage the cross-fertilization between different colonies necessary to maintain a robust and diverse gene pool. Most of the world's coral species time these events for night, when many of the reef's predators are inactive, thus giving the fertilized eggs a better chance of growing up to become a new coral colony.

Divers can now experience these nocturnal spawning events on the Great Barrier Reef in Australia, at Flower Garden Banks National Marine Sanctuary in the Gulf of Mexico, and in Hawaii. Watching coral colonies release their eggs and sperm in the beam of a dive light is very interesting, but what if you could witness this event in the daytime?

Daytime spawning is uncommon, but one species known to spawn during the day is *Pocillopora meandrina*. Called "cauliflower" or "rose" coral in the islands, this is a common species on shallow, clear-water sites around Hawaii. It is the dominant coral on Molokini's western arm, where the remarkable daytime spawning was discovered. This species produces such minute eggs, and even more minute sperm, and in such mind-blowing numbers, that a very low percentage is lost to reef animal predation, even during daylight.

Pocillopora meandrina is a widely distributed Indo-Pacific species, and presumably spawns in the daytime everywhere, but Hawaii is the only place where the timing and location of this event are known, so that divers can go and witness the spawning. Daytime spawning is much more dramatic than night spawning. Instead of watching a few colonies under your dive lights, the entire reef can be seen releasing new life.

7:20 A.M., ON THE DOT

If someone told you that all the dandelions in your neighborhood were going to release their seeds into the air at 7:20 a.m. on a certain day, you'd want to see that right? That is basically what happens with the *P. meandrina* colonies at Molokini.

At 7:15 the reef looks just like it always

does. Then, at 7:20, the first coral heads begin to "smoke," and within minutes most of the colonies are releasing their eggs and sperm. Just 15 minutes after the first colonies begin to spawn, a huge billowing white cloud engulfs the reeftop and the divers, reducing the underwater visibility to just five feet.

This remarkable event takes place once or

Pocillopora meandrina   Molokini April, 2000

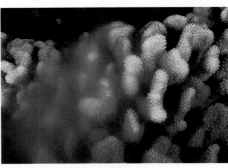

Pocillopora meandrina   Molokini April, 2000

At Molokini, the cauliflower coral spawns reliably at 7:20 a.m. for three days around the April or May full moon.

twice a year, for three days, around the April or May full moon (or both). *P. meandrina,* like many reef animals, times its spawning to the full moon, when tidal currents are strong and can quickly disperse the eggs.

So far, Molokini is the only known place where this event goes off like clockwork. *Pocillopora meandrina* spawning has been observed off of the Big Island, Oahu, and Maui, but no one has yet found a comparably reliable site on these islands to take divers. For now, at least, Molokini has the exclusive.

the current hits it, the upwelling carries enough plankton to support its own drop-off habitat community of banded and milletseed butterflyfish. Closer to the coral are other species of butterflyfish such as oval and teardrop butterflies which eat only coral polyps, a very specialized diet and one that limits where they can live. Turtles are not generally found at Molokini, but in recent years a young endangered hawksbill turtle has been living in this area.

DEEP DIVING

Finally, it should be pointed out that there are several exceptional deep dives for trained mixed-gas divers at Molokini. The most frequented deep dive is **Reef's End Cave**, a 180-foot-deep cave off the western arm. This cave has had at least one occupant, a 300-pound grouper which, as two divers approached, suddenly charged out, wedged between them, and vanished over a nearby ledge, leaving the divers in a state of profound bewilderment. Another good deep spot is the wall at **The Dark Side**, which drops vertically in the shade to 285 feet and a field of very large boulders that have crashed down from the cliffs above and rolled out onto the deep sand bottom. A third is the stepped drop-off on the Maui corner of the back wall. This drops to 150 feet, then hits a flat bench before dropping again to a boulder field at 250 feet where you can see the rare dark-finned bass living in a vertical cave at 275 feet.

Finally, there is **The Curve at Enenue**. The Curve is the most challenging dive at Molokini, reaching a depth of 312 feet on the flat sand bottom. Here there are spectacular curving walls with cracks and caves as well as beautiful black coral and lots of sharks. At the bottom is a large school of *taape*, no doubt the feeder school for the shallow water *taape*. This dive does not have the continuous wall of the other deep dives and so decompression must be well planned for divers to safely make it up the slope into shallow water.

Hawaii is blessed with two quite special endemic, deepwater basslets. The yellow anthias (Holanthias fuscipinnis, see pp. 114–115) and the sunrise basslet below. The sunrise basslet is usually found at 200 feet or more, although at Molokini they have been seen in more moderate depths. This one was photographed at 130 feet.

Liopropoma aurora Molokini 1989

(FORMERLY) EXCITING AND SILTY

Kahoolawe

Now Politics and a Slow Cleanup

ONE MORNING IN 1993, HAWAIIANS in native dress and representatives of the U.S. Navy gathered at a Maui beach called Palauea, with Kahoolawe visible across the channel. There a U.S. Navy admiral signed over the deed to an entire island to the state of Hawaii, formally returning the island of Kahoolawe to the descendants of the people who first discovered it and inhabited it for almost 2,000 years.

TARGET PRACTICE

Before World War II, Kahoolawe had been ranch land, mostly run by Hawaiian cowboys. After the United States entered the war, the Navy took over the island in the interests of national defense. After the war ended, they decided to keep it.

In the early days of World War II, the island was used to train young bomber pilots before they were sent off to the Pacific war. Later it was used for ship to shore bombardment exercises. As recently as the 1980s, the U.S.S. *Missouri* was firing its huge guns at the island, and even foreign ships were invited to use the island for target practice.

The tonnage and variety of ordnance fired at the island over the years, some of it landing in the surrounding waters, are staggering. The crowning devastation came with a test explosion so great that it was meant to simulate an atomic bomb—this left a huge crater that has now filled and become a shoreline pond.

Outrage over the Navy's occupation of Kahoolawe had always smoldered in the Hawaiian community, but when committed young Hawaiians took up the cause in the '70s, the struggle gained momentum. The plight of Kahoolawe came to symbolize the need of the Hawaiian people to reconnect with their land.

The Protect Kahoolawe Ohana was formed, and citizens from across the state voiced their support. A small group began illegal landings and occupations, peacefully asserting their right to the island. The loss of two passionate young Hawaiian men at sea while

This dry island, grazed down to red dirt and bombed relentlessly by the Navy, has now been given to the Hawaiians. The environment is being restored, and no diving is allowed. When it was, things were wild.

paddling home after one of the occupations galvanized the community in its effort, and the Hawaiians eventually prevailed.

At first, the Navy allowed limited, scheduled cultural activities and surveying of archaeological sites. Finally, President George Bush issued an executive order halting the use of the island by the military as a bombing target. And, in 1993, Congress passed a law that required the return of the island to Hawaii and directed the Navy to

Cirrhipathes sp. and Naso hexacanthus   Hawaii 1989

Deep beds of spiral black coral were one of the hallmarks of the east Kahoolawe sites. Diving off this island, although it sometimes meant facing a plague of silt, offered some of the wild, untamed feeling of Midway.

lucky few who may get a chance to dive this island.

WHAT WAS THE DIVING LIKE?

During the years of military control, divers would occasionally be allowed to dive off the island, though not officially. Whenever the surrounding waters were open for fishing (sometimes just two weekends a month), divers would go over as well. But the weather conditions didn't always cooperate, so diving Kahoolawe was always a rare opportunity.

Partly because it was so often unapproachable, and partly because of the excellent diving there, diving Kahoolawe was always special. Mysteries took longer to solve because dives there were so rare. How large was that colony of garden eels off Ule Point? Acres, it turned out. Did the gray reef sharks congregate seasonally off Halona Point? They did. What caused the circular clearings on the bottom around Puu koae? A torpedo motor and propeller finally solved that one.

Although always interesting to dive, because of the years of grazing by feral and domestic animals, Kahoolawe has been reduced in many areas to red hardpan, and when it rains the run-off stains the seas redbrown. One of my most disturbing underwater experiences was right after the island had experienced a good rain. Halfway into the dive, a massive brown shape began to draw near us. Eventually it engulfed us like a dark spirit. I tried to swim out of it, but the current kept moving it toward me. I couldn't see even one of my diving companions—all I wanted was get out of there!

Run-off has particularly affected the reefs on the shallow northwestern coast facing Lanai. Species that cannot grow fast enough to gain the size they need to withstand the occasional blanketing by silt are re-

clean up unexploded ordnance and restore the island's much-damaged environment.

The beginning of Hawaii's right to control one of its own islands signaled the end to diving off Kahoolawe for the average Hawaiian citizen. Neither commercial boats nor personal craft are allowed within two miles of the island. The entire island and its waters, now called the Kahoolawe Island Reserve, are to be forever held for education, historical, and environmental restoration, and Native Hawaiian cultural, spiritual and subsistence purposes.

While scientists and students and some Hawaiians are able to enter Kahoolawe's waters, currently the general public is not. We have included this section for those

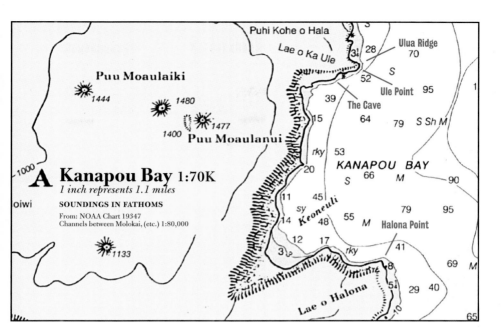

A **Kanapou Bay** 1:70K
1 inch represents 1.1 miles

SOUNDINGS IN FATHOMS
From: NOAA Chart 19347
Channels between Molokai, (etc.) 1:80,000

stricted or missing. Others, such as *Porites lobata,* had formed massive colonies before the island was so critically denuded and its soil washed into the sea. Areas of high wave action or current will stay clean, but these are generally steep upper slopes with very little area available for coral. In the deeper areas, where there is no wave action and the currents are dampened by the irregular coast, the coral ends abruptly off Kahoolawe. Here a silt desert begins, which is the reason for Kahoolawe's massive garden eel populations.

While there is good diving at many points around the island, the most accessible was the east end, centering around the two points of Kanapou Bay. A small tunnel through **Ule Point** was often occupied by an *ulua* or two. Just 200 yards to the north a dive site named **Ulua Ridge** provided many thrilling experiences. The ridge which runs perpendicular to shore is sheer on its south side and drops to over 140 feet. Black coral poked

out from ledges and long-fin anthias, and thousands of milletseed, pennant, and pyramid butterfly fish hovered along the current-swept edge. Whitemargin unicornfish—with the super long horn and flag tail—hung in the water. Anything could show up here. Schools of skipjack tuna, mantas, and eagle rays were common. Branching coral grew up to the northern edge of the ridge, but further north and toward shore the bottom was brown silt, occupied by thousands of garden eels and scattered anemones.

The entire inner slope of Kanapou Bay seemed to be ringed by endless finger coral in the shallows. The beautiful high-ceilinged **The Cave** at just 27 feet could be located by finding a small cove toward the inside of the bay from Ule Point. A huge school of needlefish hovered just below the surface at the cave's scenic entrance. Below this cave was one of the finest black coral beds around. The black coral is large and attached to the face of a cliff that seems to drop off into the abyss.

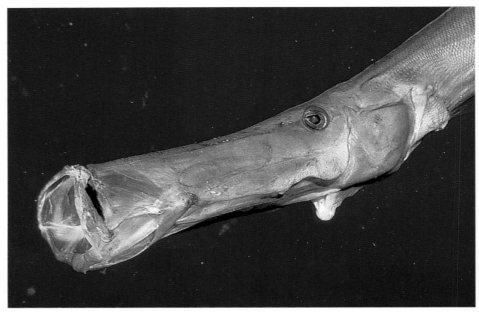

Aulostomus chinensis Makena 1989

The business end of a trumpetfish is remarkably well adapted to its task. Which, of course, is to suction up unsuspecting fishes.

Along the southern edge of the bay rare Tinker's butterflyfish could sometimes be spotted along the finger coral slope, and hammerheads often cruised by. This is the only place we have seen the great hammerhead in Hawaii. Where the coral-covered slope descended to sand, thousands of garden eels lived in the quiet deeper water.

Out around the corner in the rougher water of **Halona Point**, dramatic ledges provided the backdrop for black coral, Tinker's butterflyfish and congregations of gray reef sharks that were very territorial—even disturbingly so. Heller's barracuda schooled here by the hundreds. Inside the shallow shoreline caves here a new species of nudibranch was discovered, soon to be named for a Hawaiian goddess.

A SPECIAL PLACE

Kahoolawe is one of those places that offered excitement on every dive, regardless of the depth or the location. It had that sense of wildness much like Midway. With luck, and the implication of protective measures, Kahoolawe will retain this character.

Today, one of the most ambitious clean-up efforts in history is taking place there. Every day huge Sikorsky helicopters shuttle the 300 workers from Maui to Kahoolawe to continue ordnance removal and environmental restoration, and every evening they return. The very strong winds and lack of rain (the island is in Maui's rain shadow) make the propagation of vegetation extremely difficult, but workers and volunteers are planting native seedlings in an attempt to bring back the lowland dry forest that once covered the island. A few rare native plants remain on the island, and these are carefully monitored. At the same time various ocean surveys are being conducted to determine the rate of silt deposit, the number of game fish in the surrounding waters, and makeup of the reef fish population. And off course, policing of reserve waters is ongoing.

Lanai

Rugged Formations and Healthy Coral

THE IDLING OF OUR BOAT MOTOR WAS enough to bring the sandbar sharks up from the depths where they spent the day. We turned off the engines, and lowered the anchor to about fifty feet where it dangled in the deep water. This would be our only reference point in the open blue, so that when things got exciting we didn't sink too deep or lose track of the boat above us.

We were looking for sandbar sharks (*Carcharhinus plumbeus*), which though rarely seen by divers were the most common shark caught during an extensive research program in Hawaii during the 1960s. These sharks, which grow to seven or eight feet, are a uniform gray color, with a pointed snout and an unusually tall and wide dorsal fin placed rather far forward on the body. Perhaps these sharks had always been at this place, congregating at depth during the day and breaking up at night to feed, but this was our first encounter with them.

As soon as we got in the water they were there to greet us, firing in from every direction. The sharks would veer off at the last second, but we had to constantly watch each other's backs. Mostly they seemed attracted by the electrical currents pulsing through cameras, strobes, and even our anchor. Many times the sharks made passes at the steel anchor, testing to see if they could eat it, and no doubt disappointed when they found out they couldn't. Strobes were hit more than once.

During our surface interval the boat drifted near a ball of baitfish visible as a dark shadow below the surface. When we motored over to have a look we could see the sandbar sharks charging through the baitfish, scales and fish fragments flying everywhere. The sharks were so intent that they thumped into the boat in their frenzy. Later, photos taken while gingerly holding the camera over the side of the boat revealed a school of tuna below the baitball as well. Those tiny fish didn't stand a chance.

EXCITING AND PROTECTED

Lanai can be wild like this. The topography is bold, from the lava tubes, ridges, and pinnacles to vast expanses of healthy coral reef. Cliffs on the south and west sides of the is-

Mr. Dole's former plantation island offers divers beautiful lava tubes and formations, wild and healthy fish life, and the single largest stretch of coral in the lower islands.

land make the coast accessible only by boat, so there has been little human impact over the years. This long stretch of coastline is shared by only four dive boat operators that come over from Maui every day, meaning there is usually only one boat on a site, with the possible exception of the two Cathedrals, the island's most requested dive sites, where there might be two.

Lanai's most protected area is the southern coast. Even a south swell doesn't necessarily rule out diving here, though it can make things uncomfortable, and dives along other parts of the coastline may be better at such times. The south side dives are each defined by their particular formations. The animal life is similar across all the sites—most all have large resident moray eels, octopus, a whitetip reef shark or two and lobsters. Almost all the popular sites have moorings installed and, given the low density of dive boats, there is little impact from divers except at the Cathedral sites.

BACKSIDE LANAI

An hour-long ride from Lahaina will land you on the opposite side of the island from Maui. This is called the backside of Lanai, and thousand-foot-high cliffs, the highest on the island, meet the ocean here. Maui and Molokai protect the island's northeast shoreline from storm surf, but the southwest side faces the open ocean. Storm waves here continue to undermine the rock above, and scars from land-

slides can be seen from the boat.

Some of these cliffs were blasted in the 1920s to get building material for Kaumalapau Harbor. The harbor was built in 1926 by James Dole, who owned most of the island and turned it into the world's largest pineapple plantation. Dole needed a harbor to ship his pineapples to Honolulu for canning. Pineapple farming on Lanai has ended, but Kaumalapau remains Lanai's only inter-island shipping terminal.

Barge Harbor, just north of Kaumalapau, is not often dived because of its distance from Maui. (See Map 2.5, pp. 134–135.) This is unfortunate, because it is one of Lanai's best dives. Here there is a steep wall, raining with damselfish, and since the bottom drops away to great depth on this side of the island, open ocean animals such as whale sharks and thresher sharks have been seen here.

A light is essential on this dive. At the base of the wall on a boulder slope a few large, intensely colored Hawaiian longfin anthias hover

This species of Haminoea (there are at least 64 others) is one of the most colorful of the bubble shells, as this group is loosely called. More properly, it should be called a Cephalaspidean, but don't try to say this with food in your mouth.

Haminoea cymbalum Hawaii 1989

above the bottom, and titan scorpionfish rest in the shadows of the rocks. Along the wall, you can find hairy yellow hermit crabs, nudibranchs, and bandit angelfish living on ledges and in small openings. At the end of the dive you can explore a great cavern and cave system just fifteen feet deep.

Another backside dive, **Shark Fin**, centers around a small wall that reaches from about 80 feet to just above the surface, where its exposed tip gives the site its name. Aggregations of pyramid and milletseed butterflies and black triggerfish feed in the water column, evidence of the frequent eddying current here. Across a small canyon to the south is another short, coral-covered ridge to explore. Harems of palenose and bullethead parrotfish number in the hundreds here with courting and spawning activity easily observed in broad daylight. One of Hawaii's more colorful moray eels, the dragon eel, also lives here.

Beginning just inside little Kaunolu Bay and rounding Palaoa Point is the dive called **Lighthouse**, where several species of rarely seen fish such as saddleback butterflies, bandit angels, and Tinker's butterflies can be found. Coming up from a large group of garden eels at 115 feet, boulders cover the bottom before arriving at the coastline, a small wall 35 feet high. Along the edge of the island are small and large caves, the biggest called Volkswagen Cave for the size of its opening. Enter carefully so as not to stir up the silt on the floor of the cave, and you can find spiny lobsters, beautiful Fellows's nudibranchs, or a pair of fountain shrimp. Whitetip reef sharks often occupy the cave, but leave quickly once a diver enters.

THE SOUTH SIDE

Drifting east from Lighthouse, divers come to a dramatic formation, a V-shape cut into the cliffs

Scyllarides haanii Molokini 1997

along the shoreline. Called **Grand Canyon**, it has 40-foot walls and cuts 120 feet into the coastline. The holes and crevices of the vertical walls are full of fish and invertebrates, and Hawaiian sergeants nest on the flat rock surfaces. Out from the canyon, at 55 feet, is a field of coral, and further offshore is a deep pinnacle.

Monolith is a solid lava pinnacle the size of a four-story house. It can be dived as a spiraling level dive beginning at garden eels at 90 feet and reaching the top at around 40 feet. There is a large black coral tree at 50 feet. A yellowmargin moray named Stretch has lived here for years, although he is no longer fed by divers. A dense covering of cauliflower coral blankets the top of the pinnacle.

The ridgeback slipper lobster is said to be a very docile species, and these two certainly don't look particularly fierce. Slipper lobsters always appear to me to be some kind of holdover from the ancient oceans, but of course they are modern decapod crustaceans just like any other lobsters.

Map 2.5 South Lanai 1:80K

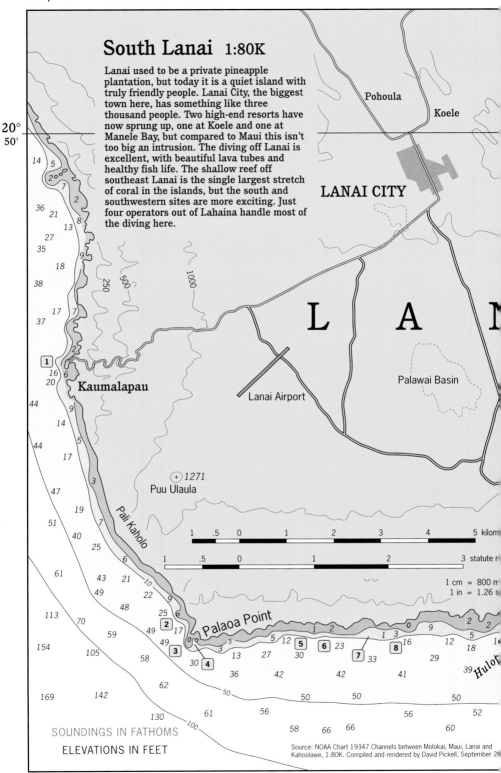

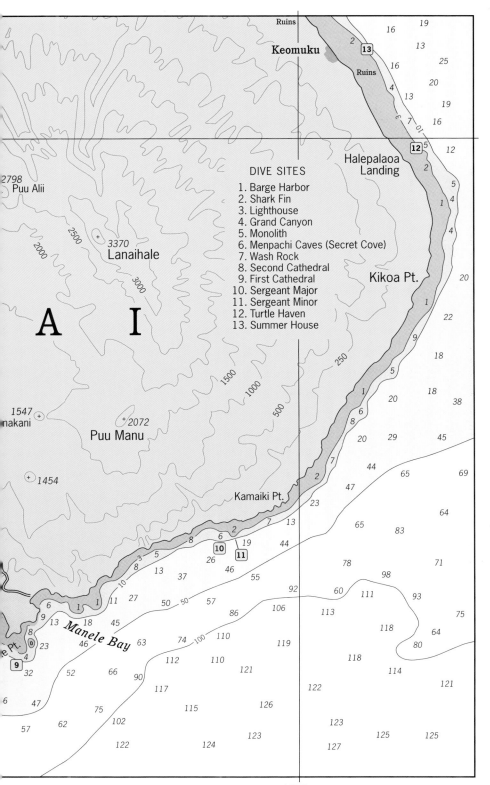

Ruins

Keomuku

Ruins

Halepalaoa Landing

DIVE SITES
1. Barge Harbor
2. Shark Fin
3. Lighthouse
4. Grand Canyon
5. Monolith
6. Menpachi Caves (Secret Cove)
7. Wash Rock
8. Second Cathedral
9. First Cathedral
10. Sergeant Major
11. Sergeant Minor
12. Turtle Haven
13. Summer House

Kikoa Pt.

2798
Puu Alii

3370
Lanaihale

A   I

1547
makani

2072
Puu Manu

1454

Kamaiki Pt.

2500

2000

3000

1500

1000

500

250

Manele Bay

e Pt.

157° 50'

Menpachi Caves (Secret Cove) is a 125-foot-long lava tube, beginning at a depth of 29 feet near the mooring and ending at 45 feet. The tube doglegs, which makes it dark enough inside to suit the rarely seen mole lobster, a species that usually lives in total darkness. Its tiny eyes are so much smaller than those of other lobsters that one wonders if

Sphyraena helleri Molokini 1997

There are several, almost identical looking small schooling barracuda species in the Indo-Pacific. The only one known from Hawaii is this one, Heller's barracuda.

they work at all. Another uncommonly seen lobster, the long-handed spiny lobster, is also found in this narrow tube. Outside are archways and holes full of invertebrates.

The site called **Wash Rock** is a large circular pinnacle from an 80-foot bottom to just breaking the surface. Great barracuda are frequently seen, and flame angelfish live in the coral to the west. Although not

endemic to Hawaii, the Hawaiian population of this species has the most beautiful coloration. It is brilliant red throughout, whereas non-Hawaiian forms are a lighter yellowish orange. This fish is extremely shy, and the color is not visible at depth—a guide and a bright light are usually required to appreciate this stunning little fish.

Although the pinnacle can be circumnavigated in little time, there is much more to see in the rubble and antler coral trees to the east, and on a large ridge that runs perpendicular to shore on the other side of the sand channel. Because the ridge is 20 feet on top, this dive can last a long time.

THE CATHEDRALS

The smell of formaldehyde hit us as soon as the door was opened. Arnold Suzumoto of the Bishop Museum was taking us on a tour of the museum's fish collection—the second-largest in the world, thanks to the indefatigable Jack Randall. Pickled fish of every size and shape, all a sickly tan color, filled shelf after shelf. Our first and only look at a deep water butterflyfish collected by Richard Pyle was here. Found off Kona and Johnston Island, this fish was a recent addition to the known Hawaiian fish fauna. This specimen had been collected by Richard at 400 feet while using his mixed-gas rebreather.

Arnold peeled back the lid of one of the five-gallon buckets stacked off to one side. Filling the entire bucket was the severed head of a moray eel, the largest moray in the world—*Gymnothorax javanicus*. The Javan moray can reach more than nine feet and weigh 154 pounds.

These giants are rarely seen in Hawaii, but one—named The Alien—has lived at **First Cathedral** for at least 15 years. In the words of Erik Stein: "All big eels are in the 'big eel' league. Then there are female Javanese eels, in the league of 'eels-as-big-as-anything-you-have-ever-seen.' Then there is The Alien—who is in another league altogether."

Morays as huge and old as this have seen it all, and The Alien spends its days resting calmly in various parts of its large territory completely unaffected by our presence. Despite the rarity of Javan morays in Hawaii, The Alien has been seen with another of its species several times over the years, mostly in the spring, a testament to the amazing abilities of animals to find others of their kind under seemingly impossible circumstances.

The Cathedral dives are the most requested on Lanai due to their beautiful formations. These are lava tubes which formed above water during a time when sea level was lower and have now been flooded by the sea. Holes eroded in the ceilings of these lava tubes allow light to stream in, and inside First Cathedral some of the beams land on a small rock at the end of the 100-foot-long cavern, giving it the appearance of an altar. If possible, spend some time alone inside the formation and take it all in.

If there is surge, divers can get flushed out through one of the openings to the outside where there is lots to see. Spectacular coral reef goes on forever with an occasional crown-of-thorns sea star digesting the coral tissue away. Frogfish of various colors and titan scorpionfish have always lived here, blending right in with the coral.

The huge expanses of coral here release an unquantifiable amount of eggs and sperm when spawning occurs among cauliflower coral colonies in the spring. Whale sharks, which apparently detect this spawn and follow it up current to the source, can be found at Lanai and at Molokini around this time. In May 2001, whale sharks were seen by various divers four days in a row off South Lanai during the week that the coral spawned—a little above the normal incidence of whale shark sightings!

Second Cathedral to the west is an even larger cavern system. It consists of two main caverns and an open area referred to as The Atrium. Rising from 70 feet to about 15 feet, its bigger openings, archways

Antennarius pictus La Pérouse Bay 1989

and more extensive network of tubes make it a stunning site. Numerous young black coral trees of several species are growing throughout, and one, an old white feathery black coral tree hanging from the ceiling, has to be the only black coral in the world to have been given a pet name—The Chandelier. Nudibranchs of many kinds, crabs, shrimps and shells are found while

This little alien is the painted frogfish. If I were him I might have picked a different spot, as a yellow sponge growing inside a colony of pink sponge looks a little suspicious.

poking around. The entire top of the cavern is blanketed with healthy cauliflower coral.

SECOND DIVES

Escorting boats along the coast is a large pod of Hawaiian spinner dolphins. There's also a good chance they'll be inside Manele Bay. Manele and adjoining Hulopoe Bay form Lanai's sole protected marine area. Nothing may be taken or injured by divers, and no vessels are allowed in Hulopoe Bay. While in the bay the dolphins use this time for socializing and resting. At dusk their activity increases and then they head out to sea for a night of feeding on fish and squid. On the point just outside and to the west of the bay are many shallow caves and grottos good for second or third dives.

The last dive of the day is often at **Sergeant Major**, home to a large population of endemic Hawaiian sergeants. A series of three parallel ridges running perpendicular to shore contains a few small caves and tubes often occupied by whitetip

reef sharks and turtles. The shallow 50-foot depth of the area means that there is plenty of bottom time to swim to the nearby ridges of **Sergeant Minor**, 100 yards to the east. A long lava tunnel here is always occupied by lobsters, often the rare and gorgeous regal slipper lobster.

THE EAST SIDE

While most eastern shores in the main islands get hammered by surf periodically, Lanai's east coast is under the protective wing of Maui, resulting in Hawaii's largest contiguous reef. Beginning at about Kamaiki Point and wrapping up and around the east side to Polihua Beach, the reef, built up of a variety of coral species, is a good place to observe inter-species coral competition and coral-eating fish. Turtles tend to be more abundant on the northeast side than elsewhere off Lanai, with many congregating off Kalakala at a dive site named **Turtle Haven**, and at **Summer House** off Keomuku where fish graze algae from their shells.

This sacoglossan lives in association with Caulerpa algae, which serves as both its food and hiding place. Caulerpa is common and widely distributed, as is this animal, which has a circum-tropical range. Some Caulerpa species are now classified as weeds, most famously in the Mediterranean, where a strain of C. taxifolia has rather hysterically been dubbed 'killer algae.'

Lobiger souverbiei on Caulerpa racemosa var. turbinata Hawaii 1991

WORTH THE LONG BOAT RIDE

Molokai
Rich Pinnacles, Hammerheads, and No Crowds

MOLOKAI IS ONE OF THE LAST OF THE main Hawaiian islands to be explored by sport divers. It is long and thin, and touches on two channels, the Pailolo Channel between Molokai and Maui and the Kaiwi Channel between Molokai and Oahu. The north shore is almost always rough, and the boat landing on the Kalaupapa Peninsula is the only place to land on the entire coast. The south shore, in contrast, is well protected and normally calm.

The south shore of Molokai has an extensive barrier reef which protects the shoreline, and here some of the only mangroves in Hawaii are found. The ancient Hawaiians also took advantage of this calm water, building long stone walls arcing out from shore to form fish ponds. Halfway along this protected shore is the town of Kaunakakai, which has the island's only commercial harbor.

To reach the north shore—and the better diving—from Kaunakakai takes as long as crossing the Pailolo Channel from Lahaina, so most Molokai diving is done from Maui. On most days, the wind and rough seas coming south down the Pailolo Channel make the crossing miserable (and even dangerous), but on a calm day it is just another long boat ride. The diving makes it worth the effort.

OKALA ISLAND

When you arrive at Molokai's remote sites you feel a dramatic sense of isolation. The beautiful green cliffs drop almost directly to the sea, and the almost constant surf forms an impenetrable barrier along the shore. The rugged and beautiful north shore of Molokai offers some of the best scenery in Hawaii.

A spectacular tunnel cuts through a small island named **Okala** to the east of Kalaupapa Peninsula. (See MAP 2.6, pp. 142–143.) The cavern is 80 feet high from its sand bottom to the surface, where an air chamber has formed inside the island. The entrance is as tall as the cavern. The sides of this 100-foot-long tube are covered with sponges, and you can find at least six different species of

> The crossing from Maui is often rough (and always long), but Molokai offers some remote and beautiful sites with very exciting diving. Then there is the Penguin Bank—where the diving is, frankly, too exciting.

lobster here, including the rare long handed spiny lobster. Outside the tube are numerous bandit angels and the bottom is blanketed with gray leather coral.

Unfortunately Okala is many miles past Mokuhooniki (see below), and the long, usually rough trip means it is rarely dived.

On the top of the pinnacle-shaped island above the cave lives a rare endemic Hawaiian plant. The plant has become extinct on the main island and this little island of

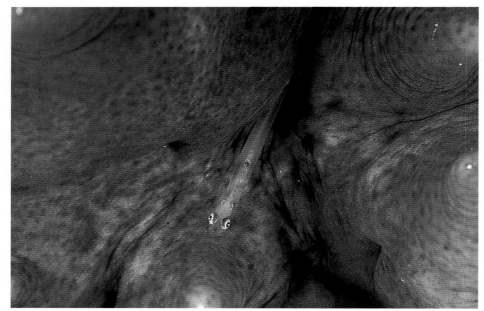

Carapus homei on Stichopus horrens   Makena 1989

This pearl fish is a commensal of sea cucumbers in the genus Stichopus (and sometimes Bohadschia). Here the little eel-like fish hides among its host's papillae, but if threatened, it will disappear, tail first, into the holothurian's anus.

rock remains one of its last refuges. Like all offshore islands in Hawaii Okala is also frequented by sea birds.

MOKUHOONIKI

The most popular site off Molokai is Mokuhooniki, just across the channel from Maui. The formation is an offshore tuff cone, eroded into two small islands—Mokuhooniki and Kanaha Rock—with a shallow bay in front. Both islands are now bird sanctuaries, but during World War II the two were used extensively for target practice, and the surrounding bottom is littered with munitions.

There are many bombs and rockets here, and a spectacular **Missile** embedded nose-first in the bottom on open sand on the Molokai side of the island. Off the southwestern end is an area that has a high concentration of rockets and even torpedoes laying on the sandy bottom. Further inshore from the island local divers have reported another F4U Corsair, half-buried in sand.

This island is most famous for its hammerhead sharks. Every year, hundreds of large scalloped hammerheads (*Sphyrna lewini*) are seen gathered near the southern end of the island at about 120 feet, on a gently sloping sand bottom that leads out to deep water. Though the sharks are said to be there year round, they seem to be most numerous in late summer and early fall. If you are lucky enough to see them it is a magnificent sight and observing them can be done relatively unobtrusively by sitting behind the boulders along the edge of the sand at the base of the island.

The sharks swim in long, lazy circles just inches off the bottom and on a good day you may see more than fifty—on a great day even more. Although big (up to 13 feet), scalloped hammerheads are not considered dangerous. Once the sun goes down they scatter out across the deep sandy bottom of the Pailolo Channel to feed, using the sense organs in their great heads to detect prey buried in the sand.

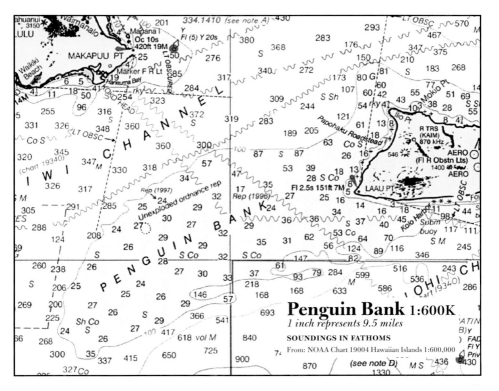

Off the northwestern side of Mokuhooniki is **The Pinnacle**, an isolated rock protruding up through a sand bottom at 110 feet on the inshore side. The rock is far enough from the island to be hard to see, and is seldom visited. Velvet nudibranchs (*Tambja morosa*) live on the shadowed walls along with some small black coral trees, and the rare Thompson's anthias hovers nearby. It is also frequently visited by eagle rays and mahi-mahi.

A long ledge runs out to the south of Kanaha rock with a sheer drop to seaward and a long slope back toward Molokai, a site called **Fish Rain** (or Hole in the Wall). The wall often has a very strong current which is forced up and over the top of the ledge gaining speed and carrying enough nutrients to keep a very healthy community of plankton-feeding fish busy as their schools merge and blend together into a cloud of colorful fish composed of milletseed butterflyfish, Hawaiian longfin and bicolor anthias, pennantfish, and large surgeonfish species.

Although you can easily anchor your boat to the top of the ledge, the current here can be so strong that it is impossible to pull yourself down the anchor line to the ledge from the boat. Once over the lip the current disappears, and you can drop down to a rubble and sand bottom at the base of the wall. At 120 feet the bottom becomes sand. An opening in the southwest side of Kanaha Rock marks this spot and gave the site its alternate name.

Passing through the plankton feeders and lingering in the current you can often see great barracuda and sometimes eagle rays gliding above the wall. Along the wall there are lots of blue dragon nudibranchs, some black coral trees and

Map 2.6 Sites on Molokai

276

Okala and Mokapu 1:10K

Mokapu I.

2

+ 360

-200-

186

Few divers (and operators) are willing to brave the long, wet run from Maui to these sites. This is too bad, because this area offers some very interesting and wild diving, particularly a spectacular tunnel that cuts into the island of Okala. Underneath the island, it opens to the air. This coast, with its sheer cliffs, also offers some of Hawaii's most spectacular scenery.

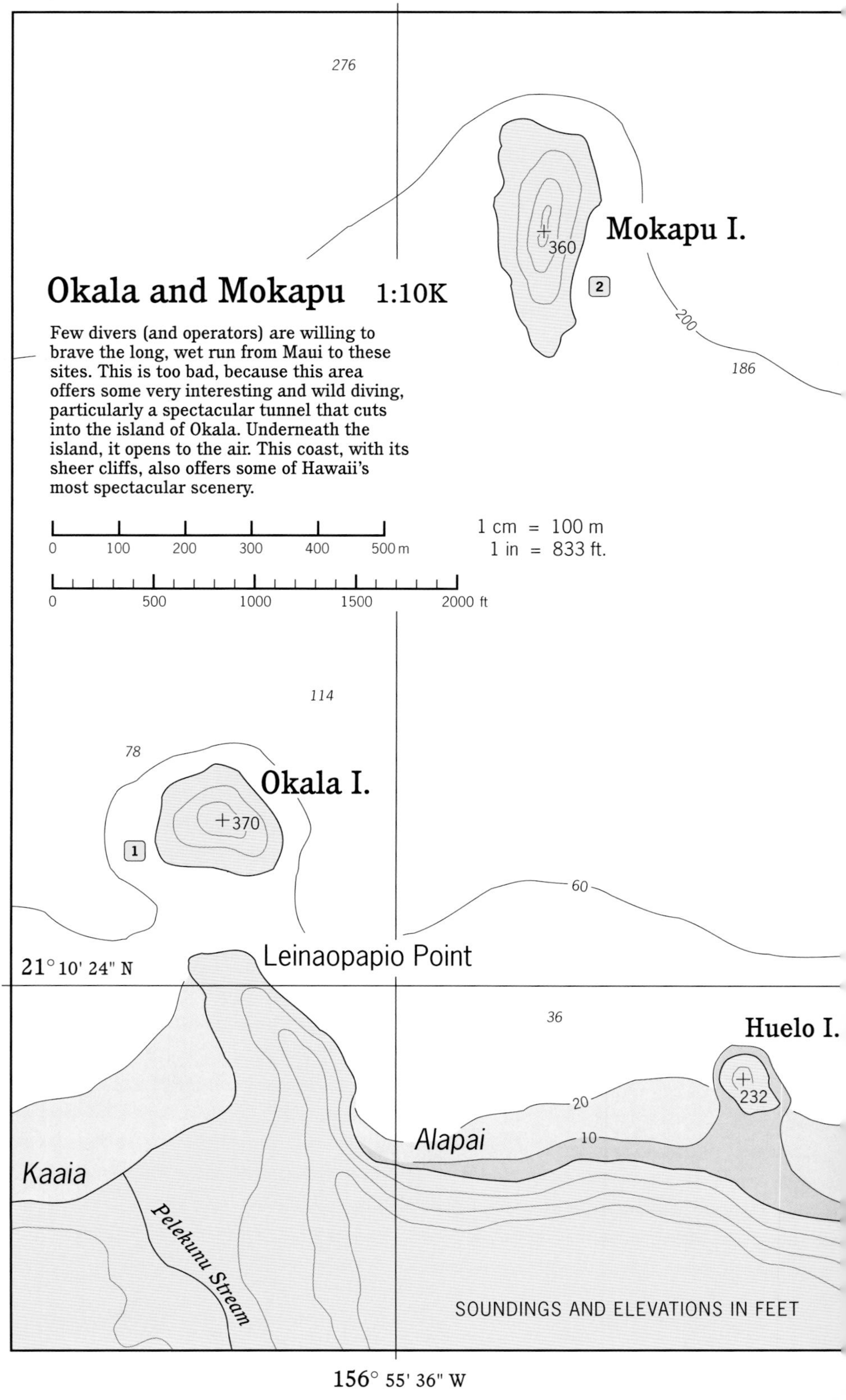

0	100	200	300	400	500 m

1 cm = 100 m
1 in = 833 ft.

0	500	1000	1500	2000 ft

114

78

Okala I.

+ 370

1

-60-

21° 10' 24" N

Leinaopapio Point

36

Huelo I.

+ 232

-20-

Alapai

-10-

Kaaia

Pelekunu Stream

SOUNDINGS AND ELEVATIONS IN FEET

156° 55' 36" W

Mokuhooniki 1:5K

This is the closest Molokai site to Maui, and thus the most frequently dived. Here there are pinnacles, walls, and other striking formations, and healthy fish life. Since the island was used for bombing practice for many years, military debris is common here, including—reportedly—an F4U Corsair. But the real attraction of Mokuhooniki are the sharks. Particularly in late summer and early fall, scalloped hammerheads gather here by the hundreds.

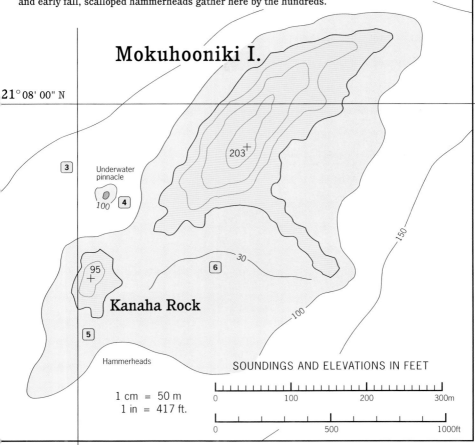

Mokuhooniki I.

21° 08' 00" N

203

3

Underwater pinnacle

100

4

30

6

150

95

Kanaha Rock

100

5

Hammerheads

SOUNDINGS AND ELEVATIONS IN FEET

1 cm = 50 m
1 in = 417 ft.

| 0 | 100 | 200 | 300m |

| 0 | 500 | 1000ft |

156° 42' 18" W

LOCATION DIAGRAM

DIVE SITES

1. OkalaTunnel
2. Mokapu Island
3. The Missile
4. The Pinnacle
5. Fish Rain (Hole in the Wall)
6. Fishbowl

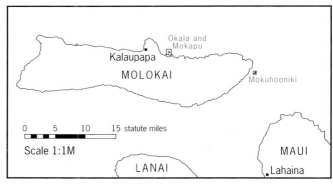

Okala and Mokapu

Kalaupapa

MOLOKAI

Mokuhooniki

0 5 10 15 statute miles

Scale 1:1M

MAUI

LANAI

Lahaina

Sources: Various, including NOAA chart 19347 1:80K. Compiled and rendered by David Pickell, September 2001.

Desmoholacanthus arcuatus, Carijoa riisei Molokini 1991

SOUTH SHORE

The south shore of Molokai consists primarily of long shallow fingers of reef separated by sand channels. It is not often dived, but it was at one time an area where green turtles were hunted extensively. Now that the practice is forbidden, the turtle population has come back, and you can expect to see them on every dive. Because of run-off, the water on the south shore is not as clear as in the north, but the coral reef community there can be quite beautiful.

THE PENGUIN BANK

Not too long ago a group of divers, including a friend of mine, headed out to the Penguin Bank, the shallow reef that sweeps out west and south of Molokai for many miles. When they reached the Penguin Bank, conditions were as they had hoped—calm seas, light current, no wind. Since the divers were all friends and very experienced, the group was somewhat fragmented. They entered the water at their leisure and fanned out, often out of sight from each other, each following his or her own interest.

Everything went normally until near the end of the dive, when the current came up with a vengeance, becoming too powerful to swim against, and almost too strong to hold on against. It practically trapped the divers in place. As they held the bottom, their bubbles trailed straight behind them, swirling in their eddy, and didn't rise. Pulling along the bottom, hand over hand, all but one reached the anchor line, and ascended to the tanks they had staged there for decompression.

Exhausted, breathing heavily, and low on air, one diver was forced to let go and begin ascending. Once in the current she was swept

The bandit angelfish is an unusual Hawaiian endemic that is the only member of its genus. It tends to deep water, usually more than 100 feet. The snowflake coral Carijoa, on the other hand, was an accidental introduction to the islands. It is thought to have come from the Caribbean, perhaps in a ship's ballast water.

wire corals and the occasional bit of leftover ordnance from the years the island was a target. When the hammerheads are in the area they can be seen approaching the base of the wall low on the sand, often with silver mackerel trailing along behind to give a sense of scale to the great sharks.

The inside of the ancient crater is called **Fishbowl**. Here the water is calm and the current is almost non-existent even on a strong day. This is a flat bottom with a thin layer of sand and supports a healthy population of reef fish and almost always has a great barracuda lingering above waiting for an easy meal. Along the shore of Fishbowl are some interesting tide pools fed by the high surf which splashes over the windward arm of the island.

across the bottom which soon dropped away out of sight, leaving only shafts of light radiating down into deep blue. The only sense of depth were the numbers on her computer. Above was the forbidden surface, and with the bottom out of sight, all sensation of speed was gone. It was an oddly peaceful circumstance, she said, except for the increasingly desperate mismatch between the amount of air and amount of time she had left. Endless minutes passed before the first hard breath announced the end of the tank—well before completing decompression.

After surfacing, it took only a few minutes for the first symptoms of the bends to appear. First her lower body grew numb, then her legs became paralyzed. The boat was nowhere to be seen, and only when lifted by each swell could she see the mountain tops of Molokai. Paralyzed and alone, on a gently undulating sea, there was nothing to do but keep looking for her boat and stay calm, as the sun sank ever lower toward the reddening horizon.

It so happens, however, that a Hawaiian couple from Molokai had also been attracted by the calm water that morning, and decided to go out on the Bank for a day of fishing. Near sunset the husband was ready to call it a day, but his wife suggested they make one last pass before heading in. It was on this final pass that they heard a voice. With the sun going down and Molokai vanishing on the horizon, a boat drew near and Susie grabbed the gunwale and was helped on board.

The Penguin Bank is the eroded summit of a sunken volcano, now a broad submarine shelf about 180 feet on top. It is capped with fossil coral and covered with sediment, which trickles down the slopes, eroding deep grooves in the limestone. The Bank is a very interesting place. It is also current-swept, unpredictable, and just plain dangerous. Some people dive this area, which is why we mention it. Please note, however, that this is not a recommendation.

The leopard blenny is stocky, and rather large (4.5 inches) for a blenny. It eats coral polyps and the males (as here) can be very territorial.

Exallias brevis Molokini 1991

Although found throughout the tropical Pacific, Hawaii's current swept environments and rocky ledges suit this species, and it is common here. The females are drab, and only the males have the blue chin and gold-edged fins.

Xanthichthys auromarginatus   Molokini 1999

Wreck of PB4Y-1 Maui 1999

Hawaii's waters offer a number of diveable wrecks, most of them of World War II vintage. Some of the most accessible of these are off Oahu, including the Mahi, which thanks to the intervention of the diving community, became the state's first planned shipwreck. This 165-foot vessel, after a long career with the Navy and as a research ship, was sunk in 1982.

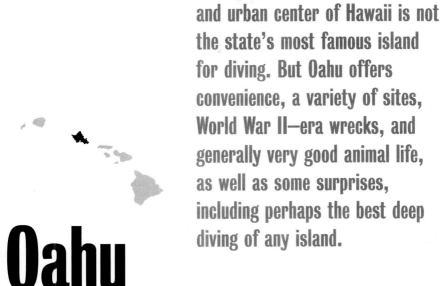

The government, communications, and urban center of Hawaii is not the state's most famous island for diving. But Oahu offers convenience, a variety of sites, World War II—era wrecks, and generally very good animal life, as well as some surprises, including perhaps the best deep diving of any island.

Oahu

OAHU IS THE MOST POPULOUS OF THE Hawaiian Islands, and its lovely people, gentle climate, and remote location have attracted the attention of such talented writers as Robert Louis Stevenson, Mark Twain, and Somerset Maugham, whose work has subsequently shaped Oahu's reputation and the expectations of visitors. In Maugham's "Rain," Honolulu was where the infamous prostitute Sadie Thompson boarded a steamer, just one step ahead of the police, only to end up in gloomy Pago Pago where, cornered by a determined missionary, she used her knowledge of human nature to devastating effect.

Honolulu is a fascinating mix of Asia, the Pacific Islands, and the West. This cultural soup is what makes the island so fascinating and complex. Oahu has been called many things, but "The Crossroads of the Pacific" and "The Gateway to the Orient" are the most common. Today, "The Gateway to America" may be the most practical nickname, as more and more Asian tourists and businesses get their first taste of the United States here.

WHY BOTHER WITH OAHU?

Traveling divers with no plans to stay on Oahu might want to reconsider. Granted, Oahu doesn't have the same bucolic charm of the less populous islands, but Honolulu, with almost 400,000 people, is the only real city in the islands—and the only place with the cultural resources of a city. Oahu offers lively cultural shows, historical tours, and of particular interest to divers, the excellent Bishop Museum, and the Waikiki Aquarium.

The Bishop Museum offers a glimpse into what makes the Hawaiian Islands so interesting. There are many cultural displays

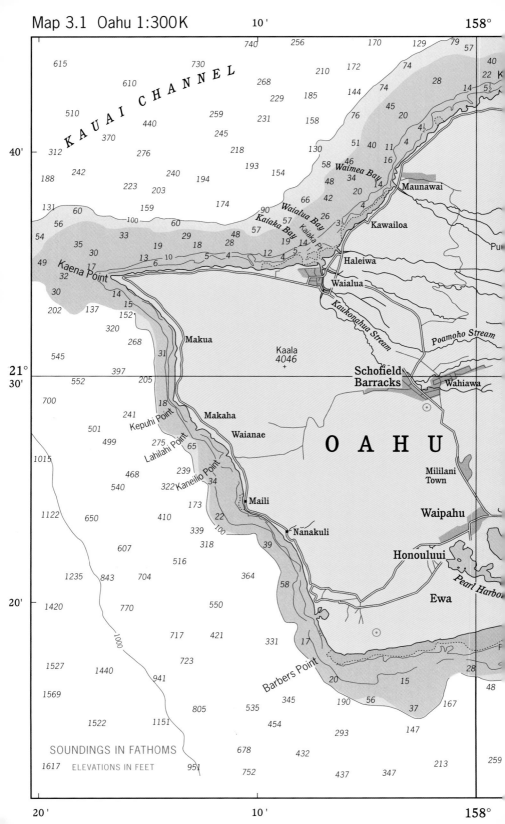

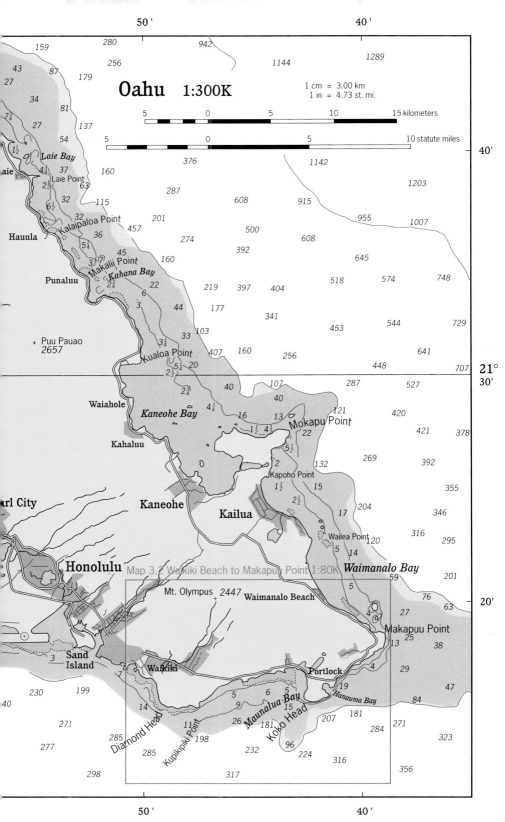

Oahu 1:300K

1 cm = 3.00 km
1 in = 4.73 st. mi.

5   0   5   10   15 kilometers

5   0   5   10 statute miles

50'   40'   40'   21° 30'   20'   50'   40'

159
280
942
1144
1289
256
43
87
179
27
34
81
7¾
27
137
54
1½
Laie Bay
376
1142
aie
37
160
Laie Point
2½
63
1203
32
6½
115
287
32
Kalaipaloa Point
201
608
915
1007
Hauula
36
457
955
5¼
45
274
500
608
3
Makalii Point
160
392
645
Punaluu
Kahana Bay
518
574
748
2½
22
219
397
404
6
544
729
44
177
3
341
453
33
103
Puu Pauao
3¾
407
160
256
641
2657
Kualoa Point
5¼
20
448
707
2½
287
527
2¾
40
107
Waiahole
4¾
40
121
420
Kaneohe Bay
16
13
Mokapu Point
421
378
Kahaluu
1½ 4¼
22
5½
269
392
2
355
132
Kapoho Point
1½
15
204
346
2½
17
Pearl City
Kaneohe
Kailua
Wailea Point
316
295
120
5
14
Honolulu   Map 3.2 Waikiki Beach to Makapuu Point 1:80K   Waimanalo Bay
59
201
Mt. Olympus
2447
Waimanalo Beach
5
76
4
63
27
Sand
Makapuu Point
3
Island
Waikiki
4
25
13
38
Portlock
29
19
3
230
199
Hanauma Bay
47
14
5
5
84
9
15
Maunalua Bay
181
271
11
26
207
181
271
Diamond Head
198
232
181
284
323
285
Kupikipiki Point
96
224
316
285
317
356
277
298

Rhinecanthus aculeatus   Maui 1997

The lagoon trigger-fish is a relatively uncommon inshore species in Hawaii. Both it and the species shown opposite are called humuhumu nukunuku apua a, the famous 'fish with the nose of a pig' in the Hawaiian tale. Officially, however, the state fish is R. rectangulus.

that range from the ancient Hawaiian culture, how they lived by farming and fishing and what their houses once looked like, to the modern influx of the Pacific Rim peoples and how their cultures have influenced the culture of Hawaii in general. Environmental displays explain the high rate of endemic species on land, as well as what animals are going extinct and why, such as the precious Hawaiian birds and tree snails. You can learn about Hawaiian geology, an important aspect for divers since it will allow you to better understand the reefs and the general structure you are seeing underwater. A stroll through the Bishop Museum and its book shop is an excellent introduction to Hawaii for anyone interested in understanding this uniquely isolated island group.

Then there is the Waikiki Aquarium. Here you can see monk seals and green sea turtles, as well as a wide assortment of rare and unusual Hawaiian fish. The displays are well-presented and the explanations will open your eyes to behavior you may not notice when diving. The reason for the high endemicity underwater is explained, and you can learn here why Hawaiian reefs are so different from the reefs of other tropical areas. Rare, deep-water fish such as the yellow anthias and the Hawaiian

grouper are on display, as well as a good assortment of reef fish, game fish, and small sharks. The Waikiki Aquarium also has an excellent book store.

And, of course, there is the diving on Oahu, which can be every bit as good at that of the outer islands. Oahu's twin mountain ranges effectively block the trade winds, forcing them up and over the long, comb-shaped summit ridges, where they acquire the faint scent of the upper forest before descending down into the central island as breezes. The lee coasts created by these ranges are excellent for boating and diving. The windward coast, from the northeast tip at Kahuku to Makapuu, is on most days uncomfortable and rough, and the dull sloping bottom here has not endeared the area to divers. But the other two-thirds of the island can be very interesting.

SOUTH SHORE OAHU

South of Waimanalo, past Makapuu, the rocky end of the Koolau Mountains reaches the coast, punctuated by the rolling knob of Koko Head. Here the shoreline becomes far more interesting with the spectacular and very popular Hanauma Bay. The bay was formed by the erosion of one side of a volcanic crater and is well protected from the wind and the surf, making it a snorkeling and diving mecca. Its clear water and excellent coral reef are a good introduction to the Hawaiian marine environments and rarely are its inner waters dangerous. Beyond Hanauma Bay are the sea cliffs of Koko Head, where the diving is done almost exclusively from boats out of Hawaii Kai. The deep blue color of the water here is contrasted beautifully against the white water cascading from the dark brown cliffs.

As you round Koko Head you feel the gusty trades, but they disappear when you enter Maunalua

Bay. The waters of Maunalua Bay are considerably calmer than the windward side. Here there are some good ledges, a lone and picturesque World War II fighter airplane, and an artificial reef of hundreds of concrete modules and other interesting items including several barges. The bay ends at Diamond Head, the final windbreak before the calm waters of Waikiki.

There is good diving off of Waikiki on some outer ledges and artificial reefs put down by the submarine tour companies. In front of the Harbor, Sand Island, and the Reef Runway, is a bleak and scoured bottom. But here you will find history in stunning profusion, from the great piles of trash and garbage once dumped in front of Honolulu (now affectionately called "The Penny Banks") to antique bottles tossed over the side from moored boats and ships.

WAIANAE COAST

Once you round Barber's Point, the water and the bottom conspire to produce what we consider some of Oahu's finest diving.

Here the water is calm and reasonably clear because the Waianae Mountains block the rain. There are many famous and secret sites along this coast, and there is some excellent deep diving on submarine ledges that at one time formed the shoreline. Deep diving on these ledges is gaining an excellent reputation, and very interesting discoveries are being made here on a regular basis.

THE NORTH SHORE

As you might imagine from what is one of the world's premier surfing areas, the North Shore is almost undiveable in winter, and the battering of the surf has limited the coral growth here. Almost no commercial operators run diving here. Still, many locals rate this their favorite area, and in the right season, there are interesting formations, very good animal life (including some rare species), and as you might guess, no crowds at all.

The Picasso triggerfish is the official humuhumu nukunuku apua a. This one is blowing on its eggs, to keep them clean and well-oxygenated.

Rhinecanthus rectangulus Molokini 1989

FEW, BUT FASCINATING

Wrecks in Hawaii

From the always elusive Spanish wreck to artificial reefs

HAWAII IS NOT ONE OF THE WORLD'S MOST FA-mously wreck-diving destinations. But over the years the islands' rough seas, high winds, storms, and occasional tsunamis have conspired to sink many ships, caught in an island chain with only very few (and widely spaced) natural harbors to run to for shelter.

Some of the earliest European ships to visit were lost in the islands, as were numerous steamships, schooners, and sampans. Later island-based training exercises during World War II resulted in the loss of airplanes and amphibious military vehicles, and modern yachts and boats have been lost during storms and surf since then. Recently, worn out barges and fishing boats have been purposely sunk to create artificial reefs throughout the state.

Divers are fascinated by wrecks. Some just want to take stuff. That is understandable, but wrecks more than 50 years old are protected by state historic preservation laws, and wrecks too recent to fall under this protection, well… good manners at the minimum suggest that you leave everything as you find it. It certainly makes future visits more meaningful if a wreck hasn't been stripped. Other divers like wrecks for the animal life they attract and as photographic subjects. Still others are history buffs, and want to know how the wreck came to rest where it is, and what questions the existence of a wreck might answer.

WERE THE SPANISH FIRST?

One gigantic question in Hawaii has always been: were the Spanish the first Europeans to visit the islands? Captain Cook is traditionally credited with being the first European to find Hawaii, but overwhelming evidence points to earlier contact between Hawaiians and the Spanish. A Spanish chart available since 1570 (and referred to by Captain Cook on his trip to the islands) shows a group of islands of similar layout to Hawaii, although well to the east of Hawaii's true location. Of course calculating longitude was fa-mously a problem in those days, and since there are no islands where those on the Spanish chart are located, common sense suggests they represent Hawaii.

Also, when Cook landed on Kauai in 1778, the Hawaiians already possessed iron and referred to it using a word very similar to the Spanish word for iron, and the resemblance of the chief's headdress and cloak to Spanish men's attire also pointed to Spanish contact prior to the arrival of the English.

None of this is certain, of course. But what if there is a Spanish shipwreck lying somewhere beneath the sands off Hawaii? If found, it could possibly include incontestable proof that the Spanish were here before Cook, and thus this is the Holy Grail of underwater archaeologists in Hawaii.

WORLD WAR II

How several World War II–era military vehicles ended up on the bottom off Makena, Maui, is a question that intrigued long-time Maui diver Scott Castile. Although there are many military vehicle wrecks in the islands, none were lost during actual battles, and the presence of the Makena vehicles was somewhat of a mystery.

The several amphibious tanks and personnel carriers—LVT (A)-4's and LVT-4's—off the Makena coast were thought by some to have been discarded intentionally after the war. This theory was bolstered by the shortened gun barrels, which would have been removed in preparation for scuttling.

Scott's research showed, however, that the gun barrels were short by design. In addition these vehicles went down with their magazines loaded and everything still on them, from helmets and tool kits to ammunition and machine guns. The value of the vehicles and their contents, and their close proximity to shore indicated that these were not intentional sinkings, but losses during training exercises (or from some other unknown mishap).

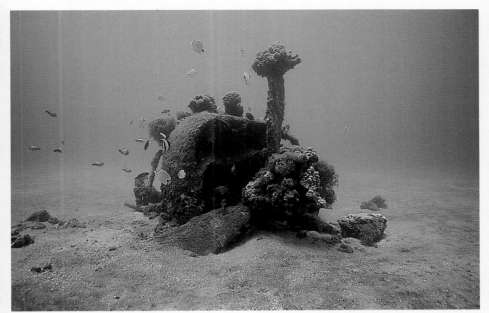

Hellcat wreckage off Kihei, Maui n.d.

This F6F Grumman Hellcat engine, off Kihei, Maui, is just one of a number of World War II wrecks scattered around the islands. These were either lost in training exercises, or sunk as they became obsolete.

HAAHEO O HAWAII

Within the last five years a whole host of questions have been answered at the site of a wreck in Hanalei Bay off the north coast of Kauai. As part of the first underwater archaeological excavations in the state, the 1824 wreck called *Haaheo o Hawaii* (it was previously named *Cleopatra's Barge*), was found by archaeologist Dr. Paul Johnston of the Smithsonian Institution and volunteers from the Sandwich Island Museum.

This 100-foot ship was the first ocean-going pleasure yacht built in the United States, and the last of her owners was King Kamehameha II, Liholiho. She was a treasured royal possession until her loss in 1824. Finding a wreck that was known to have sunk in a small bay close to shore may sound like a simple case of looking at old charts, making some dives, or watching the depth sounder as your boat passes over the bottom. But after 170 years, this wreck was five to ten feet under the sand. Sophisticated magnetic detection equipment is used in such situations, and in this case a device called a proton precession magnetometer was even brought in to help.

Because the tropical climate has left little from Hawaii's early post-contact years, *Haaheo o Hawaii* turned out to be a porthole into that period. Some early 19th century American shipbuilding techniques have been discerned from the small pieces of wood and metal, the fasteners, and even the holes made for the fasteners. To the amazement of the workers, the artifacts recovered so far have proven to be quite a cross-cultural assemblage. Copper sheeting from the hull has been traced to a company in England. Poi pounders, stone anchors, and remnants of a gourd helmet are Hawaiian. Ceramics from China and green gin bottles from Holland are also some of the finds. The dearest discovery was finding the ship's horn—a triton's trumpet shell.

PIONEER DIVER AND WRECK EXPERT

One of the key figures involved in this unbelievably exciting (and often tedious) project has been Richard "Rick" Rogers, a Boeing 717 captain for Hawaiian Airlines who in his spare time has spent 25 years studying Hawaii's shipwrecks in the field and tracking down written reports. Like many of the sport's early divers, he began his diving career under unusual circumstances, breaking in his double-hose regulator in the upper Ashley River in South Carolina diving around old plantation landings and a pre–Revolutionary War fort named Dorchester. Later he logged hundreds of hours along the East Coast of the mainland diving on Civil War blockade-runners and ironclad war ships.

Amtrac Makena 1987

One of the military vehicles off Makena, Maui. Diver and World War II buff Scott Castile has theorized that these vehicles were lost during training exercises, and not purposely sunk as some have maintained.

Rick's lifelong passion is to produce six volumes on the shipwrecks of the islands. Over the years he has compiled a list of sunken vessels from written accounts and from wrecks discovered on the bottom for which there were no written accounts. Included are modern fishing boats, yachts, sampans, inter-island barges, airplanes as well as the older coasting schooners, steamships, clipper ships, whale ships, fur and sandalwood traders. Very few of these are anywhere close to intact. Surf has pulverized some and evidence of their existence may now be buried under many feet of sand. Coral has covered and disguised others.

The first volume in his series—*The Shipwrecks of Hawaii*—is already finished. Every tidbit and legend he found out is included in this first volume which details the known wrecks of the Big Island. Rick has a mischievous streak, as readers will find out, and the book excites the imagination as much as gives information. There is always more to be discovered. As Rick says, "I'm always amazed at

what I don't know about my favorite subject."

WRECK DIVING TODAY

Today divers in the islands have few opportunities to dive historic wrecks. Aside from a couple of scattered debris fields left from early 20th-century ships on Kauai and a few intact World War II–era wrecks on Maui and Oahu, wreck diving in the islands is limited to boats and barges that have been purposely sunk and to a few pleasure craft lost during storms.

One world-class wreck dive was the USS *Bluegill*, a World War II Balao class submarine 311 feet long. The vessel was sunk by the Navy in 1969 off the coast of Lahaina, Maui, to use as a training site for its divers. It sat in the current-swept channel in clear water with its deck at 110 feet and its keel at 130 feet, and became home to rare seashells, small black coral trees, and thousands of fish. Its formidable, elegant form made it one of the most magnificent and inspiring dives in Hawaii.

By the 1980s, the Navy had stopped using the ship for training, but it had become a much loved site among recreational divers. Unfortunately, after several people got bent here, a vocal minority began clamoring for its removal. According to its agreement with the state, the wreck was to be raised and towed out of state jurisdiction when no longer needed by the Navy.

Some suggested moving the sub to an area off Kihei that had already been designated an artificial reef area, but political squabbling between the Lahaina operators, who did not want to lose business to Kihei, and the Kihei operators meant no consensus was reached.

So, in 1983, the State of Hawaii ordered the navy to raise the wreck and tow it to a site 12 miles west of Lanai, where it was sunk in 1,000 feet of water. The state's cited reason for this was liability for divers who got bent or otherwise injured while diving the *Bluegill*, although 13 years earlier the State had already begun an artificial reef program off Oahu, where barges and military vehicles were placed at similar depths.

Such short-sighted acts are unlikely to be repeated. Hawaii now realizes the value of wrecks as artificial reefs, which reduce wear and tear on more fragile natural reefs, and has spent thousands of dollars sinking objects.

South Shore Oahu

Flat, Easy, and Convenient

DIVING OFF HONOLULU ITSELF CAN BE a rather bleak affair, which is why the artificial reefs have been set out here to attract fish and entertain divers. But this ugly bottom holds a great many surprises for anyone talented enough to ferret them out. Dave Norquist had that talent in spades. His instincts were comparable to the early trappers who scrounged a living from the wilderness across the continental United States.

The first day with Dave was a bit of a surprise, when we left the harbor and set out to dive on the flat, desolate bottom outside Sand Island. Our first dive was on Comb Reef, a long pile of rocks covering an abandoned pipe. This was the old outflow for Honolulu's storm sewer, and the name came from the old plastic combs that lay around it on the bottom. Washed into the pipe by the rains and carried out to sea, thousands of combs littered the bottom around the pipe's terminus.

The combs were only a curiosity. In the early days of Honolulu, long before the pipe, ships would anchor off Sand Island and items lost overboard sank to the bottom, eventually nestling into cracks and hollows of the fossil coral beneath the sand. What Dave had discovered was that, periodically, a gold mine of antique soda and whiskey bottles, terracotta jars, and Hawaiian artifacts, would be uncovered by shifting sand. This was economically profitable work, and he had a ready market of collectors competing for his finds. He simply swam high and looked down. At the end of each dive we spent our surface in-tervals admiring the items and discussing their history.

Not long after I abandoned this lifestyle, Dave found the mother lode of all antique sites, which he called Penny Banks for an old Hawaiian coin he found there. It took him a while to figure out what the unusual rolling hills were, but in the end it dawned on him—the old city dump for Honolulu. Today, deep dumping grounds and "unofficial" artificial reefs are still scouted by some of Oahu's tech divers.

Most of the normal boat diving on Oahu's South Shore takes place

These sites, right off Waikiki Beach and Honolulu City, are perhaps not Hawaii's best, but they sure are easy to get to, and you might even find some peculiar treasures here.

off Waikiki and Maunalua Bay, where dive sites are protected from the wind. A host of wrecks have been sunk and reef areas with small caverns are populated by moray eels, a profusion of turtles, and definitely more than the island's fair share of eagle rays. Farther to the east, around Koko Head the wind becomes a big factor, limiting diving there to days of light wind or a boat of hearty divers.

DIVING OUT OF WAIKIKI

At the western end of the Oahu dive boat repertoire is a site called

Ewa Pinnacles. These are not pinnacles at all, but a series of long fossil coral reefs 20 feet high from top to bottom, lying off Ewa Beach just west of the Pearl Harbor channel. Although not known for good visibility, the animal life is good here, and it has been a reliable place to find whitetip reef sharks over the years. Frogfish and red lionfish are

Labroides phthirophagus in Gymnothorax flavomarginatus   Makena 1988

It's nice to see someone who takes his job seriously. Here a Hawaiian cleaner wrasse disappears into the gill hole of a moray eel in a thorough search for parasites.

also found with some regularity, especially by guides who dive here often. In the sand surrounding the ancient reefs at 85 feet is a colony of Hawaiian garden eels.

Sitting outside Kewalo Basin, in 120 feet of water, is a wreck sunk just two years ago, the 168-foot *Sea Tiger*. Originally built in Miezosen prefecture in Japan as a fishing vessel (the bridge equipment is in Japanese), the ship was transporting illegal Chinese immigrants when it was seized by federal marshals in 1990. Voyager Submarines obtained the necessary permits and sponsored the cleaning and sinking of this wreck for its submarine passengers to visit. The company discontinued the submarine trips a year later, so now only divers enjoy the *Sea Tiger*.

The *Sea Tiger*'s location makes it a little more protected from wind and current than many other sites, and the visibility has been described as "epic." The cauliflower corals on the wreck are about the size of cookies at the time of this writing (corals in Hawaii grow about two centimeters a year). It is already shelter to a pair of fountain shrimp, a couple of whitetip reef sharks and, of course, turtles. Single stingrays are sometimes even seen. The explosion of scrawled filefish throughout the islands beginning in 1999 has resulted in a large congregation on this wreck as well. Inhabiting the cracks of the teak deck at 104 feet are shortnose mantis shrimp which scan the surroundings for crabs or mollusks which they chase down and smash open with a blow using their thickened "elbows."

An easy shore dive right in Honolulu is found at **Magic Island**, which is part of Ala Moana Beach Park just opposite the Ala Wai Boat Harbor (and not an island at all). Divers enter at a tiny beach by the short breakwater that juts into the channel, and then swim seaward, being careful not to enter the busy boat channel itself. The wall eventually peters out and to the right is a series of shallow canyons with sandy bottoms. Although visibility is not great, there is a surprising amount of life here, including flame angels, turtles and a school of cornetfish that has lived in the same place for years. Even manta rays have been seen. Every now and then divers find something remarkably rare such as the endemic Hawaiian freckled frogfish, the whitemargin moray, or the speckled butterflyfish. One of the first three masked angelfish ever recorded was found a little further out from this spot in 60 feet of water in 1973, and many of the first sightings of Chromodorid nudibranchs were made here by Scott Johnson and Hans Bertsch in the 1970s. Indeed, if you are interested in nudibranchs, follow the boat channel wall back toward the parking lot instead of out to sea like normal divers would do. This mucky area is one of the best spots in the Islands to find them, including the large and colorful velvet nudibranch (*Tambja morosa*).

YO 257 is the catchy name for a 110-foot-long wreck off of Waikiki, formerly a yard oiler stationed at Pearl Harbor (for this and the following sites, see Map 3.2, pp. 160–161). This was originally sunk in 1989 as an artificial reef for Atlantis Submarines, and in its early days dog kibble was used to attract marine life, mostly a voracious and massive school of taape and some milletseed butterflyfish and black triggerfish. Sitting in 100 feet of water in an area of sometimes strong current, it is now doing fine without the daily feeding, and is covered in many places by snowflake coral. Good hard coral growth, nudibranchs, and frogfish are found throughout the wreck. The deck (at 85 feet) is massive. Two standing masts and their rigging, gantry structures and all kinds of gear provide great habitat for yellowmargin and whitemouth morays and great hiding places for trumpetfish. Sections of the hull and the pilot house ceiling have been cut away for animals and divers, and sometimes a whitetip reef shark is flushed when divers arrive.

When visibility is good you can see its sister wreck, the ***San Pedro***, inshore about 50 yards sitting in 90 feet of water. A smaller longliner, it parallels the YO and forms a channel so passengers on *both* sides of the submarine have something to look at. Frightening as it may sound to have a submarine cruise through while you are diving, the noise is not that offensive, and some divers find

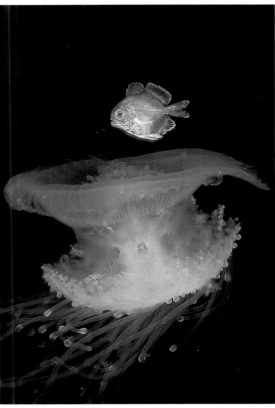

Psenes arafuraensis; Cephea cephea   Molokini 1991

it a novelty to be stared at by submarine passengers.

In keeping with the tradition of Waikiki area site names, **100 Foot Hole** is neither a hole nor 100 feet deep, but it *is* one of Oahu's better dives. This has long been a dependable Hawaiian fishing spot as evidenced by the litter of *palu* stones on the 90-foot bottom. These smooth beach stones are

This medusa fish, a juvenile, uses the drifting jellyfish as shelter. If threatened, it will swim inside the bell.

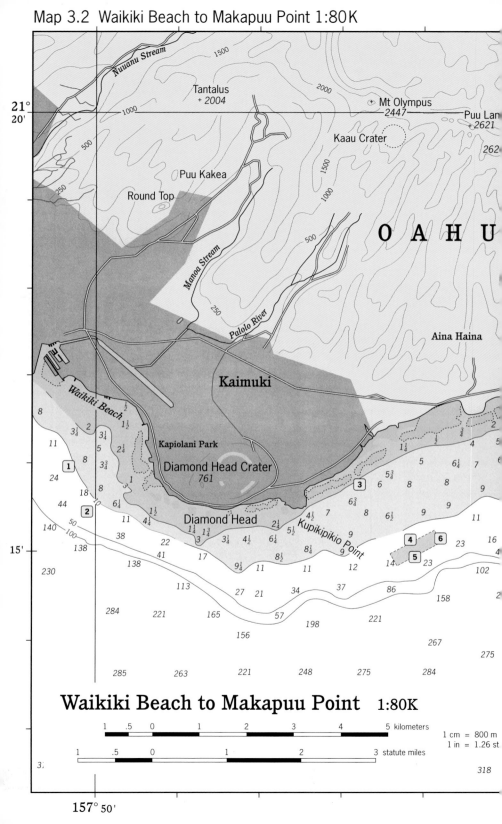

Map 3.2 Waikiki Beach to Makapuu Point 1:80K

Nuuanu Stream

1500

Tantalus
+ 2004

2000

Mt Olympus
2447

Puu Lan
+ 2621

21° 20'

1000

Kaau Crater

262

500

Puu Kakea

1500

Round Top

250

1000

O A H U

Manoa Stream

500

250

Palolo River

Aina Haina

Waikiki Beach

Kaimuki

8

3¾   2

11   5   3½   1½

1½

Kapiolani Park

3¾   2¼

3¾   3½   1¼   4

⊡1   8

Diamond Head Crater

5¾   6¼   7

24   3¾   761   6   8   8   9

18   8   3   1   6¼   3   5¾

44   ⊡2   6¼   11   1½   **Diamond Head**   4½   7   6½   9   11

140   50   4¼   2¼   5½   9

138 100   38   22   1¼   3   3¼   4½   6¼   8¼   9   12   14   23   16

230   140   41   17   8½   23   102   4

138   9¼   11   11   11   86   158   2

113   27   21   34   37   198   221

284   221   165   57   267   275

156

285   263   221   248   275   284   318

Waikiki Beach to Makapuu Point   1:80K

| 1 | .5 | 0 | 1 | 2 | 3 | 4 | 5 kilometers |

1 cm = 800 m
1 in = 1.26 st

| 1 | .5 | 0 | 1 | 2 | 3 statute miles |

3.

318

157° 50'

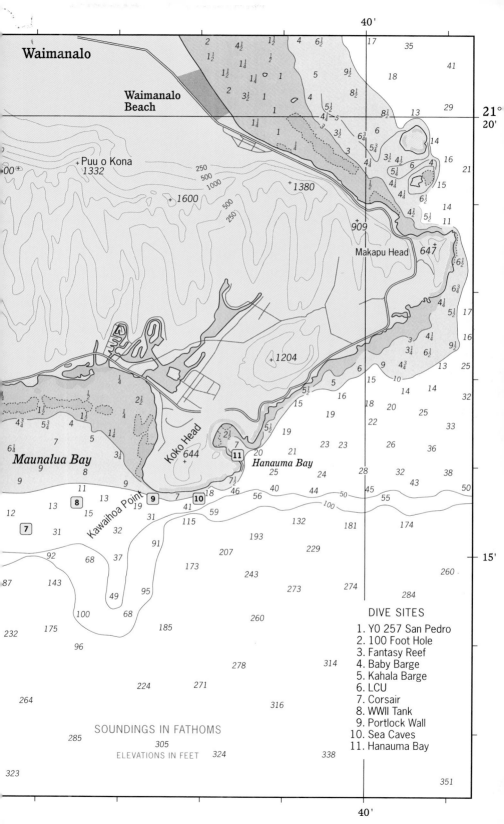

DIVE SITES
1. YO 257 San Pedro
2. 100 Foot Hole
3. Fantasy Reef
4. Baby Barge
5. Kahala Barge
6. LCU
7. Corsair
8. WWII Tank
9. Portlock Wall
10. Sea Caves
11. Hanauma Bay

SOUNDINGS IN FATHOMS
ELEVATIONS IN FEET

Octopus cyanea Hawaii 1997

The octopus has some of the most remarkable eyes in the invertebrate world, and its vision is just as acute as a vertebrate's. Oddly, for a creature with such striking powers of mimicry and elaborate color changing abilities, all chemical, physiological, and behavioral evidence suggests that octopuses are color blind.

clearly out-of-place on the hard flat bottom. Several large stone canoe anchors are also reminders that this site was known to fishermen long before the invention of scuba.

A house-size formation rising from 85 to 65 feet attracts lots of fish, including occasional predators. Although coral growth is limited, the top of the rock does have a beautiful covering of cauliflower coral. A tunnel runs through the pinnacle that divers can swim through, sometimes flushing a whitetip reef shark, and there are numerous holes and undercuts. An old cable on the Diamond Head side leads to an interesting ledge at 130 feet.

MAUNALUA BAY

One of few places on the south side where the 40–80 foot shoreline

is well-defined is **Fantasy Reef**. Erosion has created many places for fish to hide including the rare male lined *Coris*. Although live coral coverage is not that high, it is healthy and undamaged and considered one of the prettier dives in the area. Animal life is good with eels, octopus, and sometimes barracuda. Ledges and archways are big enough to attract larger turtles and sharks.

Beginning with the deposit of 549 cars in 1961, the Department of Land and Natural Resources has been involved in building an artificial reef within about a one-square mile area off Kahala. Called the Maunalua Bay Artificial Reef, some of the early items were sunk before the availability of GPS and there's no telling where they really ended up. But the area is supposed to contain four barges, a Navy LCU, and literally thousands of tons of pipes, tire modules, old pilings, and concrete shapes. The barges, between 65 and 90 feet, are all far enough apart to make them separate boat dives. All can experience strong current, which does wonders for the visibility.

The largest and deepest of these, **Kahala Barge**, is impressive just in length alone—165 feet! Although this was the first barge sunk in this area 15 years ago, coral growth is still limited, but the vessel is choked with soldierfish, which make their characteristic grunting sound when disturbed. Many eels and sometimes large crabs can be found, as well as rays and jacks. **Baby Barge** in 65 feet of water has a dozen resident turtles and also whitetips. The **Landing Craft**, a Navy LCU, was sunk three years ago and lays on its side in 87 feet of water. A Galapagos shark has recently frequented this site. In August 2000 the state added hundreds of concrete "Z" forms nearby, although they haven't attracted many inhabitants yet.

A mile off Portlock, in 108 feet of water, rests a lonely **F4U Corsair**. This was reportedly ditched in 1945 after it experienced engine problems during a training flight and the pilot, Lt. W. Holden, escaped. Recognizable by its inverted gull wings, the F4U Corsair was the first single-engine Navy fighter to exceed 400 mph, and is considered the most outstanding carrier-based fighter of World War II. The cockpit is open and occupied by two thigh-sized yellowmargin morays. The port wing is almost completely buried, but the starboard wing is intact and a day shelter for soldierfish. Because of the depth and lack of competition from light-requiring organisms, brilliant red encrusting sponge covers the fuselage, and bicolor anthias harems hover above picking plankton. Nearby in the sand are garden eels and big horned helmet shells. Careful scrutiny of the sand may reveal the well-camouflaged head of a crocodile snake eel. It remains still as a rock until a fish nears, when it explodes from the sand and grabs the fish, pulling it under the sand. Visibility is excellent here, and the plane can usually be seen as soon as you enter the water.

The other historic wreck dived on this side of the island is the remains of a World War II **Tank** in 80 feet of water. As one would expect, the vehicle has collapsed from 50 years of exposure to salt water and hurricanes, and in fact is almost unrecognizable. The lump attracts a good amount of marine life, including adult female octopus which lay and brood their eggs here. The only cover on the hard, flat bottom, the tank is used by a school of pennantfish. They feed on plankton high in the water column, but hug the tank when threatened, creating a beautiful sight of swirling black, yellow and white.

Just inside Maunalua Bay is a distinct section of the submerged shoreline and a very popular shore and boat dive called the **Portlock Wall** (or China Wall). This is a small wall that drops from 30 to 45 feet.

A spiny cowfish investigates the camera. The lumbering and comical trunkfishes are perennial favorites with divers. Their stiff body structure and skin toxins discourage any bad behavior from predatory species.

Lactoria diaphana   Molokini 1990

Moku Manu

The first time I ever heard of Moku Manu, it was the setting for a fantastic, almost Biblical, account of the sea around it turning red, from millions of small red fish. I heard this third-hand, and later, when I talked to the person who had actually witnessed the masses of fish, the story became a little less dramatic, but far more interesting.

John Earle had been out to Moku Manu that day and yes, a red area composed of millions of tiny anthias had drifted toward the boat he was diving from. Fascinated, but not wanting to miss an opportunity, he scooped a few with a hand net, and took them home thinking that they would be an excellent snack for an ever-hungry frogfish he was keeping in his aquarium. Bruce Carlson, now the director of the Waikiki Aquarium, happened to be at John's house during a feeding and noticed that there was something different about these particular anthias, and called ichthyologist Dr. John E. Randall.

When Jack arrived, he knew right away that they were an undescribed species of anthias, and the poor frogfish lost its colorful food. Jack subsequently named the fish after John, *Luzonichthys earlei*, or Earle's splitfin. This species has since been collected in other areas of Hawaii and the Pacific, but the red ball of fish drifting toward John's boat was an unusual sighting.

Population explosions like this one over the years are not uncommon. The conditions that allow this are obscure, but somehow a species is favored either in its larval stage or as adults, and for a few years there will be an unusually high number of them around. In the mid-1980s, fantail filefish were in big aggregations high off the bottom, and *ahi* tuna were being caught with their bellies full of the little filefish. This species is usually relatively scarce, but in those days, it was not uncommon to see hundreds of them on a dive. Competition for food must have been intense, and many appeared half-starved. Most recently another species of filefish, the scrawled filefish, has shown up in unusual

numbers on many wrecks and reefs. John's splitfin was experiencing such a population explosion that year at Moku Manu.

ROUGH, EXPOSED, AND RICH

Sticking bravely out off the windward coast, in rough water Moku Manu is just about the most inaccessible point off Oahu. The twin rock islands—Moku Manu means "Bird Island"—lie about 500 yards offshore from Mokapu Point. The rocks are the remains of an old tuff cone that has eroded.

The water is rough and the current can be strong, so few divers ever visit this site. When you enter the water this fact will become obvious. Fish that are scarce in more accessible areas are rich here. Large parrotfish and goatfish, *ulua* and *uku* are seen near the bottom, while hundreds of soldierfish hang near holes and caves, and schools of *kawakawa* sometimes swim by in blue water.

Several caves and caverns that have been eroded into the islands make diving here even more interesting. One cave in the seaward islet opens at a depth of about 50 feet. From the large ten foot by ten foot entrance, the cave runs for 150 feet before opening up into a vertical crack, with a stunning shaft of light streaming in. In addition to various species of lobsters, there are some unusual animals here, such as Evermann's cardinalfish, a cave-dwelling species, and rarely seen glass spine urchins live in the recesses. Nudibranchs, sponges, and many small crustaceans can also be found with a light as well.

Outside the caves cauliflower coral growth is lush because the excellent water clarity allows good light penetration, and the constant water movement brings food and carries away any sediment. The yellow, green, and tan corals house hundreds of snapping shrimp, which fill the water with their crackling sounds. Large sea turtles rest out in the open and in the protection of the cave entrances, but since they rarely see divers they tend to bolt when divers appear.

About a thousand yards north-northeast

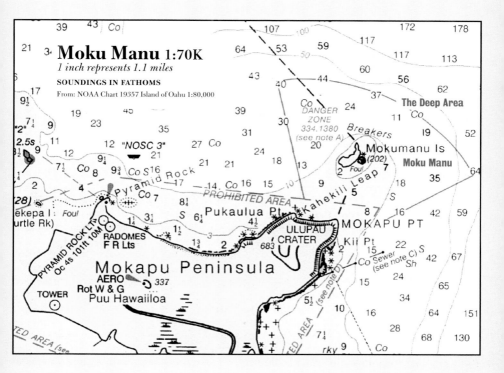

Moku Manu 1:70K

1 inch represents 1.1 miles

SOUNDINGS IN FATHOMS

From: NOAA Chart 19357 Island of Oahu 1:80,000

DANGER ZONE 334.1380 (see note A)

Breakers

Foul

The Deep Area

Mokumanu Is (202)

Moku Manu

PROHIBITED AREA

Pukaulua Pt.

Kahekili Leap

MOKAPU PT

ULUPAU CRATER

Kii Pt

Sewer (see note C)

(see note D)

PYRAMID ROCK LT. Oc 4s 101ft 10M

RADOMES F R Lts

Mokapu Peninsula

AERO Rot W & G

Puu Hawailloa

TOWER

ekepa I. *Foul*

urtle Rk)

PROHIBITED AREA (se

rky

from Moku Manu is some dramatic deep diving in an area of, naturally, very strong current. The bottom drops away from about 80 to over 200 feet, and black coral trees with long-nose hawkfish grow in abundance along the drop-off. Tinker's butterflyfish and Thompson's anthias have been seen here hovering along the drop.

Most divers will want to keep looking out into the blue for jacks and sharks. This paid off for one diver who saw a great white shark here (and this is a reliable report).

A NATURAL PRESERVE

As anyone who has been diving in Hawaii for any length of time realizes, Hawaii is not the place to see big groupers. Only two native species of groupers exist in the entire Hawaiian chain. One, the Hawaiian grouper, is seen regularly at diving depths only at Midway. The other has been seen by only a handful of divers ever. This species, *Epinephelus lanceolatus,* is called the giant grouper because it has been recorded to 9.8 feet in length, and 882 pounds.

These fish are usually very deep when seen by divers, but fishermen have been known to catch them from shore. One shore-caught fish was even propped up on the back of a pick-up truck and paraded through the streets during the Makawao Rodeo parade a few years ago, underscoring its size and rarity even to long-time residents. Stomach contents of such huge groupers have included lobsters, stingrays and even turtles.

In any case, off the drop at Moku Manu two incredibly lucky divers were able to watch one of these giant groupers for about 30 seconds as it slowly pushed its 7-foot body through the water. As an added bonus, they had each other to verify their stories.

Inaccessible islands like Moku Manu begin to give us a picture of what Hawaii's reefs and nearshore environments would be like without spearing, harvesting, and fishing pressures, or even the visits of divers. Hawaii's numerous small rock islands in windward areas are unofficial havens for many constantly hunted species, and with the help of mother nature will probably remain that way—since there are so many calmer, easier and safer areas to fish or dive.

Because they are open water fish, tuna are rarely seen by divers, but they are well known to fishermen. In Hawaii, most of the catch is ahi (either bigeye tuna or yellowfin—equal numbers are caught and the Hawaiian 'ahi' doesn't distinguish between them) with aku (skipjack) and albacore also being important. The Hawaii tuna fishery is considered quite well-run and sustainable. Of the common market tunas, ahi from bigeye tuna (Thunnus obesus) is the highest quality, whether served as sashimi, seared, or dried.

The real star of the tunas is northern bluefin (Thunnus thynnus), considered the most valuable animal on earth. On Jan. 5, 2001, at the Tsukiji fish market in Tokyo, one fine 444-pound specimen sold for $172,400. At $388 a pound wholesale, this set a new record.

It is generally protected from tradewind wrap, but is best done on an incoming tide when visibility is better. This site is loaded with moray eels, conger eels, and snake eels, and is also a good site to find Commerson's frogfish. And lots of turtles. The waters off Portlock seem to be Oahu's best area for sighting humpback whales (December through May).

Koko Head is a large tuff cone that last erupted in pre-historic times. Three-hundred-foot cliffs along the edge continue underwater down to about 90 feet, where the bottom begins to level out. **Sea Caves**, along the edge of the island, is one of the better South Shore dives. At about 45 feet a huge cavern extending 90 feet into the cliff slopes up to about 10 feet where divers sometimes surface in an air chamber above water. Leaf scorpionfish, banded and cleaner shrimp, and hundreds of bloodspot sea stars live within. Although an interested diver could spend the entire dive (with or without a light) inside

this and the smaller side caves, the dive is usually done as part of a drift in moderately strong current going west toward the Portlock Wall.

HANAUMA BAY

Picturesque Hanauma Bay is the Hawaii of imagination: a circular bay with a white sand beach and palm trees, and filled with blue and turquoise water. It is the most scenic view on Oahu.

The need to protect such a beautiful site was obvious from the beginning, and it was one of the first protected marine areas in the state, becoming a Marine Life Conservation District way back in 1967. Dives of all levels of experience can be made inside the arms of the bay.

Diving inside the bay is a chance to view a healthy coral reef and all its inhabitants in a calm and relaxed setting. There are two main areas inside the bay: the inner reef and the outer reef. Since the inner reef is an ancient fossil reef, you want to swim through one of its channels to the outer reef. Because of the pro-

Unidentified tuna   Hawaii n.d.

King of the Fishes

HAVE YOU EVER ENTERED THE RANDALL ZONE? As a diver it's possible that you have, because this is a place found only underwater. Have you ever noticed the clearing found around a natural or artificial reef? A kind of corona where the sand is bare and free of algae? There is a reason for this clearing. Grazing fish that use the reef for protection will only range so far from the security of the coral during feeding. This distance is made obvious by a boundary where the sand ends and the algae begins. This clearing has come to be known as The Randall Zone, named after the man who recognized the phenomenon—ichthyologist Dr. John E. Randall, or more compactly, "Jack."

PIONEER DIVER

From the time he was an undergraduate, Jack has known that he wanted to study fishes. It was a mission. His father was a building contractor, and had other ideas for his son's career. Jack made an honest effort at studying architecture, but he couldn't help it—he was unavoidably drawn to the ocean.

Jack made his first wetsuit by dipping his long underwear in a tub of latex. With this, he dived the cold waters of California, spearing fish to sell and capturing specimens to study in his own aquarium. Then he got it into his head that he wanted to go to Hawaii.

Some people might simply book passage on a boat or plane, but Jack bought a hull, constructed a sailboat, learned to sail, paid off the loan, and sailed it to Hawaii. In Hawaii he invented the multi-pronged Hawaiian sling spear to catch his specimens, as well as a teeny tiny version for little fish like gobies, and began the work that has made him famous.

This kind of effort might be attributable to youth, but at the age of 77 Jack is still at it. Anyone who has been on a dive trip with him—and there are many, since he has dived all over the world—has a story to tell of Jack's tireless fish endeavors. I remember getting up at dawn and eating breakfast at a dive resort restaurant on Flores, Indonesia, so I could get an early start on my day. I had just started on my coffee when I saw Jack walking up the path from the bay. He was dripping wet, in full gear, carrying specimens he had just collected on a dive in the muck in front of the resort.

Jack has even been known to scrounge through all the spent tanks on the boat, trying to find one with a couple hundred pounds left in it so he can go back down and photograph just "one more" fish.

Dr. John E. Randall

THE DOYEN OF ICHTHYOLOGISTS

Ichthyologist and relentless diver don't always go hand in hand. But thanks to Jack's efforts, the Bernice P. Bishop Museum's Indo-Pacific fish collection is now the second largest in the world. Much of his scientific work has been in taxonomy and classification, and Jack has so far described 514 species—more than any other living ichthyologist.

Jack is also a natural when it comes to teaching. He has inspired those around him for years to pay attention to the fish in the most minute detail, and his students are now some of the top ichthyologists in the world.

In addition to the much-overlooked Randall Zone, two genera and thirty-nine species of fish, as well as four marine invertebrates have been named in his honor. When you are diving in Hawaii, Randall's puffer and Randall's frogfish are two you might see. If you go to the Caribbean, you might see Randall's pipefish and Randall's goby. If you venture further out in the Pacific, you might find the colorful Randall's snapping shrimp, a red, yellow, and white shrimp that lives with its goby partner. The fact is, you can be underwater almost anywhere in the world, and it is very possible that swimming around you is a *randalli* of one type or another.

tection afforded by the crater's shape, the **Outer Reef** contains beautiful, healthy coral and is home to a great variety of reef fish and many different species of moray eels. Sixty feet is about the deepest you will get in here, and most of the dive is a lot shallower. Because of the protected location you can concen-

Unidentified crab   Hawaii 1992

This little guy has just settled out into its post-zoeal form. For sense of scale, note the size of the sand grains.

trate on watching animal behavior instead of worrying about current or the rocky exit you have ahead of you. Watch for jacks hunting the smaller reef fish, eels hunting octopus, small damselfish guarding their eggs, trumpetfish using other fish as a blind, and even turtles and sharks can be found here.

Deeper diving can be done just outside the points. One of the best dives on the island is just outside the eastern point of the bay, **Palea Point,** though it is infrequently visited by dive boats due to the wind sneaking around Makapuu Point. Right along the edge of island is a ledge at 20 feet where large stingrays have been seen periodically. A steep drop from 20 to 60 feet contains several small caverns often occupied by whitetip reef sharks. Down from the caverns, the bottom slopes away—covered by extensive healthy coral—all the way to Lanai Lookout. Dragon eels live in this maze and flame angels and frogfish have also been seen. Don't be surprised if a school of Heller's barracuda appears along the way.

The area east of Palea Point is popular with divers because the bottom drops off quickly. It can be extremely rough here, however, and this site has taken the lives of many fishermen, *opihi* (limpet) pickers and occasionally tourists. Dive here with someone who knows the area well, and only when waves are not crashing on shore.

After a good rain when the atmosphere is clear, the island of Lanai is sometimes visible from this southeast extension of Oahu, giving the name **Lanai Lookout** to this boat or shore dive just east of Hanauma Bay. The dive is along a small wall covered with bracket shaped lobe corals and wire corals inhabited by commensal gobies and shrimp. A 25-foot-high cavern reaching 40 feet into the shoreline is sometimes occupied by whitetip reef sharks and turtles. Where the wall meets sand at about 50 feet look for spotted snake eels protruding from the sand. Farther out the bottom dips to 90 feet. Keep an eye out in the blue as *ulua* and eagle rays are sometimes seen. Because this has been a popular fishing spot for eons, heavy test fishing line is everywhere, so be sure to bring a dive knife.

Waianae Coast
Artificial Wrecks, Deep Ledges, and Good Conditions

STORMS THAT PERIODICALLY BRING destruction and chaos to the shallow water ocean floor we all dive often uncover older bottom. Depending on the strength of the storm, they may reveal a bottom that has been buried for decades, sometimes resulting in exciting finds once the waves have subsided.

In 1982, John Earle watched as hurricane Iwa slammed into his home coast and favorite dive sites. Iwa was the worst storm to hit in some twenty years, bringing enormous surf. He knew this would churn the bottom, breaking coral and shifting massive quantities of sand. By the time the storm subsided he had a plan.

John headed out to the Waianae coast, the arid local side of the island where few tourists visit, and spent several days diving some of his favorite sites. Among the debris left in the wake of huge waves he found numerous freshly dead shells, including checkered cowries, a beautiful shell that is found only in Hawaii, and even then, only rarely. Their shells hadn't been tumbled in the surf, so John suspected that they had emerged from their crevices after the storm to find their habitat destroyed and their food supply diminished, and had soon starved.

A couple of days later he entered Ulua Cave, a well-known site visited constantly by divers who scan the bottom of the cave for shells. Shining his light around he saw something laying on the sand. Not a seashell at all, this turned out to be a three-inch-long Hawaiian fishhook carved out of bone.

This artifact currently resides in the Bishop Museum collection, where the specialist who catalogued the hook said that it was of an early Hawaiian design and probably hundreds of years old.

> **Most divers head to the artificial reef just off Waianae, with the wreck of the Mahi. This is easy and rich diving, but there are also some great deep ledges and drop-offs here.**

The bone had not decayed, he suggested, because it had been buried deep in an anaerobic layer of sand in the cave. The chaotic water movement created by the storm had reached well into the cave, excavating the hook which had remained undisturbed for hundreds of years.

Of course, one wonders how the hook got into the cave in the first place. Here there can be only one likely scenario. It must have been brought into the cave in the mouth of a big fish, probably an *ulua*. The hook either finally worked its way out or was spit out by one fish that definitely did get away. The hook, now resting in a place of honor, is with the few other surviving hooks of its era.

DIVING OAHU'S LEE COAST

The Waianae Coast is Oahu's protected lee side, so it is no surprise that the island's major fringing reef is off this side of the island. Oahu's

A traditional Hawaiian fishhook. These were constructed of wood and bone, with a stone weight.

leeward side is also the side with the more complex lava formations such as caves, lava tubes, and arches.

A pod of Hawaiian spinner dolphins resides along this coast, as they do on the quiet sides of most islands in Hawaii, and they often accompany dive boats during their trips.

While there is a healthy natural reef to the south, the main attraction

Paracirrhites forsteri on Pocillipora eydouxi   Hawaii 2000

Hawkfish like a high perch, and on Hawaiian reefs the scattered clumps of Pocillipora eydouxi, particularly in the deeper reef areas, tower over the dominant P. meandrina and Porites colonies.

off **Kahe Point Beach Park** is actually two parallel exhaust pipes that discharge warm water from the Hawaiian Electric power plant across the road. The pipes are about ten feet in diameter and ten feet apart, and are encased in concrete and corals. Christmas tree worms have colonized the pipe casings. A rock barrier has been placed in front of each pipe to break

up the outflowing water. This exits the pipes at three to four knots, so if you decide to go for a ride be prepared to be carried out and *up*.

Getting tossed around in this turbulent water are surgeonfish, parrotfish, and damselfish. They all try to come in from the side to pluck at the lush algae growth at the mouths of the pipes, but eventually get tumbled. Barracuda, crocodile needlefish, and eagle rays are also attracted to this outflow. This is a shallow shore dive, but very scenic!

Paralleling some frequently dived ledges off Maili Point are ledges in a much deeper range. Called **The Maili Ledge**, this area is explored mostly by local technical divers. (This and the following sites can be found on the chart opposite.) The Maili Ledge is far from shore where the current can be very strong, and the drop-off begins at 170 to 200 feet. Understandably, few divers visit, and Maili Ledge is a bragging rights dive.

A diver who is willing to try this one can expect to see sharks, usually whitetips and sandbar sharks, and can hope for more unusual species—tiger sharks, hammerheads, and thresher sharks have all been seen here.

Drift diving anywhere along this ledge is an adventure, and rare fish like Tinker's butterfly and the sunset basslet are possible. Black coral trees with longnose hawkfish are there as well. There is never enough bottom time to explore very much of this area, which includes a big cave and an island just off the ledge.

Inshore from the ledge is a dive site called **Twin Holes**. This is a comfortable drift dive along an ancient shoreline that drops from 55 to 90 feet. There are four arches and chimneys carved into the ledge, but you can only see them all on a single dive if the current is vigorous. More typically, a dive will cover only

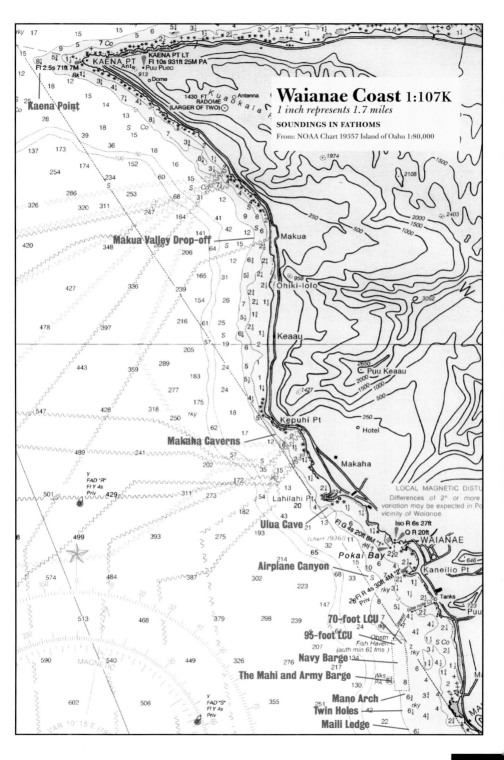

Waianae Coast 1:107K

1 inch represents 1.7 miles

SOUNDINGS IN FATHOMS

From: NOAA Chart 19357 Island of Oahu 1:80,000

Kaena Point

Kaena Pt

KAENA PT
Fl 2.5s 71ft 7M
Bk

KAENA PT LT
Fl 10s 931ft 25M PA
Puu Pueo

Ante
913
Dome

1430 FT
RADOME
(LARGER OF TWO)

Antenna

Kuaokala

Makua Valley Drop-off

Makua

Ohiki-Iolo
958

Keaau

C. Puu Keaau

Kepuhi Pt

Hotel

Makaha Caverns

Makaha

Lahilahi Pt

LOCAL MAGNETIC DISTU
Differences of 2° or more
variation may be expected in Po
vicinity of Waianae.

Ulua Cave

Fl G 4s 20ft 8M
(chart 19361)

Iso R 6s 27ft
Q R 20ft
WAIANAE

Pokai Bay

Airplane Canyon

Kaneilio Pt
646

Fl R 4s 30ft 4M
Priv

Tanks

70-foot LCU

95-foot LCU

Obstn
Fish Haven
(auth min 6½ fms)

Navy Barge

The Mahi and Army Barge
Wks
PA

Mano Arch

Twin Holes

Maili Ledge

Y
FAD "R"
Fl Y 4s
Priv

Y
FAD "S"
Fl Y 4s
Priv

VAR 10° 15' E

MAGNETIC

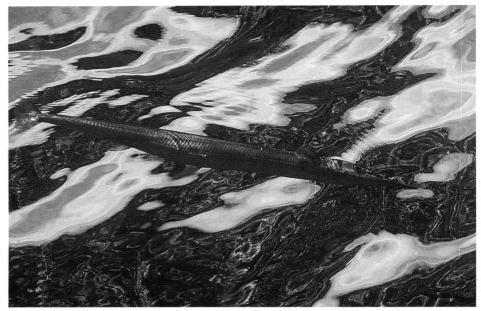

Tylosurus crocodilus ssp. crocodilus   Molokini 1989

The crocodile needle-fish is the largest of this group of fast-moving surface predators. It is aptly named, and reaching a length of four feet, not to be trifled with.

part of this three-quarter mile section of ledge.

The first three arches extend deep into the ledge with silty bottoms and darker environs. Slipper lobsters and many banded coral shrimp live on the sides of the caverns, with orange cup coral and yellow sponges covering the ceilings. Sometimes *ulua* and small jacks are flushed from the caverns. Drifting north along the ledge you will see wire corals extending into the water and some of the fish, such as Moorish idols, orient themselves upside-down to the ceiling of the overhangs.

A dive at Twin Holes winds up at **Mano Arch,** a beautiful, wide arch with a big chimney opening and lots of light streaming onto the sand bottom. On top of the ledge is a profusion of cauliflower and antler corals. From here the *Mahi* is only 150 yards offshore. About half the time the current runs the other way, so you might find yourself beginning at the arch, and drifting to Twin Holes.

If you sign up to go boat diving out of the Waianae Boat Harbor, it is almost impossible not to dive the wreck of the ***Mahi***. This is not necessarily a bad thing, as this artificial reef is not only one of Oahu's most popular dives, but one of the most spectacular. The ship has spent almost two decades on the bottom, which has resulted in good coral growth on the deck, cup coral and hydroid growth in the holds, and a lively community of reef fish and hunting jacks.

Fish feeding has created a community of tamed milletseed butterflies and *taape,* contributing to the apparent swarm of fish.

The navy originally built the ship as a mine sweeper, but the 165-foot, 800-ton vessel was used instead to lay cable, as divers can see from the modified bowsprit and cable reel. The *Mahi* was sunk in 1982, just in time for Hurricane Iwa. When diving resumed after the storm, divers found that the 800-ton ship had been turned 180 degrees, facing her streamlined bow into the tempest and out to sea.

Octopus sp. Makena 1996

Before the ship was sent to the bottom, sections of the hull and some of the hatches were removed to create habitat and allow diver access to the three decks and pilot house, which range from 60 to 80 feet. In the sand around the wreck, at about 92 feet, are garden eels and horned helmet shells.

Keep your eye out for eagle rays here, as they are almost guaranteed. As many as 14 have been seen at one time, and if not chased they will often stay in the vicinity for the whole dive, gliding in formation with graceful wings and up-turned noses. During the ascent on the mooring line notice the amazing number of porcupine and spiny pufferfish in the water above the wreck, all facing into the sometimes strong current.

WAIANAE ARTIFICIAL REEF

The *Mahi* is within an area designated the Waianae Artificial Reef which, like the similar site in Maunalua Bay, was initially stocked with junked cars in the 1960s. Later, ob-

solete military craft were sunk.

The 110-foot-long **Army Barge** lies just 150 feet to the south of the *Mahi*. Although this is within swimming distance, because of the limited bottom time at depth, diving both sites on the same dive isn't really feasible. If the *Mahi*'s regular school of eagle rays isn't present they are sometimes found over on the Army Barge.

Further north is another barge, the 170-foot-long **Navy Barge**. This vessel, sunk in 1970, was the first ship to be sunk as part of an artificial reef in the state. It rests at 112 feet and because of its age has very good coral growth. Two 115-foot Navy LCUs (Landing Craft Utility vehicles) are also located within the artificial reef boundaries, named for their depths: **70-foot LCU** and **95-foot LCU**. Coral growth is just beginning on these, but they already host a good community of fish.

The use of landing craft in amphibious assaults began during World War II. Carried aboard amphibious assault ships, landing

The Hawaiian sand octopus, like most of its brethren, is a small, secretive creature that hunts tiny crabs and shrimp in the nooks and crannies of the reef.

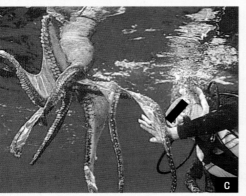

An Octopus Quiz!

GENTLE READER, I'm sure you've never chased an octopus into its hole, reached in, yanked it out, shook it until it inked, chased it some more, and finally cornered it, terrified, bleached, and in shock, panting through its spiracle in a desperate attempt to remain alive. Others have, of course, and a quick flip though some magazines and guidebooks uncovered these examples. There are many others. See if you can match the caption to the picture. —*Editor*

1. "Aw c'mon guys, that shot's ancient. Look at that regulator, for chrissakes! I haven't done that kind of thing in years. Oh, you heard about that? Okay, I'm caught. I couldn't resist. She had a buoyant personality, if you know what I mean. Anyway, let's not forget what we're talking about here: tako poke on the hoof. It's not like it's a turtle or anything."

2. "I am the sleek and masculine dancer with the underwater creatures. I am porpoise man! Go, gentle monster, go, back to your watery home. Did you get the shot, Franco? Can I exhale yet?"

3. "He wasn't very cooperative at first, but once I gave him a couple good pokes with the framer and popped him with my double 104s he settled right down. In fact, he didn't move at all after that. I like the white color—I had to bracket for that. Do you think he's dead?"

4. "Hold still, you... Damn! The ink! Vile creature, I will tear you apart with my bare hands and eat you right here and now!"

5. "All I can say is, like, AMAZING! I mean, you watch the Discovery Channel and all, but it doesn't prepare you. Like, it's alive. Know what I mean? I touched it. I wasn't sure I could do it at first. I couldn't get the air out of my BC thingy, so I pretty much stayed at the top while my girlfriend and these two, like, accountants or something from Fresno (they were gross!) went to the bottom. Then Sean, who's this hunky divemaster guy (long story—don't ask) got this octopus and brought it up to me. Cool, huh. It was like an offering or something. Tina doesn't like him, but I think he's sweet."

Answers: 1 D; 2 A; 3 B; 4 E; 5 C

Nemateleotris magnifica   Molokini 1988

craft were then launched to transport tracked or wheeled vehicles and troops to beaches or piers. LCMs (Landing Craft Mechanized vehicles) have only a bow ramp for loading and off-loading; LCUs have both bow and stern ramps. In addition to the LCUs, numerous tire modules and concrete forms have been sunk in recent years to add to the complexity of the site.

A box canyon facing west off Pokai Bay, closer to shore, is the site of a current-free dive called **Airplane Canyon**. The dive is usually begun at 92 feet, where a demolished twin-engine Beechcraft sits upside down on a sand bottom. Sunk as an artificial reef, the airplane was upright until it was tumbled by hurricane Iniki in 1992. It is missing its engines and propellers, but still attracts a school of *taape* and scrawled filefish, and an assortment of reef fish and small eels hide in the small crevices. On the slope next to it octopus move among many holes and horned sea cucumbers are usually seen.

Heading upslope and across the canyon to the north is a wall 20 feet high where eels, crabs, and large frogfish can be found. The dive usually ends in about 65 feet of water on top of the wall covered with cauliflower coral.

To the north, a quarter mile off Lahilahi Point, is a beautiful amphitheater shaped cave that cuts 40 feet into a ledge facing the sea. This is **Ulua Cave** and it is a great gathering place for goatfish, *taape*, and milletseed butterflyfish. As usual, the roof of the cave is covered in orange cup coral, and sometimes gold-lace nudibranchs are knocked from the ceiling by divers' bubbles. Soldierfish, bigeyes, sponge crabs, and lobsters all wait out the day inside or near the entrance. This dive can be done as a level dive from about 90 feet on up to the top of the ledge at 50 feet.

The **Makaha Caverns** off Kepuhi Point are often visited as the second dive on boat trips. These are lava tubes, archways, and deep overhangs in 35 to 50 feet of water.

The fire dartfish is rarely seen in Hawaii, as the islands are at the ragged edge of its range (some authors consider the Hawaiian specimens to be waifs only). It is a high strung little creature, flicking its dorsal fin up and down in a kind of nervous tic, and diving into its hideout (from which it never strays more than a foot or two) at the least sign of trouble.

The structures are occupied by whitetip reef sharks, green lionfish, and small frogfish. Deeper within the cracks, Spanish dancer nudibranchs and the bizarre, catfish-like large-eye brotula tuck away until nighttime. Schools of goatfish and huge schools of *taape* hover in the open, and mahi-mahi have even been seen here darting in from the

turtle that divers had been hand feeding. The turtle, just a teenager, grabbed a woman's short blond hair and tugged with such force that she froze in pain. The top of its beak even broke the skin of her scalp. It finally realized that its next meal was not going to come from this particular carpet of fine filaments and let go. Afterward the diver said she was amazed at how much leverage the turtle was able to generate just by flapping against the water.

NORTH WAIANAE

Another ancient shoreline is the site of a wall dive that runs parallel to shore for about a third of a mile off Makua. Called the **Makua Valley Drop-off**, the ledge is 80 feet on top and drops to 120 feet at the bottom, with undercuts and small caves along its length. Current that runs along the ledge feeds several species of black corals including tree forms and wire corals, and orange cup coral grows in the shadows. Spiny lobsters and sponge crabs can be found, and bandit angels are sometimes seen along the drop-off. Up on top of the ledge, corals grow in abundance.

Because it lies about an hour from the Waianae Boat Harbor and is inaccessible from shore, **Kaena Point**, Oahu's northwestern tip, rarely sees divers. The rough water and strong current here whittle potential diving days down even more, so that a dive up here is truly a special occasion.

The island slopes away before dropping sharply at 45 feet, and then again at 130 feet, far out on the point. Boulders in shallow water give way to the drop-offs, which are undercut, and sponge crabs, lobsters, and yellow hairy hermit crabs live in small caves eroded along the ledge. Because almost nobody ever gets out here, there is plenty of jack activity and sometimes other pelagic predators are sighted.

Parupeneus multifasciatus and Labroides phthirophagus   Hawaii 1991

In some places cleaner wrasse are called 'doctorfish,' and they deserve this designation. Their services are essential to the overall health of the reef. Regular visits to a cleaning station are as essential to a fish as finding enough to eat.

40-foot edge of visibility and quickly darting away.

Very friendly turtles familiar with divers live in the protection of the ledges. Some of these snap at divers' bubbles, and have even been known to try to eat their hair! This is not as unusual as it may sound, and we have seen this happen several times over the years.

On one occasion, it involved a

North Shore Oahu
Some Fine Diving, But Seasonal

MANY OAHU DIVERS WOULD RATE the North Shore as their favorite side of the island to dive. Millennia of gigantic surf have left a legacy of walls, tubes, ledges, and overhangs that divers love. Heavy winter surf limits access, and little commercial boat diving takes place up here. Coral growth is also limited due to the seasonal pounding this side receives, but the cavern formations are extensive, rivaling the Waianae side for Oahu's best caves.

DIVING THE NORTH SHORE

Devil's Rock is a living room sized wash rock a half-mile off the east end of Dillingham Airfield. The site provides good boat diving along its steep sides, and bottoms out at 100 feet on its seaward side. But an even more interesting dive is found across a trench with a white sand bottom clearly visible from the air. On the shoreward side of the trench is a wall that drops from 25 feet down to 85 feet, heads west and seems to be great habitat for corals. Lobe corals on this wall grow in bracket forms to capture as much light as possible, and during the day slipper lobsters can sometimes be found inverted on the undersides of the brackets. Other colonies attain huge size here. Turtles can be found throughout the area.

Extensive tubes, arches, and caverns eroded into the fossil reef off Kawailoa Beach form a dive called **Alligator Rock**. Even more extensive than the popular Makaha Caverns, its big skylights make this a beautiful dive when visibility is good. Turtles move in and out of the

caverns as they go up for air and return to the bottom. A long wall along one side runs out from shore and bottoms out at 45 feet.

Local divers are used to the five minute walk in knee-deep water over fossil reef once they enter the water at Haleiwa Alii Beach Park. The water soon becomes deep enough to swim, and after kicking out a few more minutes the dive known as **Haleiwa Trench** opens up beneath you. The structure here was created when a piece of ancient coral reef fractured away from the island creating a trench with a 70- to

Oahu's North Shore is not well known to tourist divers, but locals love the caves, tubes, and other formations here. The one drawback to this area is the pounding surf that makes diving here impossible in the winter.

100-foot sand and rock bottom. In the sand at the bottom of the trench live Randall's pufferfish, a species not frequently seen in the islands. At night, milky-colored tube anemones extend from the sand, their outer tentacles slowly and gracefully capturing food and passing it to the inner row of tentacles.

But the real highlight of this dive are the sides of the trench. About a five-minute kick across the trench is the far wall, a little less steep and covered with bracket-form lobe corals. The side of the trench closest to shore is riddled with caves and deep undercuts—"almost more cave than wall, if that can be imagined" is how Oahu diver John Hoover puts it. Orange cup coral grows in the darkened areas, along with some rare corals almost never seen by divers in Hawaii. One, the honeycomb coral *Gardineroseris planulata,* is fairly common here, with at least one colony an impressive six feet across. Nudibranchs and frogfish and many different species of shrimps also inhabit the wall. This can be an eerie, weird place when the visibility is low, but the drop-offs are dramatic and it is a great macro dive.

Dive boats sometimes visit **Puaena Point,** where a wall comes up to 55 feet from 85 feet of water. Along its convoluted face, which is overhung in places, you can find eels and some interesting crabs and shrimps. Following the wall in toward shore the top eventually comes to within 20 feet of the surface, where the real object of this dive is found. This is a heavily-visited turtle cleaning station, right on top of the wall, where as many as 20 turtles have been seen at one time.

PUPUKEA CONSERVATION DISTRICT

Within the Pupukea Marine Life Conservation District established in 1983 are two of the most popular dives in the state. As is often the case with conservation districts, limited fishing activities were grandfathered in, but as far as divers are concerned nothing naturally occurring may be taken.

Not named for the presence of sharks, **Shark's Cove** is a hugely popular dive, but mainly in the summer. Winter's massive surf makes this a very dangerous area of coastline. The cove is located on the northern side of the Sunset Beach Fire Station and includes a shallow inner bay, where visibility is not great, and an outer area about 50 feet deep with better visibility. A labyrinth of caverns and vertical and horizontal tubes is the reason for its popularity. Entry can be made from

Hawaii has its own endemic species of garden eel, which was not named as such until 1980. Since these eels stay put, plucking drifting plankters from the water with at least half their bodies still safely under the sand, they always settle in an area regularly swept by current.

Gorgasia hawaiiensis Hawaii 1997

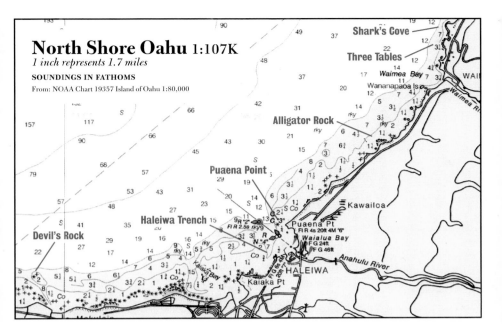

1 inch represents 1.7 miles

SOUNDINGS IN FATHOMS

From: NOAA Chart 19357 Island of Oahu 1:80,000

Shark's Cove

Three Tables

Waimea Bay

Wananapaoa Is

Alligator Rock

Puaena Point

Kawailoa

Haleiwa Trench

Puaena Pt

Waialua Bay

Devil's Rock

Anahulu River

HALEIWA

Kaiaka Pt

the beach, which requires a long surface swim or walking out on the rocks. On the walk out there is a large opening in the rock which leads to a 10-foot diameter vertical hole called The Elevator. It goes 20 feet down and then splits into three different tubes, only one of which leads out to the ocean—a good reason not to enter this way, unless you have experience at this site.

Working out along the wall on the north side of the outer bay many small, photogenic animals may be found, including lionfish, leaf scorpionfish, devil and titan scorpionfish, and harlequin shrimp. A large cavern open at both ends lies a little farther out, where you can find fountain shrimp and slipper lobsters within and cup coral covering the ceiling. Many different species of sponge-eating nudibranchs have been seen here, so look closely with a light.

This is a favorite night dive for locals, so much so that one motivated photographer, Pete May, returned for a second night dive the same night! After getting in the water at 11 p.m. and finding a spectacular red frogfish in full fishing mode just the right size for his framer, he shot the last five frames remaining on the roll. After driving back to Hawaii Kai to get new tanks and more film (an hour each way), Pete was back in the water again at 5 a.m., finding the little red guy in exactly the same place.

To the west, three flat rocks that break the surface just offshore make up a dive site called **Three Tables**. The rocks line up parallel to shore, and are just off a nice sandy beach entry. Generally the diving is done on the seaward side of the "tables," where canyons, caves and arches can be explored down to about 50 feet. Turtles and whitetip reef sharks rest in the darkness of the lava tubes. This is another favorite night dive, where many large morays, conger eels and the night octopus are regularly seen. Spanish dancer nudibranchs and many smaller species of nudibranchs can also be found out at night.

Most hawkfishes live in the shallows, perched on knobs or branches of hard coral, but the longnose hawkfish likes the deep, usually 100 feet or more, and is usually found in bushy black corals.

Oxycirrhites typus in Antipathes sp. Hawaii 1988

Monachus schauinslandi Lehua Rock 1994

The Hawaiian monk seal is one of the strangest of the extant pinnipeds, and one of the most endangered. Unlike the baying herds of the California coast, for example, this species is mostly a solitary traveler. It is very rarely seen in the populated islands, and the couple thousand or so remaining live chiefly on the banks and atolls of the northwest, from Nihoa to Kure.

Kauai is wet, verdant, and just plain beautiful. The diving here is markedly different from the islands to the southeast, with rough, rocky, coralline algae dominated reefs. Here you will also find rare reef fish species, breathtaking formations, and more sharks than you might even want to see.

Kauai and Niihau

THE PACE ON KAUAI IS SO SLOW THAT plant growth seems speedy. Which it is on the lush, green "Garden Isle." Kauai seems to produce life almost casually. As you drive through the sleepy neighborhoods of Kalaheo you can see piles of cuttings tossed from gardens and yards already sprouting, misted by a rain so fine it is more like warm fog. Wrong turns can be blamed on signs totally overgrown by vegetation. It is impossible to kill a plant here.

The island even smells wonderful. Near the coast, you can almost taste the warm central Pacific and the sweet, humid forest. Kauai is a lovely place.

THE OLDEST ISLAND

Kauai was originally a single smooth volcanic peak, but is now deeply carved by erosion, creating some of the most beautiful cliffs, ridges and valleys in the world. It is the oldest island in the southern Hawaiian chain, and there has been lots of time for this erosion. This long history has also created an island with the highest ratio of beaches to coastline. These features, along with the lush vegetation, make Kauai's main attraction its stunning natural beauty.

Kauai has a history of pre-Hawaiians, Hawaiians, Spanish, Russian, and English explorers, and finally entrepreneurs and missionaries and assorted laborers brought in to work the large agricultural holdings. The Spanish probably landed on Kauai well before the Russians and the English, as it is believed they did on all the islands, but they were thrifty people and left little tangible evidence behind, except for possibly affecting local fashions with their elegant crested helmets.

Culturally, Kauai has always

been an unusual corner of Hawaii, producing unique tools and crafts, such as the curious and practical ring poi pounder, unseen on the other islands. It also may have been home to the last descendants of the original settlers of the islands, who were from the Marquesas. The Marquesans were subjugated by later settlements of Tahitians and

Dactyloptena orientalis Molokini 1991

The flying gurnard is one of the reef's more imaginative creations. Not only does it have 'wings,' but it also has 'legs'—modified pelvic fin rays that it can use to walk along the bottom.

relegated to forced manual labor, giving rise to Hawaiian legends of a tribe of little people known as *menehune* who inhabited the islands before the Polynesians. It is believed that the word "menehune" arose from the very similar Tahitian word for outcast. While legends of *menehune* exist throughout the islands, they are most alive on Kauai, where people listed themselves as *mene-*

hune as late as the mid-1800s. A visit to the Kauai museum in Lihue is fascinating.

THE DIVING COAST

Kauai's low mountains and practically round shape have left the island with little lee coast. Like other islands, the largest concentration of hotels will tell you where the most protected side is, and this also tells you where most of the diving is done. In the case of Kauai this means the south coast from Poipu west to about Hanapepe. Not that the diving is better here than the rest of the island, but it is more comfortable and there are more divers staying close by.

Beyond Barking Sands, where the U.S. Navy operates a missile range facility and the largest underwater listening device in the world, the wind begins to become a little less reliable, though there is still excellent diving along a drowned barrier reef off Polihale State Park, known as the Mana Crack.

Continuing north, the flat low coastal plains give way to the mountains and the remote, isolated valley of Kalalau comes into view, once home to a large Hawaiian settlement. A cultural landscape of stone structures indicates these now isolated places were once thriving communities. In the 1960s the Kalalau Valley was occupied again when hippies moved in. They found paradise intact, but were themselves unprepared for the life they dreamed of. Eventually they retreated, coached along by the authorities, who disapproved of certain of their crops.

Further to the north, the coastal cliffs are even more dramatic. This is the famous Na Pali coastline, where the cliffs end right at the sea and the valleys look inaccessible. A quick glance from a hovering helicopter will show acres of ancient agricultural terracing and the remains of the foundations of canoe sheds, houses and other structures from a time when this remote and windswept coast was home to thousands of Hawaiians. Hiking, kayaking, or boating this coastline is a feast for the eyes—vertical folding cliffs, deep green valleys, and the wind and wave sculpted shoreline—as well as great exercise.

The cliffs of the Na Pali Coast come to an end at Kee Beach. Here there is a road, the first one since Barking Sands. Shore diving becomes possible again, and one of the most popular dives on the island is here, off Tunnels Beach at Haena. There are also excellent offshore sites, but since commercial boat launching on this side of the island has been prohibited for some time, those without their own boat are likely to dive only from shore (and then only seasonally). Just past Haena is Hanalei, the famous home of Puff the Magic Dragon, and the staging area for the hippies hiking into Kalalau.

Moving east, past the planned luxury communities and golf courses of Princeville, is Kilauea Point, a national wildlife refuge and seabird sanctuary. Few large seabirds nest in the developed main Hawaiian Islands and this is a rare opportunity to see red-footed boobies and Laysan albatross, beginning in the fall on through to the following summer. Great frigatebirds can be seen soaring above the point year-round, though they do not nest here, and Hawaii's endangered goose, the *nene*, can also be spotted in the refuge.

KAUAI FROM THE AIR

Kauai is a phenomenal place to take a helicopter ride. It is the best way to see the sea cliffs, remote beaches and fringing reefs along the Na Pali coast. One such beach, Nualolo Kai, is ringed with cliffs and one of several accessible only from

the sea. For decades Jack Harter, Kauai's master helicopter pilot, has seen large green sea turtles hauled out on the beach during the day basking and sleeping. This unusual behavior for green sea turtles in Hawaii usually requires areas of extreme isolation, and thankfully such places still exist. They also nest on Kauai slightly more than they do on

Hippocampus fisheri Hawaii 1989

other islands for the same reason.

Flying inland, razor-thin mountain ridges, deep valleys, and waterfalls in an endless variety of configurations are on the flight plan. The spectacular Alakai Swamp, considered the highest swamp in the world, contains plant species found nowhere else. The sight of Waialeale Crater, with 3,000 feet of waterfalls on three sides, just might

Fisher's seahorse is poorly known. It may be pelagic, accompanying bits of floating weed. Two of the rare museum specimens came from the bellies of fish: a mahi-mahi and a jack. Other than one specimen from Lord Howe Island and a few in poor condition from New Caledonia, it is only known from Hawaii.

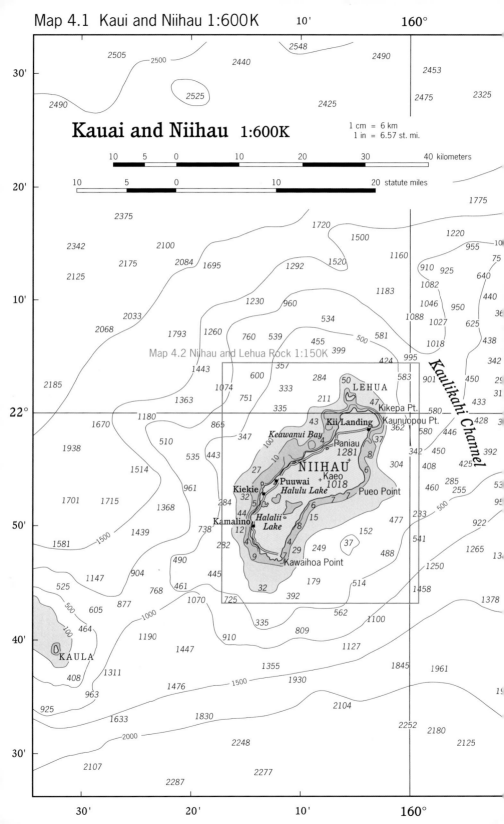

Map 4.1 Kaui and Niihau 1:600K

Kauai and Niihau 1:600K

1 cm = 6 km
1 in = 6.57 st. mi.

10 5 0 10 20 30 40 kilometers

10 5 0 10 20 statute miles

Map 4.2 Niihau and Lehua Rock 1:150K

Kaulikahi Channel

LEHUA
Kikepa Pt.
Kaunuopou Pt.
Kii Landing
Keawanui Bay
Paniau
1281
NIIHAU
Kaeo
1018
Puwai
Halulu Lake
Kiekie
Pueo Point
Halalii Lake
Kamalino
Kawaihoa Point

KAULA

30'
20'
10'
22°
50'
40'
30'

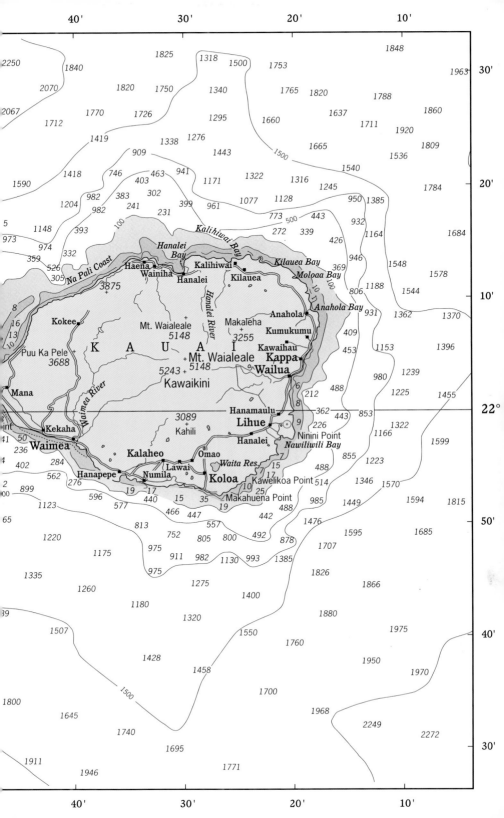

leave you speechless. The falls are the product of Mount Waialeale above, the wettest spot on earth, which gets 37 *feet* of rain a year!

NIIHAU AND LEHUA

Not far off the west coast of Kauai lies the privately-owned island of Niihau, the smallest of the in-

Kauai 1988

No visitor is immune to Kauai's intoxicating natural beauty.

habited islands, although it is a little bigger than Kahoolawe. Unlike Kahoolawe, Niihau has been occupied, mostly along its long westerly shore in the lee of Paniau, since long before contact with Europeans. The island lies in the rain shadow of Kauai, and is semi-arid. Surprisingly, it has the largest naturally occurring lake in Hawaii, Lake Halalii,

although it is often dry. There are large areas of ancient sand dunes to the south and the hills in the east, facing Kauai, end in impressive cliffs.

Although Hawaiians had lived there for centuries, King Kamehameha sold Niihau to a Scottish woman in 1864 for $10,000 in gold. She began a sheep and cattle ranching operation that continues today under the direction of her descendants, the Robinsons. The Robinson family has lost money on this enterprise for years, but has hung onto the island mainly to protect the Hawaiian way of life for its residents. Hawaiian is the primary language spoken, but English is taught as a second language in the two-room schoolhouse. While it is popular to disparage this kind of feudalistic situation, the residents seem to appreciate their unique isolation, and join the Robinsons in resisting outside interference.

Fortunately the waters around Niihau are not privately owned and divers can make day trips over from Kauai, though going ashore is prohibited. Caves, caverns, arches, and large animal encounters entice divers to make the usually rough crossing.

Lehua Rock, to the north, is a crescent shaped tuff cone much like Molokini, although much larger (291 acres vs. Molokini's 19) and higher (710 feet vs. 165 feet). Lehua was formed in a much larger volcanic event. The eruption produced vast amounts of steam and wet ash which was blown downwind, creating the crescent-shaped rim of the cone that is exposed today. The steep slopes of the island continue underwater and are even vertical in places. The walls and the clear blue water are the backdrop for some incredible Hawaiian diving. Though comparatively few people dive Lehua, for those who do, it is a reliable source of once-in-a-lifetime diving experiences.

Kauai

Laid-Back, Remote, and Some Rarities

YOU KNOW YOU ARE STARTING TO GET out on the edge when you meet in the morning for your first day of Kauai diving. The divemasters are a little more laid back, the equipment a tad more weathered, and the wind is blowing a bit already. Diving around Kauai has become a little more tame since commercial boat launching was prohibited on the north shore several years ago. Now the vast majority of diving occurs along the more protected south shore where the two commercial boat harbors are.

Kauai's small size does not completely block the wind, and wind wrap affects diving on all sides of the island, although somewhat less on the south. Even on this side conditions are rough enough to cancel boat dives about 14 days a year. An old shoreline that drops from about 50 to 100 feet occurs around about two-thirds of the island, and many boat dives are conducted along this drop. Extensive lava ledges, arches, tunnels, and caves are the backdrop for most of the dives. The somewhat cooler water here limits the growth of coral and results in more coralline algae growth. In this regard, Kauai begins to look like the reefs at Midway Atoll.

The island was slammed by hurricanes in 1982 and 1992, which dramatically changed the reefs. Car-size boulders were thrown 50 to 100 yards onshore, and sand from entire beaches was deposited up on land. Two morays that had been fed by beginning diver classes at Koloa Landing, a popular shore dive, were found hanging in bushes onshore. These changes will not be noticed by divers visiting today, but local divers remember.

What you *will* notice are species of fish rarely seen in the other main islands, an abundance of enormous green sea turtles, interesting formations, and the occasional encounter with unusual species of sharks. Even monk seals and (otherwise un-

> **Niihau and Lehua Rock are justly famous, but Kauai offers some good diving as well—sharks, an occasional monk seal, lots of turtles, great formations, and some rare animals.**

heard of in Hawaii) loggerhead turtles have been sighted by Kauai divers in the summer.

SOUTH SHORE

Much of the diving along the south shore of Kauai is along an ancient shoreline ledge, which creates a visually interesting bottom. Just out from Hanapepe the ledge drops from 50 to 75 feet and a scenic arch begins a dive known as **Amber's Arches**. The flat-topped arch, 50 feet wide and 20 feet high, was carved by waves when the sea level was lower and it is now submerged. Orange cup coral covers the ceiling and frogfish can often be found hunkered in among it. Continuing along the edge of the shoreline the ledge is concave and full of holes where we have seen bicolor anthias hovering, slipper lobsters, black coral and monster red lionfish. On top of the ledge are a profusion of cauliflower and antler corals, but only along the edge.

Just out from Maka o Kahai Point is a great dive site called **Turtle Bluffs**, where holes and tiny caves in the old shoreline create a myriad of places for animals to hide. Dropping to the base of the ledge at 90 feet, whitetip reef sharks are sometimes seen in small caves. Moving offshore onto the flat sand bottom helmet shells can be found, and boarfish can be found huddling under a small arch, where they are easily photographed. Hovering in the water along the ledge are a school of *toau* (blacktail snapper) and, an even rarer sight, spotted knifejaws, a fish almost never seen in the main Hawaiian Islands. Sleek unicornfish approach the ledge to be cleaned by forcepsfish—an unlikely cleaner in Hawaii.

Up on top of the ledge, in about 40 feet of water, is an unremarkable area where very old turtles congregate to be cleaned by surgeonfish. These turtles appear to have seen it all and seem absolutely unaffected by divers' presence. Continuing west along the ledge, an area called **Fishbowl** is home to nesting Hawaiian sergeants. At different dive sites across the islands one finds different fish attacking Hawaiian sergeant eggs. Here the attackers are black triggerfish and milletseed butterflies—the contrasting black and yellow fish feeding on one small patch is visually stunning.

Over the years this ledge has proven to be an optimum spot for big animal encounters. Eagle rays, feeding monk seals, schools of hammerheads, and occasional pelagic sharks have all been seen out from here. Dolphin encounters and annual humpback whale sightings are also typical.

There's a dive on every island that operators are pestered about daily due to advertising, and on Kauai, that dive is the **Sheraton Caverns**. A series of caverns in a V shape with paralleling cracks just

Lehua Rock is one of the very few places in the southeastern end of the chain where one can more or less regularly find monk seals.

Monachus schauinslandi Lehua 1994

out from the Sheraton Hotel, it is the one dive where you might find another boat besides yours. It is calmer here than many other sites, and moorings make tying off easy. Ranging from 35 to 65 feet, the caverns house frogfish, resting sea turtles, and sometimes whitetips. From time to time a Hawaiian monk seal even makes an appearance. Crevices house pairs of brilliant red Baldwin's pipefish, the males carrying tiny pink or silver eggs on their underbelly.

Out from the caverns is **Deep Pinnacle**, which begins in 90 feet of water. Black coral grows from the sides with hawkfish in every tree, and anthias harems hover along the steep slopes. If you look carefully you can sometimes see the outlines of large stingrays on the sand at 180 feet. Since this site is rarely visited *ulua* are usually startled from a cave.

Two ledges running perpendicular to shore are part of a site known as **Ice Box**, a favorite of some local dive leaders, but considered hit and miss by others. Small caves and overhangs along the ledges, which slope from 65 to 85 feet, house whitetip reef sharks and tons of soldierfish. It was this site's reputation as a hunting ground for spearfishermen that earned it its name. Schools of *taape*, surgeonfish, and sometimes Heller's barracuda hover in the water. Divemaster Kim Davenport and six divers were here when a seven-foot tiger shark whacked a school of whitebar surgeonfish with its tail and then circled back to devour those that it had stunned. Before the divers finished their tanks they watched the shark do this four more times!

EAST KAUAI

Because of rough seas and distance from permitted commercial harbors, diving on the east side of Kauai, like diving the east sides of most of the main Hawaiian islands,

Niihau 1994

is done mostly from shore. This is unfortunate because there is some wild and beautiful diving to be had. The Analoa/Moloa area alone, surveyed by USGS for the Navy, was found to have the highest number of caves and caverns in the state. Unfortunately it couldn't be in a worse place: right at the rough northeastern tip, far from any harbor.

The island's best-known wreck dive, the ***Andrea F. Luckenbach***, sits about 300 yards off Wailua in 30 feet of water, making it accessible by boat or from shore. After running aground on a submerged reef in 1951, the 435-foot freighter remained partially exposed for the next 20 years before disappearing beneath the surface. Storms have reduced it to a debris field of chain, huge anchors, a propeller, and part

Great, black, clefts and other dramatic formations are the hallmarks of Niihau and Lehua. Lehua is the 'other Molokini.' It has a similar shape, but a very different feel. Wild, untamed, and exposed to the brunt of the weather, this wonderful site is paradise for shark lovers. In a way, Niihau and Lehua are where the Northwestern Islands begin, and this rarely dived area has a frontier feel.

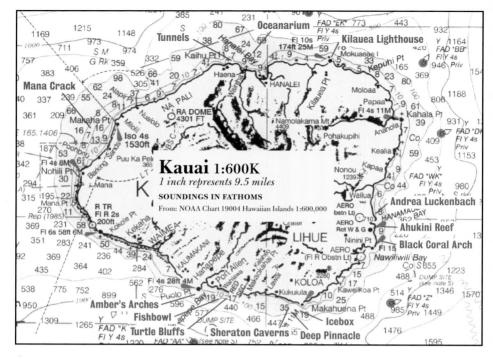

1169 1215 1148 385 241 231 80 67 Oceanarium FAD "EK" 773 443 932
1000 711 973 S 90 Tunnels 38 24 FI 10s Priv Kilauea Lighthouse Y 1164
757 383 406 974 332 59 Kaihu Pt 2 174ft 25M 59 Mokuaeae I Kepuhi Pt FAD "BB" Priv
S M G Rk 359 98 305 41 7 10 1 Y FI Y 4s 946
Mana Crack 62 526 66 20 10 7 Haena 165 369 FIY 4s 154
40 337 289 55 24 Alapii 37 NA PALI RA DOME Moloaa 806 1188
361 209 66 8 11 4301 FT 10 7 Papaa 9 61 Kahala Pt
Makaha Pt 16 Nualolo BSC Namolakama Mt 4409 Pohakupihi 39 931 FAD "DI
F 165.1406 16 13 9 Iso 4s Miloli Pohakupihi Anahola Co 409 FI Y 4s Priv
187 Poohono 1530ft LT Kealia 59 453 1153
342 FI 4s 8M 61 Puu Ka Pehu Kauai 1:600K Nonou 1239 Kapaa 41 FAD "WK"
Nohili Pt 30 Mana 1 inch represents 9.5 miles K 980 Priv
315 195 22 R TR SOUNDINGS IN FATHOMS Wailua 6 Andrea Luckenbach
Mana Pt 270 FI R 2s From: NOAA Chart 19004 Hawaiian Islands 1:600,000 AERO Rot W & G
Rep (1985) 11 200ft 58 LIHUE 9 Ahukini Reef
369 231 241 50 44 39 Crater Ninini Pt FI 15 Black Coral Arch 13
351 283 236 24 AERO Nawiliwili Bay
92 369 364 402 284 (FI R Obstn Lt) Co S 855 1223
435 Hanapepe Port Allen 15 488 DUMP SITE
538 775 752 562 276 FI 4s 28ft 4M KOLOA 17 (see note S) 1346 1570
899 Puolo Pt Kukuiula Kawelikoa Pt 514 Y FAD "Z"
950 Amber's Arches 596 Makahuena Pt 985 FI Y 4s 1449 Priv
1309 1265 Fishbowl 577 440 15 35 Icebox 488
FAD "K" Turtle Bluffs DUMP SITE 466 447 Deep Pinnacle 1476
FI Y 4s Sheraton Caverns 5 1595
(see note S)

---

of the boiler room (which reaches to within ten feet of the surface). The wreck covers a huge area and feels like a treasure hunt.

When a south swell is rolling in, **Ahukini Reef** becomes the back-up for shore diving on the island. Just out from Ahukini Landing, those who know this area well rave about the variety of special creatures to be found such as frogfish, scorpionfish, and cleaner shrimp. Also regularly sighted are dolphins and amberjack, and eagle rays and even small tiger sharks have been seen.

The south and east sides of Kauai possess one of the state's major black coral stands in deeper water, and even in shallow water just about any site here has scattered black coral. **Black Coral Arch**—a huge majestic arch 50 feet wide—anchors black coral trees on its underside as well as beautiful and rarely seen raspberry colored cup coral. Part of the ledge line—60 feet on top and dropping to 140 feet—

the arch and ledge are occupied by three species of anthias, and huge schools of bigeye jacks have cruised past, a rare sight in Hawaii.

NORTH SHORE

The North Shore's most popular shore site, **Tunnels**, is a shallow dive affected by tide and the sometimes strong current. It is infinitely more enjoyable if done with an experienced guide (who is carrying a light). Like most north shore sites, winter is not the time to dive because of the big surf, and even in the summer visibility is not spectacular. About 100 yards out, a series of caverns pierced by beams of light form a barrier which is open to the sea on the left. Water is held in a channel where a school of big-eye scad, sometimes harassed by amberjacks, and a school of Heller's barracuda are frequently seen. An inner area of caverns, overhangs, and one big archway runs along shore and drops to 60 feet. Cup corals,

Hawaiian Monk Seals

SEVERAL YEARS AGO NOW, TWO FRIENDS TOLD me about an encounter they had with a Hawaiian monk seal when they were just boys. At the time, they were on a camping trip to the rough, windy Kanaio Coast of Maui. The seal was a huge, gray, amorphous blob lying up on the rocks. At first they crept quietly up around the rocks, afraid the animal would bolt. When it didn't respond, they grew bolder, getting closer and closer. As the days passed, they began experimenting, trying to get this sleeping creature to do something—anything. Since they were still afraid of it, and not quite ready to actually touch the monster, they started throwing tiny stones at it in an attempt to get a reaction. Finally, the slumbering beast opened its eyes and looked at the boys, barely one-fifth its size. Placidly, it waddled down to the water and left. As far as they know, the seal never returned.

We have heard other stories such as this over the years and everyone seems to draw the same conclusion, that the Hawaiian Monk Seal is a docile, easily approached animal. If left undisturbed they seem happy to sleep through just about anything. On Midway a monk seal lay sleeping on the boat ramp as boats were launched right beside it.

The Hawaiian monk seal simply has no instinct to flee from a land-based threat. This animal has lived for so long in a chain of islands free of large land predators that it lacks a flight response—one of the reasons it suffered so dramatically with the arrival of man.

Although traditional Hawaiian hunters certainly took a toll, the seal's population was hit hardest in the 19th century by European whalers, fishermen, and seal hunters. One ship, landing in Honolulu in 1859, was said to be carrying 1,500 skins. This cargo represents more monk seals than are currently estimated to exist.

Monachus schauinslandi Hawaii 1993

The monk seal is an intelligent, swift, and agile hunter, chasing down fish while risking tiger shark attack. Well, some of the time.

AN ENDANGERED SPECIES

The Hawaiian monk seal (*Monachus schauinslandi*) was listed under the Endangered Species Act in 1976, and appears on the IUCN Red List and in Appendix 1 of CITES. Current population counts list 1,300 to 1,400 animals, with an uneven sex ratio of three times as many males as females. Despite this protection from hunting and harrassment, the population continues to decline by about four percent a year, because of entanglement in fishing gear, shark predation, ciguatera poisoning, and deaths of females from "mobbing" by aggressive males trying to mate.

The seals live in the Northwestern Hawaiian Islands, from Kure to the French Frigate Shoals. Small populations can be found at Necker and Nihoa Islands, and a few are seen at Niihau and Kauai. Only very rarely are they seen in the main Hawaiian islands. The females reach seven and a half feet in length and 600 pounds, and the males are slightly smaller. Unlike most seals they tend to keep to themselves. The breeding season runs from December to August, and the seals are not particularly fecund. Females reach sexual maturity at 5–6 years of age, and live 20–25 years. Monk seals eat fish, squid, and crustaceans.

Monk seals require isolation from humans, which is why the uninhabited islands of the northwest Hawaiian chain are essential to their survival. Mothers who normally spend six weeks onshore nursing their pups have been known to abandon them if repeatedly disturbed by humans. Leaving them alone is the minimum we can do. If a seal is hauled out on the beach, a distance of at least 100 feet must be maintained.

THE TROPICAL SEALS

The monk seals are the world's only tropical seals, and three species have been identified: the Hawaiian, the Caribbean (*Monachus tropicalis*), and the Mediterranean (*Monachus monachus*). All of these show adaptations to warm water, and their populations are separated by huge distances. Hawaii's species, despite its endangered status, is in the best shape of any of these.

The Mediterranean monk seal has been known since at least the time of the ancient Greeks, who respected the seals and placed them under the protection of Poseidon. The Romans were not so thoughtful, and by the Middle Ages the species was already in serious decline. Today a mere 300–500 survive, and because of the density of population in the Mediterranean, these shy animals are forced to pup in caves and along remote areas of the Western Saharan coast. This species may soon go extinct.

The Caribbean monk seal was the first animal to be described from the New World. Columbus encountered these "sea wolves" off Santo Domingo (and promptly had eight of them shot). Like the Hawaiian and Mediterranean monk seals, these animals were mild-mannered and easily approached, and their population was decimated in the 17th and 18th centuries. By the 20th century, just a handful were left, and the last confirmed sighting was on Seranilla Bank southwest of Jamaica in 1952. Expeditions to investigate reports of later sightings were launched as recently as 1993, but in 1996 the Caribbean monk seal was formally declared extinct.

ISOLATED BY GEOGRAPHY

Despite the minimum 3,000 miles that separated the species of *Monachus*, all are believed to have evolved from an ancestor of the Caribbean monk seal. In those days, monk seals are thought to have lived in a near continuous population around the northern Atlantic Ocean, ranging from southern Europe to what is now North Carolina and around the southern tip of the North American continent to what is now the Pacific coast (at this time North and South America were not joined).

This more or less continuous population of warm water seals was first split in two as the earth's climate cooled. Lowering temperatures in the North Atlantic eventually caused the North American and European populations to separate at their northern extreme. The European population, geographically and genetically isolated from the North American population, began to evolve into the distinct Mediterranean monk seal.

In North America, the monk seal population remained continuous until the eventual closing of the isthmus of Panama 3.5–4 million years ago split the population into two groups, one becoming isolated along the west coast of North America.

With the joining of the North and South American continents, warm currents that once flowed freely from the Atlantic to the Pacific Oceans were interrupted. Cool water currents were then able to flow south and north along the west coast of the Americas while the Gulf Stream continued to fill the Caribbean basin with warm water. The American monk seal population on the east coast survived to become the Caribbean monk seal, but the population on the west coast did not adapt to the new conditions and eventually became extinct.

Before this happened, however, it is thought that a few individuals reached Hawaii, where they established a population that eventually evolved into the Hawaiian monk seal.

MONK SEALS AND DIVERS

In recent years Hawaiian monk seals have been seen with increasing regularity on beaches of the main Hawaiian Islands, with some females calving annually on remote beaches on the same island. Many of the seals are tagged, and valuable information has been gathered from re-sighting records. Hawaiian monk seals have also been seen more frequently by divers, although whether this is due to more divers or more seals in the main Hawaiian Islands is not known.

Several once-in-a-lifetime monk seal encounters have occurred over the years at Molokini off the coast of Maui. It is known from stomach contents studies and from "seal cam" footage that Hawaiian monk seals eat reef and bottom fishes, octopus, eels and even spiny lobsters, sometimes going as deep as 600 feet to catch them. One morning at Molokini, in about 60 feet of water, a small group of surprised divers watched a monk seal slurp down a very unlucky yellowmargin moray, head-first. This happened as the hapless eel was being fed by a dive leader. When the photos were developed, the three-foot moray looked like a strand of spaghetti, so dwarfed was it by the size of the seal.

Even more remarkable was a young male seal that joined groups of snorkelers and divers at Molokini over a period of seven months in 1997. Appearing to crave companionship, the seal swam among snorkelers for hours, periodically hauling up on the rocks to rest. Many times the seal grasped snorkelers from behind, wrapping his flippers around them, vocalizing, and biting their backs, sometimes softly, sometimes not so softly. Those with wetsuits were definitely more inclined to rate the experience favorably! The feeling of being held by another animal is indescribable. Identified by a small scar above his right eye, this seal has been seen

Monachus schauinslandi Hawaii 1993

Do you mind? I'm trying to get some sleep here.

since. He is much bigger now, and thankfully, less amorous. He has also surprised us on occasion by appearing suddenly and hauling up on the back swimstep of boats.

While encounters cannot by law be sought out, because of the endangered status of the seals, divers on every island have had experiences where monk seals not only approached them, but interacted with them mammal-to-mammal. If this happens, divers should consider themselves among an incredibly lucky few.

sponges and nudibranchs occupy the ceilings and dark overhangs, and whitetip reef sharks rest on the bottom in the early morning. Several turtle cleaning stations are a highlight of this dive.

Straight out from Lumahai Beach is a boat dive known for its variety of animals. **Oceanarium** is a group of pinnacles which rise from about 130 feet to 60 feet on top. Cracks which spiral around the pinnacles house pipefish, angelfish, and many crabs and shrimp. Thick black coral growth creates habitat for green lionfish in the shadows. Among the rare species seen here are morwongs, boarfish, and even stripies—*Microcanthus strigatus,* an unusual butterflyfish-like species whose family has long confused taxonomists. Hundreds of Hawaiian longfin anthias hover at the deeper parts of the dive and titan scorpionfish are guaranteed.

A boat dive out from the scenic **Kilauea Lighthouse** is done among many arches and caves. Only 15–50 feet deep, you can expect it to be surgy most days. Inside the caves and arches are lobsters of various species and *ulua.* Outside in blue water hang schools of yellowfin surgeonfish, and parrotfish. Dolphins, thresher sharks, and monk seals have been seen here.

MANA CRACK

A drowned barrier reef called **Mana Crack** extends for 11 miles along Kauai's west side. The reeftop lies at 40 feet, and drops off on both sides. Amazing coral coverage, including an *Acropora* colony six feet across, was recorded from this area about ten years ago.

Since it takes just as much time to reach as the much requested Niihau, Mana Crack is rarely visited by dive operators. This is unfortunate, as Mana Crack is one of the most interesting dive sites in Hawaii. Dramatic structure in clear water and the opportunity to dive a place where very little exploration has gone on are reason enough to go, even if it weren't for the hammerheads, gray reef sharks, and rays.

The spotted boxfish is the largest and most colorful of the trunkfishes. The males are the peacocks of the species (females are black with white spots) with the younger specimens, like this one, having the brightest colors.

Ostracion meleagris ssp. camurum (male) Molokini 1989

DISTANT, ROUGH, AND SHARKY

Niihau and Lehua Rock
For Some, The Holy Grail of Hawaiian Diving

THE LIFELONG GOAL OF MANY OF Hawaii's resident divers is to dive off Niihau and Lehua. A flight to Kauai and a long, 17-mile channel crossing through usually rough water are required to arrive at this very isolated place that has been billed as "Hawaiian diving as it used to be." Only since 1984 have divers been able to sign up for regularly scheduled summer trips to dive with the untamed and untouched. An eye-opening conversation I had with Shauna Bail revealed the nature of this remote area. When I asked her what sharks she had seen over the years as the daughter of a well-known dive boat operator on Kauai, she began to list them in "ascending" order: "whitetips . . . hammerheads, tiger sharks—oh yeah, and my mom has seen great whites off Lehua."

Like many places not frequented by divers and fishermen, Niihau and Lehua are havens for sharks. In addition to the species mentioned above, gray reef sharks, Galapagos sharks, blacktip reef sharks, thresher sharks, and silky sharks have all been seen here. Note that their presence is because of our absence, so don't be too disappointed that there are no scheduled trips during the particular time you are visiting Kauai. Remember that it is a good thing overall, and when you are able to make the trip one day, your dives will be better for it.

LEHUA

Lehua is the product of an underwater eruption just off Niihau's northwest end. The two islands are so close to each other and offer such complementary diving that a dive trip usually includes some diving off both. Summer is the time when the winds are calmer, so most trips to the islands are made then. The crossing can last anywhere from an hour-and-a-half to two-and-a-half hours, depending on the boat and how rough the water is.

Hawaii's "other" little crescent-shaped island, Lehua, survives in a much different environment than does Molokini. With no protection from any other island, Lehua faces into the heaviest weather Hawaii can

Trips to Niihau and Lehua are few, but these sites have gorgeous structure, clear water, and lots of big animals. You like sharks? Even great whites have been seen in these rarely dived and untamed waters.

offer. To give an idea of the conditions that Lehua must regularly endure, it is known that during Lehua's formation ash was blown and deposited as much as eight miles to the south. Because of this the northern side of the island is scoured by wind and waves and the protected coral reefs that thrive inside Molokini are absent.

But in their place are sharks—and lots of them. In an area divers call **Lehua Gardens**, inside the western tip of the crescent, gray reef sharks,

Niihau 1994

Lava tubes are one of the more interesting underwater formations created by Hawaii's vulcanism.

dles directly in line with the eastern tip of the crescent begin a dive called **Stairway to Heaven**. The distant needle tops out at 60 feet, the next one at 28 feet, and then the rim itself is reached, and the dive continues along the east side of the island. Hard corals cover the tops of the needles, but this dive is about looking for swim-bys: dolphins, mantas, eagle rays, and even whales have been seen. The dive ends in the shallows among schools of banded butterflies and surgeonfish.

Nothing is more striking upon first seeing the wall below **Keyhole** than the thousands of abandoned sea urchin burrows carved into every inch of the island. Rock-boring urchins typically don't live below about 60 feet, so the presence of empty burrows at depth indicates that Lehua has subsided and that it existed during times of lower sea level. These urchins can be seen within their current burrows in shallow water. Excavating a channel using their spines and feeding apparatus, the urchins carve out a place in which to anchor themselves for the times when there is great surge, and feed on the algae that grows within the channel.

blacktips, and hammerheads are regularly seen. The bottom is blanketed by a huge amount of velvety gray leather coral. This coral, *Sinularia abrupta,* is in the same family as the soft corals divers are used to seeing farther out in the Pacific, but looks completely different. Like light gray felt with fingers, this soft coral covers every surface in a way we have never seen anywhere else in Hawaii. An erosional feature in 25 feet of water that adds to this strange scene are several perfectly tubular wells that bottom out at 65 feet. Deep off the point there is a good chance of seeing gray reef sharks, especially if there is current.

Across the bay off the eastern point of Lehua, the bottom is even more battered, since the point faces directly into the weather. Two nee-

Hovering along the wall are schools of the small and almost never-seen Earle's splitfin (*Luzonichthys earlei*), a type of orange and magenta anthias. The large keyhole-shaped crack in the wall ends at 40 feet with light beams shining into it and beyond. Nudibranchs, including such rarities as the "jolly green giant," have been found on the vertical sides of the crack along with multi-colored sponges and orange cup coral. Like Molokini, at Lehua several species of fish that are normally found in much deeper water are found within diving depths. The yellow anthias and Earle's splitfin, both plankton-feeders, are two.

Monk seals are a probability on any of the dives, as they prefer uninhabited areas like Niihau and this is closer to their breeding grounds in the leeward Hawaiian Islands. Curious and unafraid, they sometimes hover above divers as interested observers for a good part of the dive before anyone even notices that they are there.

On rare occasions divers have seen them feeding—several times on eels, and once at the surface a monk seal was seen tossing about an inflated spiny pufferfish, as if trying to deflate it. From the boat they are frequently seen hauled out on the rocky wave benches surrounding Lehua, resting and sunning themselves.

Drifting along the western wall, divers eventually arrive at the southwest corner of Lehua, which extends sharply out into blue water. Called **Pyramid Point** for the huge schools of pyramid butterflies hovering in the water column, anything can swim by here, from sharks of various species to a school of big-eye jacks. Orange cup coral covers the darker areas.

Upon surfacing from a dive here one time, divemaster Jennifer Anderson was surrounded by a flock of brown boobies all swooping down around her. Lehua, with its steep slopes and lack of predators and human disturbance, provides nesting habitat for hundreds of seabirds, some of which you are likely to see during your surface interval, or as in Jennifer's case, as soon as you hit the surface.

Vertical Awareness is a huge underwater pinnacle within swimming distance, but not within sight, of the southwestern point of Lehua. "Mind-expanding" is how longtime Kauai diver Linda Bail describes this site. Along the sheer walls are black coral trees, Tinker's butterflyfish, and Hawaiian longfin anthias. Even the yellow anthias is seen here. Many crevices, lined with furry black hydroids, can be explored for smaller animals. *Ulua* school up in a large horizontal crack and are flushed when divers appear, and schools of big-eye jacks often hang between the pinnacle

The stenopids are cleaner shrimp, a fact advertised to their clients by the long, white antennae. They also have the charming (to humans) habit of living together as mated pairs. This species has a strangely disjunct range, being found in Hawaii, the South Pacific (New Caledonia, New Guinea) and Mauritius, halfway around the globe in the Indian Ocean, but nowhere in between.

Stenopus pyrsonotus Molokini 1989

Map 4.2 Niihau and Lehua Rock 1:150K

Niihau and Lehua Rock   1:150K

1 cm = 1.5 km
1 in = 2.4 st. mi.

10 Kilometers
6 Statute miles

160°
50'
22°

KAULAKAHI CHANNEL

Lehua Rock
Kikapa Point
Kaunopou
Kii
Puukole Point
Lehua Landing
1281 Paniau
Palikoae
Kaununui
Keawanui Bay
NIIHAU
Kaeo
Palioli

583
424
357
751
1074
342
362
304
47
50
211
37
8
6
4
43
347
27
335
100
10

1 2 3 4 5 6

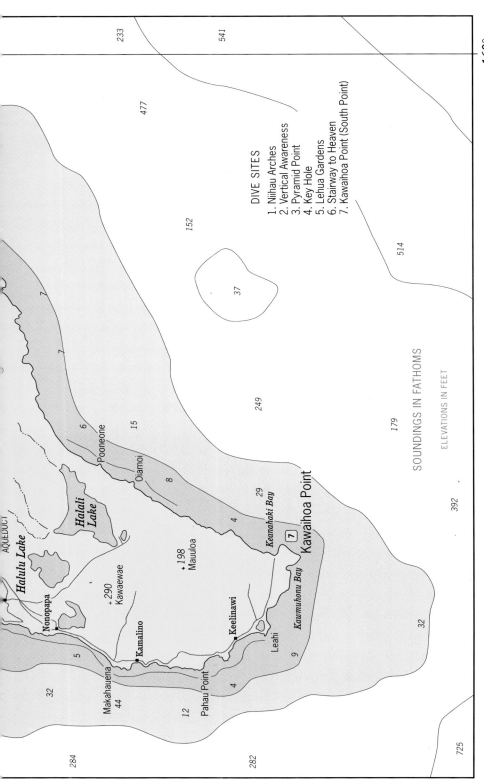

160°

AQUEDUCT

Halulu Lake

Halali Lake

Nonopapa

+290 Kawaewae

Makahauena
44

32

■ Kamalino

Pooneone

Oiamoi

6

7

7

15

8

+198 Mauuloa

5

■ Keelinawi

12

Pahau Point

4

Leahi

4

29

Keanahaki Bay

9

Kaumuhonu Bay

[7] Kawaihoa Point

37

152

249

477

179

514

DIVE SITES
1. Niihau Arches
2. Vertical Awareness
3. Pyramid Point
4. Key Hole
5. Lehua Gardens
6. Stairway to Heaven
7. Kawaihoa Point (South Point)

SOUNDINGS IN FATHOMS

ELEVATIONS IN FEET

392

32

233

541

284

282

725

and Lehua. The top of the pinnacle reaches 35 feet, ideal for level diving. On the flat spread is another striking example of an area previously occupied by burrowing urchins, their convoluted burrows a reminder of the dramatically different place this was years ago.

A CRAB AND SHARK STORY

Truly one of the strangest experiences we heard about while researching this book occurred off Lehua. In fact, if we hadn't heard this from Linda Bail, we would not have had the nerve to print such a wild story.

Linda was just ascending the wall at Lehua and kicking onto the flat area to finish her dive in the shallows when she noticed movement in a small cave up ahead. As she got closer she could see that it was the tail of a shark, but not a whitetip reef shark as one would expect after so many dives in Hawaii, but the tail of a gray reef shark. The gray reef needs to swim constantly in order to breathe, so how could it be wedged in a crevice and still be alive?

The shark continued to jerk wildly and Linda realized that it was in the crevice upside down as well. When she shined her light into the cave the scene became even stranger. An orange swimming crab had gotten hold of the shark's eye, and was *eating it!* Each time the crab plunged its claw into the eye, the shark jerked.

Somehow this poor shark had gotten itself wedged in this small cave, and in trying to escape had wiggled upside down and stuck there. Realizing that sharks can't swim backwards, she slowly pulled the shark out of its torture chamber tailfirst. Its eye, which by this time was partly hanging out of its socket, was still firmly held by the crab. She turned the shark upright and before she could do anything else it flicked its tail and swam off, sending its torturer freefalling.

It was a young shark, maybe a year old in her estimation, when it became a one-eyed gray. She has watched for this acquaintance of

This triggerfish likes its water cold, and can be found in the Pacific both north and south of the tropics, but not in the tropics themselves—for example, you can find it at Easter Island and Japan, but not Indonesia or New Guinea. In Hawaii, it is most common in the Northwest Islands.

Xanthichthys mento (male) Midway 1993

hers for a couple years now, but has never seen him again.

NIIHAU

Ash blown downwind during Lehua's formation landed between Lehua and Niihau, as well as farther to the south. These finely bedded layers of ash have since been carved into by varying sea levels and are now submerged, forming the memorable, fluid structure at a dive called **Niihau Arches**. Eight majestic, wave-carved arches, a 200-foot-long tube, and a chimney that can be entered at 15 feet and exited at 80 are covered with orange cup coral and house lobsters, fountain shrimp, and nudibranchs. The swirling formations here are so striking that even if you see sharks or a manta or even a monk seal, the unusual formations are what you will remember most.

Niihau Arches is just a primer for the even more elaborate formations at **Puu mu**, named for the hundreds of bigeye emperors (*mu*) that school here. On the underwater bridge connecting Niihau and Lehua is a series of ten relatively low-ceilinged, flat-topped caverns, between 70 and 20 feet, with groves of three species of black coral growing down into the water from the top of the caverns. Hitch-hiking on the branches are black coral oysters, which use the branches to hold them out in the water where they can feed. Away from bottom-dwelling predators and competition, they thrive. Whitetip and baby gray reef sharks inhabit the caves during the day, swimming around in agitation, silhouetted against the blue, when divers enter. Two lava tubes more than 150 feet long contain several species of cowries and tons of spiny lobster. The giant Javan moray, only a handful of which have been recorded in Hawaii, has been spotted here.

As expected from a site named

Stenella longirostris   Kanaio 1989

South Point, this site is current-swept and sharky. Niihau's southern cliffs, towering 700 feet above, continue underwater, creating a wall dive in sometimes strong current. The reason to travel all this way is simple: sharks. Resident gray reef sharks congregate here. They seem to have learned that spearfishermen mean a possible meal. Several divers have been forced to give up their catch and been chased out of the water by these sharks, perhaps emboldened by their previous successes. One diver estimated that as many as 60 grays and whitetips were in the vicinity of one such free-for-all. If you're not spearing, they should not be a problem. This is also a great jack dive, a ball of blue jacks being sighted here regularly, as well as several other jack species.

Encountering a pod of spinner dolphins underwater is a rare, and usually brief, experience. They tend to be found on the lee sides of the islands, particularly in bays that are protected from fishing and other disturbances.

The Galapagos shark is curious, gained 3 m pounds, and can be dangerous. While exciting at first, once you get six or eight of these big guys around you, the author says, it can begin to work on your nerves.

Carcharhinus galapagensis with Kyphosus sp.   Midway 1997

Taenianotus triacanthus Hawaii 1992

Pretending to be a bit of sea wrack swaying in the surge, the leaf scorpionfish continually rocks its body with an undulating movement, as hinted at in the photograph here. The behavior is hard-wired, and the fish will do this even if placed in a still aquarium. Though sometimes drab, in addition to the red shown here, they can be bright yellow, pure white, or lime green.

On land you literally have to step over albatross chicks. Underwater, you have to decide if your tolerance level is four Galapagos sharks, or forty (or one big tiger shark). It's this simple—if you get the chance to visit and dive Midway, you would be a fool to pass it up.

Midway

I LOOKED UP IN TIME TO SEE Pauline's legs disappear out of the water, in one smooth motion, followed by the thump of her tank hitting the deck of the boat. Then I noticed there was no ladder where she had gotten on board. Interesting as this was, I returned to my immediate concern, which was trying to keep my camera between me and the closest Galapagos shark. I was now alone in the water, the boat was drifting away, and the milling sharks were getting bolder.

But my biggest worry was out of sight. We had been stalked the entire dive, although we didn't know it until I entered a small cave and turned to see a gray silhouette as big as a water buffalo just beyond Pauline, half invisible and not moving. The instant I looked away it vanished, and we never saw it again.

The people on the boat did. They had been watching, helpless-ly, as a big tiger shark followed us from the time we first entered the water and swam into the shallows, where the boat could not follow. When we separated, they watched it approach Pauline, only to move away when I returned. The shark was staying near the surface, out of our sight.

I heard all of this once I was back on board, and how Al was so worried he reached over the gunwale and simply lifted Pauline, still wearing all of her equipment, up onto the deck of the boat.

The next day I saw Al again while I was walking to breakfast. He was waving a finger at a Laysan albatross chick and giving it a lecture. The chick was leaning all the way back on its heels, ready to topple over. This was usual. Every morning the chick clacked at Al and every morning the burly navy chief lectured the downy chick on snapping

PAULINE FIENE-SEVERNS Midway 1997

Midway's Sand Island, looking due south, from the lagoon side. Although a trip here is a bit expensive and troublesome to arrange, this old military outpost is a wonderful place to visit and offers absolutely remarkable diving.

at people and sitting in the middle of the road.

At breakfast Al told us the story of the sinking of a tug off Midway years ago, and the sharks that came, and of lifting terrified men from the water, one after another.

A FORGOTTEN CHILD

Midway is the forgotten child of Hawaii, and until recently has been off limits except to the few people with good reason to be there. Now that the U.S. Navy has closed its Midway base, the U.S. Fish and Wildlife Service, working with Midway Phoenix Corporation, has made Midway accessible to divers and ecotourists. They are working hard to find that rare balance between the needs of visitors and protecting the wildlife.

Under the Navy, access was greatly restricted. So much so that when we first visited Midway, while it was still under Navy control, we met people who had lived on Sand Island for six years, and never even visited Eastern Island. Eastern Is-

land, it must be said, lies exactly 1,700 yards from Sand Island.

In the Navy days, very few people were allowed to dive beyond the reef line, but in the last four years divers have been going there regularly. Everyone who has been to Midway has fallen head over heels in love with it. Most seem completely frustrated in their attempts to describe the experience. But the strangest thing of all are the divers that come back talking as much about birds as fish.

Birds normally take one look at me from a hundred yards away and begin planning their escape. I am also used to birds flying in daylight. Imagine my surprise when a white tern landed on a friend's shoulder right next to me, and then, on a nightime walk, I was bombarded by fast, and fortunately nimble, petrels. All of this was within my first 24 hours on Midway. The most confounding sight of all though were the white terns. While we rode our bicycles around the island, they always hovered over Pauline's head and not mine, as if she were a saint and I were something else altogether!

Modern history began on Midway on the morning of June 5th, 1942. Japanese sea based aircraft attacked the American defenders of what is essentially a sand bar. In an aerial assault on the island lasting only an hour and fifteen minutes, and three days of ensuing sea battle, Midway made the history books. Then it slipped once again from the public's eye for 50 years.

Midway's islands consist of three sandy spits, although it was once a massive volcanic peak, probably three or four thousand feet high. This volcano now lies 500 feet beneath sea level. The ancient island is crowned with a cap of coral, and in true Hawaiian tradition, ringed with a lei of breaking waves.

Every year, 800,000 Laysan albatross arrive at Midway, seek out their life-long mates, and produce "chicks," sharp-beaked fluff balls that weigh as much as a thanksgiving turkey. The birds are monogamous and very long lived. Some of the birds nesting on Midway today may have even witnessed the battle of Midway. Other species nest here as well, in total more than a million birds. All are dearly loved by Midway's 130 residents.

This is an extraordinary place. The roads are closed when the albatross chicks hatch in the spring and stay closed until they fledge. Everyone walks or rides a bicycle, and the few necessary motorized vehicles are parked at sunset.

AND, OF COURSE, THE SHARKS

Diving at Midway can be spectacular. When you get in the water at Midway you are going to see a shark. During some dives we were circled, cruised, and generally explored by three or four curious Galapagos sharks. On other dives the number of sharks present was almost unbelievable.

Phoebastria immutabilis Midway 1997

One of these latter dives was in the entrance channel to the lagoon. There I laid down on the bottom, alone, on an incoming tide. I watched as many as 40 sharks at a time passing overhead. It was mesmerizing. Not all of Midway's sharks are so relaxing. During the winter and spring the tigers make their appearance, to be on hand when the albatross chicks are fledging—and crash landing into the sea.

The shark stories are endless around Midway, but the incidence of attack is almost nonexistent. We heard of no direct attacks on people, though there was one mysterious disappearance in the 1950s. Still, it is not advisable to dive at night, nor do they want you swimming after dark, even in the lagoon. There is no reason to tempt fate, and besides it

The Laysan albatross now rules Midway without interference from Uncle Sam, and every square foot of available space is a nesting site.

Map 5.1 Hawaiian Chain 10M

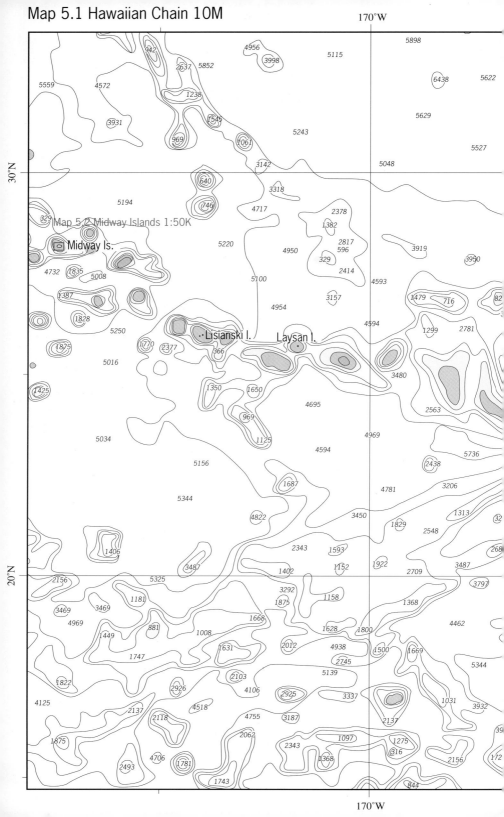

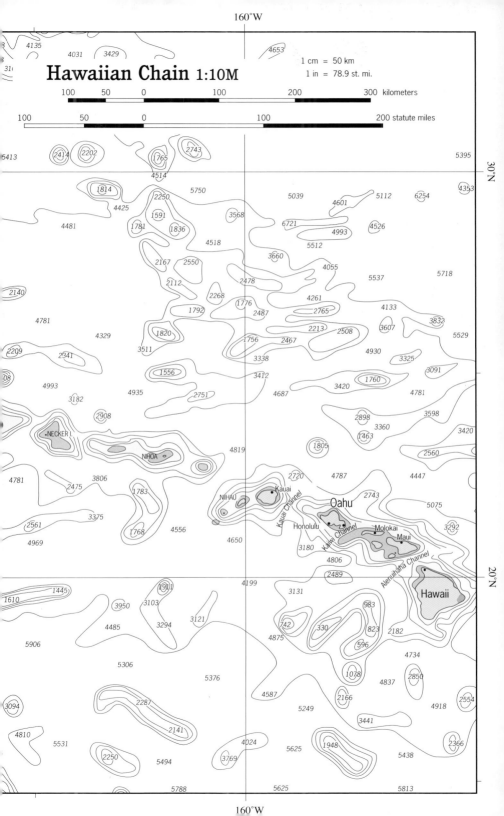

Hawaiian Chain 1:10M

1 cm = 50 km
1 in = 78.9 st. mi.

100   50   0   100   200   300 kilometers

100   50   0   100   200 statute miles

160°W

30°N

20°N

Kauai
Oahu
Honolulu
Molokai
Maui
Hawaii
NECKER I.
NIHOA
NIIHAU

Kauai Channel
Kaiwi Channel
Alenuihaha Channel

160°W

Carcharhinus galapagensis   Midway 1997

This is not a reef whitetip. The Galapagos shark is fast and aggressive, and deserves respect. They're not used to seeing divers in the water at Midway, and frankly, it's not clear they are particularly happy about the situation.

is free to play pool at the All Hands Club in the evening.

Our diving usually consisted of two dives in the morning and one in the afternoon. The best meal served at The Galley (the former navy mess hall) is lunch, and you can only get it between 11 a.m. and 1 p.m. The entire population of Midway organizes its day around this event. Fifteen minutes before the Galley opened for lunch our boat captains began to look toward shore. It was a rare day that we did not find ourselves in the chow line for lunch.

For more discerning diners, there is a French Restaurant on Midway that offers elegant dinners and wine along with a charming view across a wide white sand beach and out over the turquoise lagoon. Nearby are Charlie and Baker, the two BOQ buildings that now visitors (in relatively elegant comfort) and residents (in less well appointed rooms on the upper floors). Transportation on the island

is provided by bicycles. Not those new, fancy mountain bikes, but tried and true one-speed bicycles that you back pedal to stop, and which have a big soft seat that doesn't leave calluses on your rear-end like a racing saddle. The old bikes suit the islands' 1940s ambiance.

RARE, FEARLESS FISH

The wildlife at Midway, whether underwater or on land, does not shy away. There is an endemic grouper found in the Hawaiian Islands, a rare relic of cooler times that lives very deep in the main islands. In Midway, where the water is cooler, the *hapuu* is found shallow.

The groupers had no fear and seemed perpetually hungry, even to the point of looking into my camera housing for food. They were so fearless and curious that it was hard to get a shot. Finally, in desperation, I simply reached out, and placing my hand beneath the grouper's belly, moved him over in front of Pauline for the shot. He didn't mind at all!

Diving Midway
Where Humans are the Strangers

JUST GO. THAT'S OUR ADVICE. DON'T ask how good the dive operations are (there's only one), or how good the food is (for heaven's sakes) or how much the trip costs (it's a bit pricey). Just go.

Midway is a unique opportunity. Basically, because this was a Navy base, there is enough infrastructure still in place to make it possible to visit and dive of the most interesting and remote islands on earth. To get any farther west in the Hawaiian chain requires your own private boat or a rare spot on a research vessel. This is a side of Hawaii very few people get to see, and the diving is just the icing on the cake.

As if numerous endemic species of fish posing for your camera weren't enough, there are all the larger animals, including an abundance of Galapagos sharks, manta rays, and even monk seals. New discoveries are being made here all the time, including new species of nudibranchs and previously described species of fish that have never been recorded from Hawaii before.

Diving is done both inside and outside the lagoon by boat with some shore diving along the piers inside the lagoon. Outside the lagoon visibility is often spectacular. Since Midway is an atoll, all the formations are fossil coral, not lava. During the last ice age this fossil coral was exposed to the erosive forces of rain and wind, and now submerged once again, the caverns and overhangs form the basis of most of the dives. Almost all dives are subject to current at some

point, and night diving is not allowed due to shark activity. The sites below can be found on MAP 5.2, pp. 214–215.

WEST END

Out on the west end is a dive called **Peek-a-boo**, popular for its extensive bottom formations and concentrated fish life. Inhabiting the overhangs and ledges from 30 to 60 feet are several species of fish not typically seen in the main islands such as knifejaws, boarfish and the whitescale soldierfish (*Pristilepis oligolepis*), a red soldierfish with

> ## The comical albatrosses, the tumbledown charm of the old Navy base, the sharks, the rare species, the history, the intoxicating sense of being on the far edge of the Pacific... What more could you want?

stripes of distinct white spots. A brilliant yellow form of the normally drab *nenue* (*Kyphosus* sp.) has also been seen here recently. Sometimes a school of big-eye jacks swirls over the canyons, flashing silver as the fish turn in unison.

Chromis Corridor is a scenic dive through canyons, caverns, and small tunnels ranging from 35 to 90 feet. The site is named for the huge aggregations of oval chromis that hover in the water picking plankton, almost like anthias do farther west in

Map 5.2 Midway Islands 1:50K

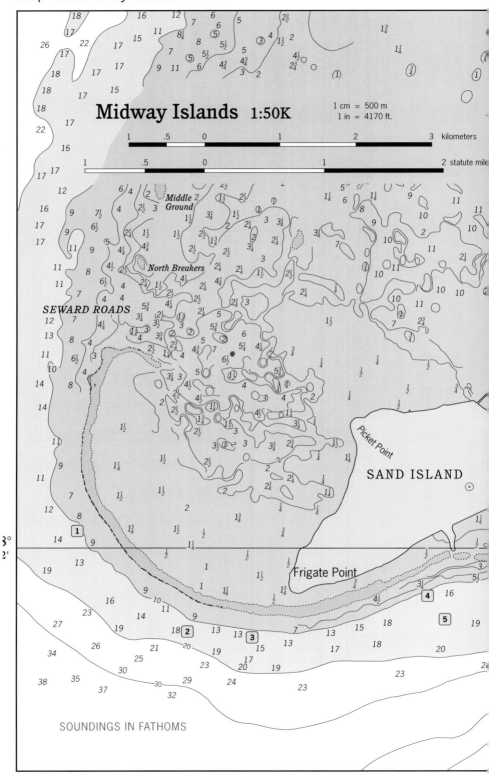

Midway Islands 1:50K

1 cm = 500 m
1 in = 4170 ft.

Middle Ground

North Breakers

SEWARD ROADS

Picket Point

SAND ISLAND

Frigate Point

SOUNDINGS IN FATHOMS

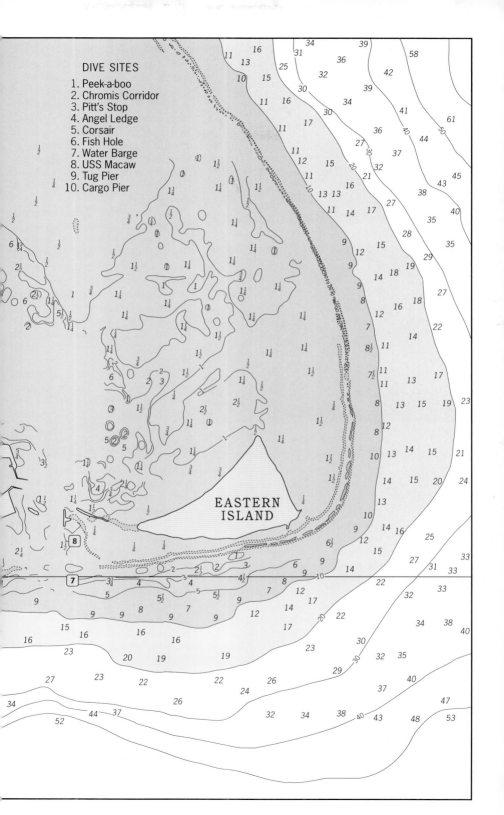

DIVE SITES
1. Peek-a-boo
2. Chromis Corridor
3. Pitt's Stop
4. Angel Ledge
5. Corsair
6. Fish Hole
7. Water Barge
8. USS Macaw
9. Tug Pier
10. Cargo Pier

EASTERN
ISLAND

Bodianus sanguineus Midway 1998

Cheilodactylus vittatus Midway 1998

Midway has a higher percentage of endemic fish species even than Hawaii overall (some 50 percent) and it is the place to see some rare beauties unknown from the southeast islands, like the sunrise hogfish.

The Hawaiian morwong is easy to see in the northwestern islands, but very rare in the southeast. The only place there where you will find it is Kauai and Niihau. At Midway, of course, it is easy to see.

the Pacific. Shaded areas are occupied by Hawaiian burnt murexes and nudibranchs, many of which are not seen in the main islands, and several species of nocturnal fish, including the rare sunset basslet. A recent addition to Hawaii's known fish fauna can be found here, but you really have to know what to look for beforehand. The redfin soldierfish (*Myripristis murdjan*) has blood red on the distal half of the dorsal fin, but it is easier to identify it by its eyes, which have no bar through them like Hawaii's other soldierfish.

Although Midway's *ulua* population has taken a serious hit from the fishing charters allowed at the otherwise strictly protected National Wildlife Refuge, **Pitt's Stop** is one place to see a school of 60–100 pounders being carried about in the

surf zone at only 20 feet. Seaward, in 55 feet of water, is a spectacular cavern the size of a two story garage, with canyons that lead down to 70 feet. In and around the cavern live titan scorpionfish a foot-and-a-half long, another endemic Hawaiian fish that is uncommon in the main islands, but ubiquitous at Midway. Whitescale soldierfish and red Hawaiian lionfish also live in dimly lit areas.

Although Midway is a breeding area for monk seals, and they can be seen hauled out on the beaches here, divers are not necessarily more likely to see them on a dive off Midway than they are off Kauai. Pitt's Stop and Bulky Dump, two sites near a beach where young seals rest and forage, have been the more likely sites to see them over the years. Right after weaning in the summer, young seals often join other juveniles 1–2 years old to hunt and play together. This is the time that divers are sometimes included. As many as three seals at a time have joined divers here. During one dive a seal came face to face with divemaster Keoki Stender, then suddenly bit him on the head! Fortunately, Keoki had been wearing a hood, or the game would not have been nearly as fun.

Rediscovered in 1997 by Ken and Linda Bail, an **F4U Corsair**, the famous gull-winged fighter from World War II, has become one of Midway's more popular dives. The wreck was the result of a mid-air collision during a training mission in 1943, and Midway's Coral Kings Dive Club had known about it for many years. But a storm dislodged it in the 1970s, making its location a mystery until Ken and Linda found it again. A portion of the fuselage and wings rest inverted on a 116 feet sand bottom, with the engine inshore from the wreck and the tail missing altogether.

The real attraction of this dive

Caprodon schlegeli Midway 1997

though is not the wreck, but the life! Japanese angelfish, Schlegel's groupers, Hawaiian longfin anthias, and large Potter's angelfish hover above and below the wings, like colorful little jewels. A pair of blue-spotted scorpionfish (*Rhinopias xenops*), one of the rarest sights in Hawaii, rests within the darkened areas of the plane. Edmondson's pipefish (*Halicampus edmondsoni*), known only from the main Hawaiian Islands until 1997, and beefy dragon morays, whitemargin morays, and slipper lobsters can be seen with a light. Out over the sand a few coral heads dot the bottom, thick-lipped jacks school, and harems of Thompson's anthias hover right out in the open.

Angel Ledge isn't much to look at, but it quickly became one of our favorite dives for the incredible variety of unusual fish. Dropping from about 70 to 110 feet and running parallel to shore, it is crossed by three communications cables, the easternmost one of which leads out to the Corsair (during the war such

undersea cables allowed the Navy on Midway and Oahu to communicate with each other in secret, since radio communication could have been monitored by the Japanese). This pock-marked ledge houses all the smaller reef fish species from masked and Japanese angelfish to Thompson's anthias and Schlegel's grouper. It was here that we watched the extremely rare sunrise wrasse clean milletseed butterflyfish, and a host of fellow endemics, its screaming yellow and red coloration an apparent advertisement of its membership in the cleaner alliance.

On top of the ledge a huge woolly octopus had arranged good-size rocks in a huge circle around its hole and sat surveying the flat expanse around it. On one dive, just after divers had passed by, a green lionfish, obviously flushed from its hiding place, set out over the bottom in apparent search for a new shelter. Within seconds a blacktail wrasse had it in its mouth—venomous dorsal spines oriented toward the

Schlegel's grouper is never seen by divers in the main Hawaiian islands, for the simple reason that it lives at a depth of 500 feet. A fisherman on Maui once brought the photographer one that he had caught on a deep line, but Mike couldn't photograph a live specimen until he got to Midway. The photograph above was taken at 115 feet.

Midway's Albatrosses

I WILL ALWAYS REMEMBER MY FIRST GLIMPSE OF Midway as we approached from the air. Every square foot of ground was occupied by what looked like furry bowling pins, hundreds of thousands of them, neatly spaced, everywhere we could see. Of course I had read that this was the largest Laysan albatross colony in the world, but the scene from the airplane was beyond anything I had envisioned.

Things got even stranger when we landed. The old navy truck that took us and our luggage to the former Bachelor Officer's Quarters could travel only a few feet at a time before the Sri Lankan driver had to get out of the truck and move a turkey sized chick out of the way. It was a test of patience only someone of strong faith could endure. On the return trip the chicks were be right back in the way.

In one of the most desirable parent and offspring arrangements ever evolved, the chick sits exactly where its mother laid the egg for the entire first five-and-a-half months of its life, which explains the continual need for Midway residents to move them from their assigned positions.

Twenty minutes and a quarter mile later we reached B.O.Q. Charlie, and had to run another gauntlet of chicks covering the sidewalk, the steps, and even the landing of the first floor. Not being overburdened with intelligence, the chicks all acted as if they had never seen a person before, clacking their oversized beaks and shuffling around as we begged to pass. Some would make half-hearted lunges, all hard-wired responses and nothing to take personally.

And then there was the smell… who could possibly be prepared for that? Not horrible, exactly, just the signature smell of Midway in spring, one whiff of which imprints you for the rest of your life.

SOME CALL THEM GOONEY

An amazing bird with an amazing life history, the Laysan albatross (*Phoebastria immutabilis*) is a beautiful animal with a neck and head of groomed white feathers. Both the males and females spend the summer and fall at sea in the rich waters of the northern Pacific. Because they fly too fast to be able to feed while in the air, they settle onto the water, sometimes in huge aggregations, and pluck food from the surface. In late autumn they begin to gather on Midway, reuniting with their lifelong mates in the male's territory, often mating within hours of reunion.

Younger birds attempting to mate for the first time participate in an elaborate courtship ritual of bobs and stretches, clacks and honks, that have become the signature sights and sounds of Midway. It is said that the English albatross nickname "gooney birds" (particularly for the black-footed albatross), and the Japanese equivalent "fool birds," arose from these entertaining displays.

After fashioning a nest on the ground and laying one egg, the two parents take turns brooding it. They average one week on, one week off, although the male takes the first shift which lasts three weeks. Throughout the entire two-month incubation the parents "talk" to the egg with a three syllable *eh-eh-eh*, which helps the developing chick recognize the voices of its parents. Once hatched, they both attend to the major task of feeding the voracious chick. Hunting far out at sea, each parent makes about 75 trips offshore for food, sometimes traveling 2,200 miles away, returning to the same view we had from the airplane, somehow going right to their chick among the hundreds of thousands of look-alikes. Once the chick is found the parent stands over it and the chick begs incessantly until the parent regurgitates a mixture of squid and stomach oil—the ultimate source of Midway's memorable odor.

Not all is perfect in this scenario. Albatrosses are attracted to any bright object floating on the surface of the ocean, which today includes such items as disposable lighters, toothbrushes, and bits of plastic and fishing line. All of this is ultimately regurgitated to the chicks. Although the chicks are able to throw up indigestible squid beaks and small-

Phoebastria immutabilis Midway 1997

With the competition for nesting sites on Midway so fierce, a cut-off utility pole will do just fine.

er bits of plastic, some of the larger plastic items are too big. If too much indigestible trash accumulates in the chick's stomach, it may eventually starve, its corpse in a month or so revealing a garbage-filled lump where the stomach had been.

Sometimes the parents quit gathering food before the chick is ready to fledge. These chicks get weaker and weaker, and eventually die in place, to be picked up later on the daily sweep by workers paid to keep Midway presentable. By the end of the season, these workers must love the healthy chicks even more than their parents do.

FLYING THE COOP

As they mature, sometimes thousands of chicks can be seen facing into the breeze, wings outstretched to catch the wind and strengthen their flying muscles. The stronger chicks can be seen rising an inch or two off the ground while practicing, and landing back down in the same place. Later they can be seen with their elegant long wings outstretched, practicing their take off runs for a few yards, then returning to their starting place to try again. At last, after much wing ex-

ercise, the chicks are strong enough to get airborne, and once aloft, they head right out to sea, not to return for over five years.

Even some of these strong, healthy chicks do not make it. If their first attempts land them in the water, they may not be able to get airborne again, and soon become a meal. People fishing these exhausted young birds from the water have sometimes gotten to them only seconds before a shark—and sometimes a very unnerving second too late. Researchers estimate that tiger sharks get one out of every ten fledglings that land in the water.

When they are sexually mature at 7–9 years, they will return to Midway to perform the enchanting courtship dance and find a life-long mate. After claiming a plot of land to call home, they raise one giant chick every year for as long as they live which, if they are lucky, could be more than 40 years.

For those who find such a commitment amazing, consider: since they spend their non-breeding summer months apart and alternate care of the chick, a mated pair spends no more than 5–10 days together each year. An albatross marriage of 35 years thus means being apart 34 of those 35 years.

Genicanthus personatus (female) Midway 1993

Genicanthus personatus (male) Midway 1993

The masked angelfish is very rare in the southeastern islands, where it lives in very deep water, but relatively common (and shallow) at Midway. This stunning species, endemic to Hawaii, was first named by Jack Randall in 1975.

wrasse's throat. When the wrasse couldn't fit the whole lionfish in its mouth it dropped it, and immediately a host of fish closed in. Working together with the wrasse, they tore the poor thing apart right in front of us.

Nearby, in 104 feet of water, rest the Corsair's engine and propeller, themselves home to lionfish, dragon eels, and magnificent snake eels.

One of the most frequently visited sites is called **Fish Hole**, where table-like formations at a maximum depth of 60 feet provide shaded areas for sponge growth and shelter for lots of fish, such as titan scorpionfish, morwongs, boarfish, spotted knifejaws, and the delicate pastel lined coris. Schools of yellowfin goatfish crowd this site, but look closely. Swimming among them are a few juvenile thicklipped jacks,

their yellow body stripe making them blend right in with the goatfish. Schools of the adult thick-lipped jacks sometimes surround divers, very unlike jack behavior elsewhere, and Galapagos sharks show up frequently.

EAST END

If the water is very calm you can dive around the mostly emerged **Water Barge**, a Midway landmark, all the way down to 20 feet, its maximum depth. A casualty of a broken tow line, the barge ran aground in 1957 and has been slowly rusting away ever since. Schools of goatfish and flagtails swarm the wreck, and some rare fish such as knifejaws are also seen.

Shoreward in the channel, a 250-foot Submarine Rescue Vessel (ASR-11) named the **USS *Macaw*** stretches from 25 feet, where the bow looms, to 60 feet at the stern, listing on a 45 degree angle to port. The rescue vessel ran aground while salvaging a submarine in 1944 and was deposited in its current location during a later storm. To clear the channel the Navy blasted the wreck, leaving the bow intact, as it was close enough to the edge of the channel not to obstruct ship traffic.

In addition to the Galapagos sharks that are sure to be seen nearby, lobsters, turkeyfish, and octopuses occupy the many holes and crevices, and a small group of morwongs hangs out under the bow. This has also been an excellent spot for finding two rarely-seen Hawaiian endemics: Steindachner's moray and the yellowbar parrotfish.

Even the channel itself is a dive. On an incoming tide when the water is clear you can sometimes see manta rays just by looking over the side of the boat. Jumping in one day with his rebreather and lying quietly on the bottom, Mike watched more than 40 Galapagos sharks facing casually into the current in a po-larized procession.

INSIDE THE LAGOON

While the better diving is outside the lagoon, sometimes the weather forbids venturing outside the reef line. In this case, diving within the lagoon is better than no diving at all. Although visibility is lower, there are areas of excellent coral growth, and some of the northwest island species that you have probably not seen in the main islands, including morwongs and various nudi-branchs. Monk seals, turtles, and dolphins also enter the lagoon.

If the wind is howling and there are no boats leaving the dock, even for the lagoon, a 30-foot dive under the **Tug Pier** inside the harbor or a 40-foot dive off the much larger **Cargo Pier** in the lagoon are op-tions. Like many piers, these are both killer macro dives. In addition to the life encrusting the pilings, in-cluding jumbo Chromodorid nudi-branchs, there is the chance for see-ing larger animals such as turtles and big jacks. Schools of fish use the pilings for protection and whitetip reef sharks sometimes cruise by. Definitely bring a light.

OUT ON THE EDGE

In 1997 the Pacific Ocean de-posited a gift on Midway's northern barrier reef. A huge whale carcass had drifted in, and big waves threw pieces and bones up on the exposed reef to bleach and, mercifully, be cleaned of rotting meat in the sun. Without the jaw there was appar-ently some question as to what species it was. Bones were sent off to be identified and the ID came back as a sperm whale.

Snorkeling along the outside of the reef one day we came upon the jaws, fist-size craters showing where the teeth had been. When we got the photos back the jaw dwarfed the free-diver in the photo.

Two of the ribs are now mounted on the wall at the Midway Mall.

This side of the atoll is rarely vis-ited by the dive boats due to its ex-posed facing. A beautiful, memo-rable area called the **Reef Hotel**, however, has been explored by divers from time to time. Several tun-nels occur in the spur and groove reef edge and at about 30 feet is the

Midway 1998

entrance to the main tunnel where 100-pound *ulua* have lived for years. The tunnel cuts 300 feet into the fossil reef here. Eventually the ceiling opens up to a hole in the reef where you can actually surface and check up on the boat captain. The view from here is one-of-a-kind. Turquoise water as you look toward the atoll, and nothing but the wide blue ocean as you look seaward.

Unlike the southeast islands, the bottom structure at Midway is all fossil reef. There is old volcanic rock underneath the atoll, but it is at least 500 feet down.

Chaetodon tinkeri
MOLOKINI

Contents

Travel Advisory

More than six million people a year visit Hawaii, and by some measures it is the most popular dive destination in the world (and certainly the most popular in the United States). With its balmy climate, relaxed pace, and great diving, for most people Hawaii is the quintessential island getaway.

General

TOURIST INFORMATION

The Hawaii Visitors and Convention Bureau has representatives in the following countries:

Australia c/o Sales Team, Suite 2, Level 2, 34 Burton Street, Milsons Point, NSW 2061, Australia. ✆02-9955-2619, Fax: 02-9955-2171.

Canada c/o Comprehensive Travel Industry Services, Suite 104, 1260 Hornby Street, Vancouver, BC V6Z 1W2 Canada. ✆604-669-6691, Fax: 604-669-6075.

China c/o East-West Marketing, 38 Da Pu Road, Hai Hua Garden, No 4 Building 27C, Shanghai 200023, China. ✆21-6466-1077, Fax: 21-6466-7501

Germany c/o American Venture Marketing, Siemensstrasse 9, 63263 Neu Isenburg, Germany. ✆610-272-2411, Fax: 610-272-2409

Japan Kokusai Building, 2nd Floor, 1-1, Marunouchi 3-chome, Chiyoda-ku, Tokyo 100, Japan. ✆3-3201-0430, Fax: 3-3201-0433

Korea c/o Travel Press, Seoul Center Building, 12th Floor, 91-1 Sokong-dong, Chung-ku, Seoul 100-070, Korea. ✆2-773-6719, Fax: 2-757-6783.

New Zealand c/o Walshes World, Dingwall Building, 2nd Floor, 87 Queen Street, Aukland, New Zealand. ✆9-379-3708, Fax: 9-309-0725.

Taiwan c/o Federal Transportation Company, 8th Floor, 61 Nanking East Road, Section 3, Taipei, Taiwan. ✆22-506-7043, Fax: 22-507-5816.

UK Box 208, Sunbury on Thames, Middlesex TW16 5RJ United Kingdom. ✆ 0181-941-4009, Fax: 0181-941-4011.

VISAS

Canadian citizens must show proof of citizenship, such as a citizenship card with photo ID or a passport. All other foreign visitors must have a valid passport and most also must have a US visa.

Under a reciprocal visa-waiver program citizens of certain countries are allowed visa-free entry to the USA for non-extendable stays of 90 days or less. A round-trip ticket that is non-refundable in the USA is also required. Currently these countries are: Andorra, Argentina, Australia, Austria, Belgium, Brunei, Denmark, Finland, France, Germany, Iceland, Ireland, Italy, Japan, Liechtenstein, Luxembourg, Monaco, Netherlands, New Zealand, Norway, Portugal, San Marino, Singapore, Spain, Sweden, Switzerland, the UK and Uruguay.

All visitors should bring their driver's licenses as all US airlines, including the inter-island carriers, require passengers to present a photo ID at check-in.

CUSTOMS

US Customs allows one US quart of liquor and 200 cigarettes to be brought into the USA duty-free by each person over 21.

Agricultural Inspection

Because of Hawaii's unique and fragile ecosystem, there are strict regulations about what cannot be brought into the state. The State of Hawaii Department of Agriculture requires inspection of plants, plant parts, animals, soil or microorganism cultures. A Plant and Animal Declaration form must be filled out before de-planing and any of the above must be presented to the Plant Quarantine Inspector in the baggage claim area to make sure they are free of pests or are not potential pests themselves.

Most plants are permitted after inspection, however some are prohibited unless a permit has been acquired beforehand. A list of prohibited plants and animals can be obtained from the State of Hawaii Department of Agriculture Plant Quarantine Branch, 701 Ilalo Street, Honolulu, HI 96813.

For similar reasons, fresh fruits and vegetables and some plants cannot be taken out of Hawaii bound for the mainland or other countries. Pineapples and orchids are two fresh Hawaii products that can be purchased at the airport already inspected and packaged for export.

CONSULATES

All are in Honolulu on the island of Oahu:
American Samoa 1427 Dillingham Boulevard, Suite 210, ℂ 847-1998.
Australia 1000 Bishop Street, ℂ 524-5050.
Austria 1314 S. King Street, Suite 1260, ℂ 923-8585.
Belgium 745 Fort Street Mall, 18th Floor, ℂ 533-6900.
Brazil 44-166 Nanamoana, ℂ 235-0571.
Chile 1860 Ala Moana Boulevard, Suite 1900, ℂ 949-2850.
Denmark 1001 Bishop Street, Suite 2626, ℂ 545-2028.
Federated States of Micronesia 3049 Ualena, Suite 408, ℂ 836-4775.
Germany 2003 Kalia Road, ℂ 946-3819.
India 306 Hahani Street, ℂ 262-0292.
Italy 735 Bishop Street, Suite 201, ℂ 531-2277.
Japan 1742 Nuuanu Avenue, ℂ 523-7495.
Kiribati 850 Richards Street, Suite 503, ℂ 521-7703.
Korea 2756 Pali Highway, ℂ 595-6109.
Mariana Islands 1221 Kapiolani Boulevard, ℂ 592-0300.
Mexico 677 Ala Moana Boulevard, Suite 501, ℂ 524-4390.
Netherlands 700 Bishop Street, 21st Floor, ℂ 535-8450.
Norway 1314 South King Street, Suite G4, ℂ 593-1240.
Papua New Guinea 1154 Fort Street Mall, Suite 300, ℂ 524-5414.
Philippines 2433 Pali Highway, ℂ 595-6316.
Sweden 737 Bishop Street,

Suite 2600, ℂ 528-4777.
Switzerland 4231 Papu Circle, ℂ 737-5297.
Thailand 287A Kalihi, ℂ 845-7332.
Tonga 220 South King Street, Suite 1230, ℂ 521-5149.

LOST PASSPORT

Make photocopies of your passport, visa and driver's license and keep them separate from the originals so that you can prove your identity in case of theft or loss. It is also a good idea to leave a set with someone at home.

TIME ZONE

Time in Hawaii is GMT-10, 2 hours behind Pacific Standard Time (3 hours behind during Daylight Savings Time, which Hawaii does not follow.)

ELECTRICITY

Electricity is 110/120 V, 60 cycles. Flat two-pronged American-style plugs are the norm but there are also 3-pronged plugs for use with grounded outlets.

SECURITY

Violent crime in Hawaii is very low but car and condo break-ins do occur. Keep your condo doors locked and your car doors unlocked, so thieves are not tempted to break the glass. And don't leave anything in the trunk. Walking alone at night is not recommended.

EMERGENCY

Police, fire, and ambulance services are reached by dialing 9-1-1 from any phone.

Climate

Squeaking in at the northern edge of the tropics, the main Hawaiian Islands offer just

about the most ideal climate imaginable. Tradewinds keep the islands from getting too warm and provide just the right amount of humidity, although this varies radically from one side of the island to the other. Desert-like conditions in some leeward areas contrast with windward exposures such as Mt. Waialeale on Kauai, the wettest spot on earth. Because the islands are also mountains, average temperatures at the summits can be near freezing, but in lowland areas where most visitors stay will range from 78 degrees F (25.6 C.) in the winter to 85 degrees F. (29.4 C.) in the summer, with nights about 10 degrees cooler—ideal for sleeping.

WHAT TO PACK

Hawaii's year-round comfortable weather means simple light-weight clothes are mostly what you'll need. Shorts, a T-shirt and a pair of rubber slippers are really all that's needed during the day. In the evening or if you go upcountry (a higher elevation on the mountain) you'll want a jacket or sweatshirt, and of course bring a rain jacket with a hood. Temperatures on the summits on two of the islands, Maui and the Big Island, can reach freezing, so bring long pants if you plan on going up there. There are many hiking opportunities in the islands so bring good tennis shoes or hiking shoes. For dinner, aloha shirts and slacks for men and simple cotton dresses for women are the norm, but really, there are very few places which require anything more than shorts and shirt.

WATER AND SURF CONDITIONS

Water temperature near shore varies a noticeable 8 degrees from summer (82°F/28°C) to winter (74°F/23°C), making a wetsuit *not* optional. Most divers wear at least a 3mm (eighth-inch) full wetsuit and smaller people 5–7 mm. A few dive guides on the Big Island even wear *dry suits*! (We won't name names.)

Hawaii's surf is infamous, both for its spectacular surfing opportunities and also for the danger it poses. Surf can occur along any coastline, but occurs more regularly along the northeastern coasts of the islands, particularly during the winter months. Generally, if one side of an island is experiencing big surf, another will be calm. It cannot be overemphasized that Hawaiian surf should be taken seriously. Every year lives are lost when even fishermen who have lived their entire lives in Hawaii are swept from rocks, never to be seen again. Shore divers in particular are at risk since they must exit the water perhaps an hour later then they entered. Surf conditions should be checked, warning flags noted and the entry/exit point studied for at least ten minutes before getting in.

Money

The US dollar is the only currency.

CHANGING MONEY

Money can be changed at the Honolulu International Airport and at major banks.

TRAVELER'S CHECKS

If you plan on buying traveler's checks before traveling to Hawaii you will find it easier if the checks are in US dollars. US dollar traveler's checks are accepted as cash almost anywhere in Hawaii.

CREDIT CARDS

VISA, Mastercard and American Express are the most commonly accepted credit cards in Hawaii, but Discover, Diner's Club and JCB are also used. They can be used for almost any purchase except smaller activity companies, B&B's and road-side vendors. Some small condominiums, especially if booked through a rental agency, also do not accept them.

ATM'S

Most Automated Teller Machines in Hawaii accept bank cards from both the Cirrus and Plus systems. ATMs are found at all major banks, in many grocery stores and convenience stores.

TAXES AND TIPPING

Hawaii has a 4.17% sales tax that is added onto almost everything. In addition there is a 7.24% room tax, adding a total of 11.41% to your accommodations bill. A $2/day road use tax is collected at the car rental agencies. Tipping is customary for services and the same as on the US mainland. Waiters are tipped about 15%, taxi drivers, hair stylists, etc. about 10%. Bellhops are usually tipped $1/bag and valets $2–$3.

PRICES

Like any small island group, almost everything including fuel must be imported. Hawaii's extreme isolation means even longer barge and flight times, translating into high prices. A gallon of milk for instance (we don't drink milk but that seems to be the American standard for price comparison), costs $5 on Oahu and goes up to $6 on the outer islands. In addition, some of the islands such as Maui are rated so highly by travel magazines that they are almost fully booked year-round—not much of an incentive to lower prices.

Because of the high cost of living in Hawaii some businesses offer what is called a *kamaaina* rate to people who live here—a Hawaii driver's license being the "proof" in most cases. These rates are usually not offered for necessities such as food, clothing, gasoline, but more for luxuries such as a night at an island hotel (a rare treat for island residents) or inter-island flights (a necessity for business, medical treatment) or car rental. Some visitors get all worked up when they hear about the "special" rate offered to residents. Keep in mind that residents pay higher prices year-round partly because their islands are in such demand and this is a very small and rarely used discount. Hawaii's larger grocery stores offer member discounts, so if you will be here for a couple weeks you might want to sign up.

Communications

TELEPHONE

Hawaii has one area code, (808), which need not be dialed except if you are calling from out of state or island-to-island. For directory assistance for the same island dial 1-411; for other islands dial 1-(808)-555-1212.

For international calls dial 011+country code+area code +number. For operator assistance dial 0.

Faxes

Faxes can be sent and received through the front desk at most hotels and some condos. Business centers such as Kinko's (www.kinkos.com) also offer fax services.

E-MAIL AND INTERNET

If you are traveling with a laptop you can usually connect in your hotel room and for the cost of a long distance call access your e-mail through your local internet service provider. An account with a major ISP such as AOL or CompuServe which has dial-in nodes throughout the USA saves the long-distance charges.

If you did not bring a portable computer; you can check your mail at public access points such as Internet cafes or 24-hour business centers such as Kinko's. You will need to know incoming (POP or IMAP) mail server name, your account name and your password.

Free Web-based e-mail accounts such as HotMail (www.hotmail.com) and Yahoo! Mail (mail.yahoo. com) are also popular with travelers.

POSTAL SERVICE

The US Postal Service (✆ 800-275-8777. Web: www.usps.com) is extremely reliable but its rates have increased steadily in recent years. As of this printing 1st class letters sent and delivered within the USA are 34¢ for the first ounce and 23¢ for each additional ounce. Standard-size postcards are 23¢. Packages mailed anywhere in the USA are $3.95 up to 2 pounds for Priority service.

Health

DRINKING WATER

Tap water in Hawaii is generally safe to drink. If hiking, bring plenty of bottled water and never drink water from freshwater streams or pools. A bacterial disease called leptospirosis can be contracted either by drinking untreated water or by exposing cuts or open wounds to fresh water.

COMMON AILMENTS

Sunburn

Because of the numerous outdoor activities and Hawaii's location in the tropics, sunburn is probably the most common health complaint. Wear waterproof sunscreen with an SPF (sun protection factor) of at least 15. A hat is especially important for fair-skinned people. Don't be fooled on overcast days. While it doesn't seem so, the sun's rays are just as strong.

Cuts and scrapes

Hawaii's tropical climate is the perfect environment for bacteria, and cuts and scrapes should not be neglected. Coral cuts are particularly nasty as bits of coral tissue sometimes get into the wound. Keep cuts clean, apply an antiseptic such as Betadine, and an antibacterial ointment twice a day. Keep a bandage on the area during the day to keep it clean and leave it uncovered at night so it can dry.

Heat exhaustion

Dehydration and/or salt deficiency can cause a condition known as heat exhaustion, and in extreme cases can result in vomiting and diarrhea. Drink plenty of liquids, especially in high temperatures and make sure you are getting enough salt.

Heat stroke

Lengthy exposure to high temperatures can sometimes result in heat stroke which in some cases can be fatal. Avoid strenuous physical activity in open sun or take frequent breaks in the shade while participating in such activities.

Seasickness

Many people do their first boat dives in Hawaii and a few are unpleasantly surprised to find themselves seasick before they even get in the water for the first dive. Others, despite previous experiences with seasickness, forget to take anything or forget how miserable they were and think it won't happen to them again. If there is any doubt, take something before the trip. Non-drowsy formulas of popular seasick medications are now available, but must be taken several hours beforehand. The most effective preventative, the Scopolomine "patch," requires a doctor's prescription. Other deterents include wrist bands that work on the premise of pressure points and ginger taken orally by capsule or in dried form.

To lessen chances of seasickness, eat something light before the trip, sit toward the stern where the ride is more stable and keep your eyes on the horizon. Stay away from cigarette smoke and engine fumes, and don't try to read. Whatever you do, don't go down in the head. The confining space with no steady visual reference will just send you farther down the path. If you do end up getting seasick, go to the downwind side of the boat and lean over the side. Drink non-caffeinated liquids as soon as you feel able.

Ciguatera Poisoning

This is a serious illness caused by eating reef fish carrying ciguatoxin. Herbivorous fish acquire this toxin from the algae they feed on, and it is concentrated in the fish that feed on them. Restaurants do not typically serve reef fish, so you are only likely to get it if you are spearfishing for your dinner and do not know which fish to avoid.

Symptoms of ciguatera poisoning include nausea, stomach cramps, diarrhea, paralysis, tingling and numbness of the face, fingers and toes and a reversal of temperature sensations. Extreme cases can result in unconsciousness and death. Seek immediate medical treatment if you suspect this illness.

Sea urchin punctures

Other than coral scrapes this is probably the most common undesirable marine animal encounter experienced by divers. Sharp-spined sea urchin spines typically break off and lodge in the skin. Spines usually dissolve or work themselves out and wounds usually heal in a month. If embedded spines are from a thick-spined urchin or if the spines are in a joint or nerve or if there are signs of infection, then see a doctor.

MEDICAL TREATMENT

There are many medical clinics throughout the islands, some with 24-hour service and some even specialize in treating tourists. The four main islands have modern, fully-staffed hospitals, but for very serious conditions or specialized treatment, Neighbor Island residents often prefer to fly to Oahu.

DCS EMERGENCIES

While the Navy operates a chamber on Oahu, there is only one hyperbaric chamber center that treats divers in Hawaii. Since it too is located on Oahu, all DCS cases are flown there from the outer islands by helicopter or small plane traveling at low elevation. Divers suspecting a diving-related illness may call the hyperbaric facility on Oahu and speak to them directly or may go first to the nearest hospital emergency room and make arrangements

after speaking with the doctors there.

Hyperbaric Treatment Center 347 N. Kuakini St., Honolulu, HI 96817. ©587-3425. Four multi-place chambers and a staff of doctors and nurses specializing in hyperbaric medicine are available 24 hours a day. A progressive treatment developed by Dr. Edward Beckman in the mid-'80s uses mixed gas and deep dive tables to achieve what the center believes are better results, due to the much slower ascent rate and higher nitrogen differential.

Diver's Alert Network (DAN) Peter B. Bennett Center, 6 West Colony Place, Durham, NC 27705. Membership services ©(800)446-2671. Web: www.diversalert network.org. This highly respected non-profit organization has been providing medical advice in the case of diving injuries, researching diving medicine and promoting diving safety for a long time. They are often the first organization called by local emergency personel in the case of a diving accident.

The organization publishes the bimonthly *Alert Diver* magazine which is distributed to members. DAN offers yearly membership for $29, and three different dive accident insurance packages for an additional $25 to $70 a year.

The organization maintains a medical information line for questions about diving health and problems ©(919) 684-2948 and a 24-hour hotline for diving emergencies only ©(919) 684-8111 or ©(919) 684-4326 (you can call collect).

Altitude after diving

Most divers are aware that waiting at least 24 hours after diving before flying is a good

idea to minimize the risk of decompression sickness. But many don't realize that the same waiting period should apply before taking a helicopter flight or driving up Hawaii's mountains. When scheduling activities, keep this in mind. The islands peak at thousands of feet and require the same consideration as going to altitude in an airplane.

Transportation

All foreign travelers must enter Hawaii through either Honolulu International Airport on Oahu or Kona International Airport on the Big Island. Domestic travelers may fly directly to these islands as well as to Maui and Kauai. Lanai, Midway, and Molokai require a stop on Oahu and a change of planes before continuing on.

INTERNATIONAL AIRLINES

The following airlines have scheduled flights to Hawaii:
Air Canada ©(888) 247-2262
Air New Zealand ©(800) 262-1234
All Nippon Airways ©(800) 235-9262
America West Airlines ©(800) 235-9292
American Airlines ©(800) 433-7300
Canadian Airlines ©(808) 681-5000
China Airlines ©(808) 955-0088
Continental Airlines ©(800) 523-3273
Delta Air Lines ©(800) 221-1212
Hawaiian Airlines ©(808) 838-1555
Japan Airlines ©(808) 521-1441
Korean Air ©(800) 438-5000
Northwest Airlines ©(800) 955-2255

Philippine Airlines ✆(800) 435-9725
Qantas Airways ✆(800) 227-4500
Singapore Airlines ✆(800) 742-3333
TWA ✆(800) 221-2000
United Airlines ✆(800) 241-6522
US Airways ✆(800) 428-4322

INTER-ISLAND TRANSPORT

Flying between the islands is as routine for island residents as commuting to work is on the mainland. The main inter-island flights range from a quick 27 minutes between Oahu and Maui to an hour and a half from Hilo on the Big Island to Kauai (including a stopover on Oahu). The two primary carriers, Aloha Airlines and Hawaiian Airlines typically post identical fares in the range of $150–$160 for round-trip inter-island flights. Smaller airlines service the smaller islands of Lanai and Molokai.

No matter who you go with, you are bound to experience the world's fastest beverage service, a service that the airlines apparently pride themselves in, as not one of them will dispense with it, even on the shortest of flights. Both Aloha and Hawaiian have passes available which allow unlimited flying for a specified period and there are often discounts offered on their websites.

Aloha Airlines ✆(800) 367-5250 (US Mainland), (808) 484-1111 (Interisland). Web: www.alohaairlines.com.
Hawaiian Airlines ✆(800) 367-5320 (US Mainland), (800)882-8811 (Interisland). Web: www.hawaiianair.com.
Island Air ✆(800) 323-3345 (US Mainland), (800)652-6541 (Neighbor Islands), (808) 484-2222 (Oahu). Web: www.islandair.com.

Ferries

Daily ferry service is available in the islands only between Maui and Lanai and between Maui and Molokai. (See Maui practicalities).

ON-ISLAND TRANSPORT

Buses

Regularly scheduled public bus service is available on Oahu from The Bus–Oahu Transit Services, Inc. ✆848-5555. Limited public bus service is available on Kauai and the Big Island of Hawaii. There is limited private bus service on Maui.

Taxis

Taxis and shuttles are available on all the islands at a rate averaging $10 per 5 miles.

RENTAL CARS

If you've come to Hawaii to dive, you will most likely want to rent a car. Only Oahu dive operators or the largest dive shops on the Neighbor Islands have hotel pick-up and because hotels and harbors can be quite far apart, taxi fare will quickly exceed the cost of renting a car. Fortunately, rental car rates are competitive ($150–$200/week), sometimes even cheaper than on the mainland. This is quickly made up for, though, by outrageously high-priced gasoline, reported to be the most expensive in the country on some of the Neighbor Islands (over $2/gallon).

While many of Hawaii's roads are two lanes only, the local attitude toward passing other vehicles and speeding are summed up by the bumper sticker "It's an island. What's the rush?" More often than not, the car you passed will be right behind you at the next stoplight.

Leaving anything of value

in your car is a big mistake. While violent crime is extremely uncommon, breaking into tourist cars is an *art form* here, especially at well-known tourist attractions. Leaving your car unattended for even a few minutes is enough time for your window to be broken and your trunk popped. Your best bet is to take everything of value with you and leave your car doors unlocked and your trunk *empty*.

Seat belt use is required by law in Hawaii, so buckle-up!
Alamo Rent-A-Car ✆(800) 327-9633.Web: www.goalamo.com
Budget Rent-A-Car ✆(800) 777-0169.Web: www.budgetrentacar.com
National Car Rentals ✆(800)CAR-RENT.Web: www.nationalcar.com
Avis Rent-A-Car ✆(800) 331-1212. Web: www.avis.com
Dollar Rent A Car ✆(800)367-7006. Web: www.dollarcar.com

Motorcycle rental

Dive bag lugging may rule this out as an option, but motorcycles are available for rent on the four major islands for $105–$130 a day, with multiple-day rates available.

Accommodations

Accommodations in Hawaii range from campgrounds to the most award-winning, stratospherically priced hotels in the world. While hotels and condos are the norm, each island also has a few hostels and many B&Bs. With some searching, picturesque cottages with earth-shattering views in rural areas away from everything can still be found. The accommodations we've listed in the practicalities section for each island are all close to the harbors and launching ramps that the dive boats leave from. Whenever possible we've listed some one-of-a-kind accommodations in addition to large luxury hotels. There are of course many many more. We have included a range of accommodations for each island and given the list prices, but in many cases discounts are offered through websites or at certain times of year, generally April to mid-December.

Food and Drink

"Onolicious" is the local way to describe good food. Like the word—a combination of the Hawaiian *ono* (delicious) and the English "delicious"—island food is a blend of the island's different cultures. For instance, a favorite local meal, "plate lunch," consists of teriyaki beef or chicken, two scoops of rice, and macaroni salad. A "loco moco" is another popular item, consisting of rice topped with a hamburger and a fried egg, and smothered in gravy.

In addition to the more mainstream Mexican, Chinese, and Thai dishes, ethnic favorites can be found at luau and fairs, in restaurants, small markets, supermarkets—even the island McDonalds, which serve *saimin* and a Portuguese sausage breakfast with rice. So chance 'em and try some of the following.

Hawaiian

Poke Literally "to slice crosswise into pieces" this cold salad is mostly cubed raw fish marinated with soy sauce, oil, seaweed, green onion and chili peppers.
Kalua Pig The final product of pig cooked whole underground in a rock-lined pit

(*imu*) for hours, sometimes overnight.
Laulau Often cooked with the pig in the imu, laulau is cooked as a neat package of inedible ti leaves wrapped around pieces of fish, pork or chicken which have been wrapped in edible taro leaves.
Poi The consistency of gray wallpaper paste (and some would say the flavor as well) poi is the product of pounding the tuber of a plant called taro and is the staple starch of the Hawaiian people.
Lomi salmon Salted salmon mixed with chopped tomatoes and onion and served cold.
Chicken luau A stew made from chicken, taro leaves and coconut milk.
Haupia A firm, white pudding made from coconut milk, sugar and corn starch.

Japanese

Sushi Usually rice and fish or vegetables wrapped in a sheet of pressed, dried seaweed.
Sashimi Sliced raw fish served with shoyu (soy sauce) and wasabi (Japanese horseradish).
Saimin Noodle soup with meat or vegetable broth.
Teriyaki Beef marinated in soy sauce, often with ginger and garlic.

Portuguese

Portuguese soup A thick, rich soup, usually spicy, made with kidney beans, vegetables and Portuguese sausage.
Portuguese sweetbread Sweet white bread served in a round loaf.
Malasadas Deep fried wheat dough similar to a donut, but without the hole.

Chinese

Manapua Kind of a hot sandwich to go, this is the Hawaiian version of a Chinese char siu bau, marinated pork in a

bun, but now with many variations.

Korean

Kimchi Traditionally just salted cabbage and turnips, now with a variety of added seasonings, vegetables and even sometimes seafood.

Local favorites

Shave ice Similar to a snowcone but made with more finely shaved ice, this is an island tradition. Sometimes there are ice cream or sweet azuki beans at the bottom of the cone.
POG A blend of passion fruit, orange and guava juices, you can find this canned or refrigerated in a carton. There are also other tropical fruit juice combinations available, but POG is an island tradition.

Small mom and pop restaurants of every ethnicity can be found in Hawaii—more on Oahu than the outer islands. Many high-end hotel restaurants and gourmet restaurants serve what is called "Pacific Rim" or "Hawaiian Regional" cuisine. Chefs combine seafood or island-raised beef or chicken, with fresh island ingredients, such as ginger, herbs, upcountry greens, taro and tropical fruits. The vast majority of the fish served in these restaurants is caught in Hawaii, but prices are high ($20–$30 for an entree). Most of these fish are sold fresh in the supermarkets, so you could also buy and prepare your own. The selection is so good, you could try a different fish every night of your stay. We've listed a range of restaurants from local to ethnic to luxurious Hawaiian Regional Cuisine and tried to include mostly those with open-air or ocean-side settings that you would not experience at home. Price ranges listed are entree prices only.

FRUITS

Hawaii is a great place to try tropical fruits that are not carried by your local supermarket at home and most are available year-round. Fruit stands usually sell several varieties of each fruit. Island varieties of bananas are smaller and have a much better flavor than commercial bananas. Visitors love them! Papayas and pineapples are also available year-round. In the summer you might be able to buy watermelon grown on Molokai and shipped to the other islands. Mangos are also mostly available in the summer and considered the fruit of the gods.

Shopping

There is a big difference between shopping at the resorts and shopping centers (Gucci, Tiffany, Louis Vuitton) and bringing home gifts that are uniquely Hawaiian.

GIFTS FROM HAWAII

Hawaiian products and crafts vary somewhat from island to island and many are uniquely Hawaiian. Some processed agricultural products such as 100% Kona coffee are considered among the best in the world. Other popular local products are macadamia nuts, taro pancake mix or chips, raw sugar and fresh pineapple. Wines and beers, jams and jellies, Maui onions, Maui catnip, Hawaii dog biscuits are a few other edible Hawaii products.

In addition to souvenir and trinket stores selling everything from carved tikis (*not* a Hawaiian craft), T-shirts, key rings, clothes and children's items, high-quality, beautiful island crafts can be found at local artist shops, the Historical Society and museum shops and in the island's many fine art galleries. Gorgeous Hawaiian woods are used in jewel boxes, bowls, and furniture. Niihau shell lei are the most highly prized shell necklaces in the world. Hawaiian quilts (even if made in the Philippines) are stunning and of a distinct style reflecting Hawaii's rich cultural heritage using island plants and flowers. X-mas tree ornaments, Hawaiian music and jewelry are available on all the islands, and you could even adopt a whale in someone's name!

Diving

Planning a dive trip to Hawaii for the first time requires a bit of decision-making, when all you might feel like doing is making a phone call to a dive resort and letting them take it from there. Unlike some dive destinations, where there is only one island, in Hawaii there are four main island groupings to choose from. And there are no "dive resorts," so you also have to decide where to stay and with whom to dive.

You must first decide which island or islands to visit. The island where you might find your favorite diving may be too busy or quiet; the island with the right flavor on land might not have the diving you prefer. You need to decide which is more important, the diving or the ambience of the island. Hopping around to the four main diving areas during a two-week stay can be done, but there are so many things to do on these mountainous islands that one week per island is not even enough. Flight time between most of the islands is 30–45 minutes, but you know how it is. Once you pack up, check out, fly, arrive, check-in and unpack, half your day is gone already. If all you have is one-week of vacation we would suggest spending it on one island. If you have two weeks then maybe visit another.

Once you have decided which and how many islands you are determined to visit then you should choose a dive operator. If you are a serious diver we recommend that you stay at least a week on each island. It's common sense that the longer you dive with a particular operation the more they have invested in your satisfaction, and you may get to see more off-the-beaten-path sites.

We have gathered information on some operations that we know to have good reputations. Well kept boats, good equipment, and safe procedures are obvious criteria, but also important are long-term crew, detailed briefings, respect for the marine life, and bottom time limited only by your computer or your air consumption. Divemasters who rip octopus out of their holes, bang on their tanks, or otherwise muscle their way through a dive can be avoided with some research. Prices given are one-day rates including equipment. There are often discounts for having your own equipment and for diving multiple days.

Finally, once you know who you're going to do most of your diving with, choose where to stay, unless you don't mind driving, which on some islands can be a very early one-hour drive to get to an operator on the opposite end of the island. Don't let such a drive keep you from diving with the best operator you can find, however.

Periplus Diving Guides

Each book: US$24.95

Diving Indonesia (3rd edition)
ISBN 962 593 314 X

"Diving Indonesia has got to be the most fascinating book published in the last year."

BBC World

"Diving Indonesia comes described as, "A Guide to the World's Greatest Diving," and lives up to its promise. This guide features over 120 color photographs, up-to-date travel information, maps of all major dive sites, essays on reef life and ecology, charts of all site conditions, plus information on local geography, history, and lore."

Ocean Realm

Diving Southeast Asia (3rd edition)
ISBN 0 7946 0076 X

"Perhaps no other region in the world presents such clear waters and abundant undersea life as Southeast Asia. The azure seas, a bounty of reefs, submerged wrecks and fabulous coral gardens should get even the most hardened land lover into a wetsuit and mask.

This guide to the best dive sites in Malaysia, Indonesia, the Philippines and Thailand maps out the watery worlds that await the enthusiastic diver. The detailed information – whether it's a walk-in dive, a night dive, diving in remote locations or from live-aboard boats – provides everything you need to take the plunge: the visibility, the current, the type of fish, the quality of the coral, the choicest spots."

Going Places

Diving Australia
ISBN 962 593 104 X

"An unbelievable collection of dive sites and information brought from renowned dive authors, Neville Coleman and Nigel Marsh. This handy book covers every state with detailed information on the sites. Every site has a map and an icon-based guide to tell you what you can expect to see, the reef life, the visibility, reef and pelagic fish, drop-offs and pinnacles. It has over 200 lovely colour photographs and, most importantly, is easy to follow.

Basically, there is an awesome amount of information in this book. As a general guide to diving in Australia – this is the business."

Scuba Diver

Periplus Diving Guides are available at bookshops and travel stores around the world. If you cannot find them where you live, please write to us for the name of a distributor closest to you.

New

ISBN 962 593 323 9

New

ISBN 962 593 499 5

Periplus Editions c/o Berkeley Books Pte Ltd
130 Joo Seng Road #06-01/03 Olivine Building Singapore 368357 tel: (65) 6280 1330 fax: (65) 6280 6290

Other titles from
Periplus Editions

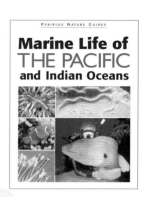

Marine Life of the Pacific and Indian Oceans
ISBN 962 593 948 2
US$16.95

This handy reference guide showcases 350 of the most colourful and commonly encountered species in the region. Features photos from many of the world's best underwater photographers.

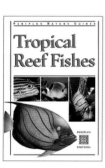

Tropical Reef Fishes
ISBN 962 593 152 X
US$9.95

Tropical Marine Life
ISBN 962 593 157 0
US$9.95

Written by leading authority Dr Gerald Allen, these two handy field guides are essential for snorkelers and divers alike.

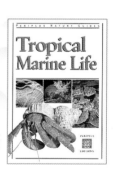

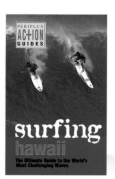

Surfing Hawaii
ISBN 962 593 540 1
US$24.95

Hawaii's awe-inspiring waves are among the most challenging in the world. Let Periplus' team of surfers and photographers take you on an action-packed surfing adventure!

If you cannot find these books where you live, please write to us for the name of a distributor closest to you.

Periplus Publishing Group c/o Berkeley Books Pte Ltd
130 Joo Seng Road #06-01/03 Singapore 368357 tel: (65) 6280 1330 fax: (65) 6280 6290
email: inquiries@periplus.com.sg

The Big Island

Between Hilo and Puna, the Kona Coast, and Kohala, divers have three very different areas to choose from on Hawaii. The accommodations and atmosphere are different as well. Kona is of course the most famous (and justly so) but there are some interesting surprises at the other areas.

Hilo and Puna

DIVE OPERATORS/SHOPS

Hilo diving is almost all done from shore or from kayaks with limited diving from a chartered boat if a minimum number of divers request it. **Aquatic Perceptions** 111 Banyan Drive, Hilo, HI 96720. ℂ935-9997. Web: www.gtesupersite.com:80/multisport. Email: kayakscuba @aol.com. 1-tank shore dive incl. equipment $60. Specialize in kayak dives. **Nautilus Dive Center** (est. 1975) ℂ935-6939. Web: nautilusdivehilo.com. Email: derooy@gte.net. 2-tank shore dive incl. gear $75, 2-tank boat dive not incl. gear $85 (6 diver minimum). This is a full service dive shop that rents equipment including kayaks, can repair just about anything, and can give you expert advice on where to shore dive. If you want a guided dive, owner Bill De Rooy delights in taking the time to show divers the wildlife along his favorite coastline.

MEDICAL TREATMENT

Hilo Medical Center 1190 Waianuenue Ave., Hilo. ℂ974-4700. 24-hour emergency service.

ACCOMMODATIONS

Hilo Hawaiian Hotel 71 Banyan Dr., Hilo, HI 96720. ℂ(800) 367-5004, 935-9361. Web: castle-group.com/HHH. Email: info@castle resorts.com. Hilo's nicest hotel, this is a 285-room highrise right on Hilo Bay. Most rooms have private lanais and some have kitchenettes. $119 standard to $360 1BR suite with kitchenette and ocean view.

Hilo Seaside Hotel 126 Banyan Dr., Hilo, HI 96720. ℂ(800) 367-7000, 935-0821. Simple rooms in two-story buildings with air-con and small refrigerators. The deluxe ocean wing rooms are recommended over others. They are away from street noise and have lanais overlooking Reed's Bay. $60–$80. **Shipman House Bed & Breakfast Inn** 131 Kaiulani St., Hilo, HI 96720. ℂ(800) 627-8447, 934-8002. Web: www.hilo-hawaii.com. Email: bighouse@bigisland.com. A renovated Victorian mansion once visited by Jack London and Queen Liliuokalani it is full of antiques and much of the original furniture. There are three rooms in the main house and two in the guest cottage, all with private bathrooms. $145–$175 depending on room, includes continental breakfast served on the lanai overlooking a gulch with tropical vegetation.

RESTAURANTS

Cafe 100 969 Kilauea Ave., Hilo. ℂ935-8683. Very popular with the locals, traditionally heavy local food including many kinds of loco moco, burgers, stews and plate lunches. Open for breakfast, lunch and dinner, you can eat inside or at outdoor tables. $5–$7.

Cafe Pesto 308 Kamehameha Ave., Hilo. (in the S Hata Building). ☏969-6640. Bright and open, this is a place you'd consider for a business lunch or quiet dinner. The menu is Italian with unusual wood-fired pizzas such as kahlua pig, as well as pasta dishes, calzones and salads. Lunch $9–$15, dinner $12–$29.

Harringtons 135 Kalaniana-ole, Hilo. ☏961-4966. A small waterfront restaurant overlooking Reed's Bay, this is peaceful and romantic setting for dinner. Steaks and seafood. Lunch weekdays $8–$12, dinner nightly $20–$30.

Kona

DIVE OPERATORS

With a long protected coastline to dive off of, Kona dive operators meet at a leisurely 7:15–7:45 a.m. for their morning dives. Boats launch from Honokohau Harbor, Kailua Pier and Keauhou Bay.
Dive Makai (est. 1974) Box 2955, Kailua-Kona, HI 96745. ☏329-2025. Web: www.divemakai.com. Email: tom@divemakai.com. 31-foot boat, 12 divers divided into two groups. Certified divers only. 2-tank dive incl. equip./computer & tax. Dive Makai's reputation is phenomenal. The knowledge and extreme enthusiasm of their guides, their skill as dive leaders and their range of dive sites combine to make this operation one of the best you will ever experience. Launch from Kailua Pier.
Pacific Rim Divers (est. 1977) Box 4602, Kailua-Kona, HI 96745. ☏988-4830. Web: pacificrim-divers.com. Email: primd-vrs@gte.net. 26-foot boat, 6 divers. Certified divers. 2-

tank dive incl. equipment $94.95. Owners Frank and Patrice Heller take out all trips personally, providing a super high-quality experience as they tailor the trips to divers' requests. One of the few 6-passenger boats in the islands, these guys care so much about the trip they offer that Patrice sometimes stays up late making brownies! Launch from Honokohau Harbor.

Dive Shop

Jack's Diving Locker (est. 1981) 75-5819 Alii Drive, Kailua-Kona, HI 96740. ☏(800) 345-4807, 329-7585. Web: www.divejdl.com. Email: divejdl@gte.net. A friendly 5-star dive shop located right on the waterfront in Kona. They have a well-stocked shop, Nitrox. Sea & Sea MX10 $50/day incl. film.

LIVE-ABOARD

Kona Aggressor Box 1470 Morgan City, LA 70381. ☏(800) 348-2628, (504) 385-2628. Web: www.aggressor. com. E-mail: kona@aggressor. com. 80-foot catamaran, 10 divers. This is Hawaii's only live-aboard. Diving along 90 miles of leeward coastline, they show some of the same sites that the day boats visit, but on the live-aboard you can explore much more during a six-day trip. Handicapped Scuba Association–approved barrier-free dive boat. $1,895/5.5 days of diving all-inclusive. Camera rentals, E-6 photo lab.

MEDICAL SERVICES

Kona Community Hospital Haukapila St., Kealakekua. ☏322-9311. 24-hour emergency service.

ACCOMMODATIONS

Kona Tiki Hotel 75-5968 Alii Drive, Kailua-Kona, HI

96740. ☏329-1425. A 2-minute drive to Kailua Pier. If you don't mind an older hotel, call the Kona Tiki first. With only 15 rooms it is probably booked, but when you're in Kona you'll see why. For the price, this is THE location—virtually at the water's edge. 5-minute drive to Kailua Pier, 10 minute drive to Honokohau. $58 for hotel room, $65 w/ kitchenette.

King Kamehameha's Kona Beach Hotel 75-5660 Palani Rd., Kailua-Kona, HI 96740. ☏(800)367-6060, 329-2911. Web: www.konabeachhotel. com. Email: reservation@hth-corp.com. A 30-second walk to the Kailua Pier, 5 minute drive to Honokohau. Once the site of King Kamehameha's residence, this older hotel is on the only beach in town (and it's a small beach). The lobby itself is a mini-museum and the staff are genuinely friendly. $120–$195 depending on the view.

Royal Sea-Cliff Resort 75-6040 Alii Drive, Kailua-Kona, HI 96740. ☏(800)922-7866, 329-8021. One of the nicest and newest condo complexes in Kona, it is also right on the water. 5-minute drive to Kailua Pier, 10-minute drive to Honokohau. $210 1BR–$240 2 BR.

Holualoa Inn Box 222, Holualoa, HI 96725. ☏(800) 392-1812, 324-1121. Web: www.konaweb.com/hinn. Email: inn@aloha.net. A beautiful upscale B&B on a 40 acre coffee plantation. The 6 charming guest rooms, some with stunning views, each have a private bath. There is also a 2-room suite available. Swimming pool, hot tub, fireplace (for those chilly Kona nights?) and cooking facilities are some of the amenities. 10-minute drive to Kailua Pier, 15 minutes to Honokohau. $150–$195, with discounts for multiple night stays.

Bianelli's Gourmet Pizza and Pasta 75-240 Nani Kailua Dr., Kailua-Kona (in the Pines Plaza). ✆326-4800. If it's good enough for Iron Man athletes it should be good enough for us divers. All you can eat pasta specials for about $9 in addition to a huge selection of gourmet pizzas in a casual sports-theme atmosphere. $7–$13 for lunch or dinner.

Huggo's 75-5828 Kahakai Rd., Kailua-Kona. ✆329-1493. A great location for a sunset dinner. Some of the deck tables are almost right on the rocky shoreline. Pasta, steak and seafood are well-prepared and served in an open-air setting. There is also a beach-side bar with live entertainment. Lunch $8–$11 and dinner $19–$46.

Ocean View 75-5683 Alii Dr., Kailua-Kona. ✆329-9998. Occupying one of the most desirable locations in Kona since 1937, across from the seawall looking out over Kailua Pier, this family-owned restaurant is the best local restaurant in town. They serve everything from pancakes to Spam to loco mocos and Chinese dishes. Highly recommended if you want to sample local food and surroundings. Breakfast $3–$5, lunch $3–$11 and dinner $5–$14. Closed Mondays.

Sibu Cafe 75-5695 Alii Dr., Kailua-Kona. (in the Banyan Court Mall). ✆329-1112. This outdoor cafe serves delicious and healthy Indonesian dishes including curries, satays, and ginger and garlic preparations. Lunch and dinner, $8–$13. Cash only.

FILM DEVELOPING

Longs Drug 75-5595 Palani Rd., Kailua-Kona. ✆329-8477. Print processing only.

Zac's Business Center 75-5629 Kuakini Hwy., Kailua-Kona. ✆329-0006. In-house print processing and 2-hour E-6 slide processing.

Kohala

Boats that dive the Kohala area launch from Kawaihai Harbor and meet around 7:45 a.m.

DIVE OPERATORS/SHOP

Aloha Dive Company Box 4454, Kailua-Kona, HI 96745. ✆(800)708-5662, 325-5560. 28-foot boat, 6 divers. Owners Mike and Buffy Nakachi were born and raised in Hawaii and share their local knowledge and Hawaiian legends and stories with divers. Kawaihai Harbor is just one of the areas they launch from. 2-tank dive $105, 2-tank remote dive $150, 3-tank remote dive $210, all including equip. and computer.

Kohala Divers Kawaihae Shopping Center, Box 44940, Kawaihae, HI 96743 ✆882-7774. Web: www.kohaladivers.com. Email: h2osport@kohaladivers.com. The only dive shop in Kohala, it has all the basic necessities, including tank rental and gear repair. 36-foot boat, 9 divers divided into 2 or 3 groups. Certified divers, introductory divers and snorkelers. 2-tank dive incl. equipment $102.50. SeaLife ReefMaster $15 not including film.

ACCOMMODATIONS

Big luxury resorts with man-made beaches isolated from each other by miles of black lava are the norm between Kona and Kohala.

Outrigger Waikoloa Beach 69-275 Waikoloa Beach Dr.,

Waikoloa, HI 96738. ✆(800) 668-7444, 886-6789. Web: www.outrigger.com. Email: owb.reservations@outrigger.com. This hotel already had the perfect location on a spectacular beach on the Kohala Coast, but after a multi-million dollar renovation it is even more highly recommended. $315 (garden or mountain view) to $535 (cabana).

Vista Waikoloa 69-1010 Keana Place, Waikoloa, HI 96738. ✆(800)822-4252, 885-4944. Web: www.southkohala.com. Email: info@southkohala.com. A condo complex managed by South Kohala Management that has distant views of the ocean, but nice rooms, a pool, hot tub and daily maid service. $255–$315 2 BR units only.

RESTAURANTS

Tres Hombres Beach Grill in the Kawaihae Shopping Center. ✆882-1031. Specializes in Mexican food with a tropical South Pacific theme. Open for lunch $8–$18 and dinner $12–$23.

Cafe Pesto in the Kawaihae Shopping Center. ✆882-1071. Pasta, gourmet wood-fired pizzas, salads. Lunch $5–$12, dinner $9–$25.

The Bay Terrace in the Mauna Lani Bay Hotel. ✆885-6622. A beautiful open-air setting, this restaurant has breakfast buffet daily ($22) a seafood buffet on Fridays and Saturdays ($40) and a Sunday brunch ($39). A la carte is also available: breakfast $10–$15, dinner $20–$40. No lunch is served.

FILM DEVELOPING

Zac's Photo King Shops Waikoloa. ✆885-0047 Print processing only. 4-day E-6 slide processing done at their Kona store. Sometimes faster service.

Maui Nui

Maui gets more than twice as many visitors per year than it has residents, and there are enough hotel rooms, restaurants, and tourist services on this island to satisfy anyone. For many people, Maui's combination of relaxed island feeling and an established tourist infrastructure is just about ideal.

Maui Nui's signature diving areas are Molokini and Lanai, with the South Shore Maui and West End Maui sites serving as weather backups and second dives. This means the operators (and attendant tourist facilities) are concentrated in two areas: Kihei and Wailea, for the Molokini and South Shore sites, and Lahaina and Kaanapali, for the Lanai and West End sites. The Windward Maui sites are shore dives, and you'll want a car, a good guide, and a sense of adventure to tackle those. You can stay on Lanai (we recommend at least a visit if you can spare the time), and even dive in a limited way from one of the resorts, but if you are serious about diving the best sites off this island, work with the Lahaina operators. Molokai, when conditions allow, is dived from Lahaina. Another very interesting option would be to stay on Molokai, and dive with Bill Kapuni, the island's only local operator and one of the few native Hawaiian owned and run dive businesses in the islands.

Maui

MEDICAL SERVICES

Maui Memorial Hospital 221 Mahalani, Wailuku, HI 96793. ©244-9056. 24-hour emergency service.

Doctors on Call ©667-7676 Web: www.docmaui.com. 3 locations: Hyatt Regency, Westin Maui, and Ritz-Carlton. Specialize in treating visitors in the Lahaina, Kaanapali and Kapalua areas. The doctors are very familiar with diving related medical issues. **Urgent Care Maui** 1325 S. Kihei Rd., Suite 103, Kihei, HI 96753. ©879-7781. Open 365 days a year, hours are 6 a.m.–midnight. Will make hotel house calls.

GETTING AROUND

In addition to inter-island flights, daily ferry service is available between Maui and Lanai and between Maui and Molokai.
Expeditions Lahaina/Lanai Passenger Ferry. ©(800) 695-2624, 661-3756. Web: www.maui.net/~paradise/expeditions/expeditions.html. Daily service between Lahaina, Maui and Manele, Lanai. Adult $50 round-trip. Child $40 roundtrip. Five trips are offered daily. Travel time is about one hour. Rental car, hotel and activity packages are available.
Molokai Princess Lahaina/Molokai Passenger Ferry. ©(800) 275-6969, 667-6165. Monday-Saturday service between Lahaina Harbor, Maui and Kaunakakai, Molokai. Adult $80 round-trip. Child $40 round-trip. This service is used by workers commuting from Molokai to Maui so

the ferry departs Molokai at 6:00 a.m. arriving in Maui at 7:15 a.m., then departs Maui at 5:15 p.m. returning to Molokai by 6:30 p.m. Additional trips are offered on Wednesday and Saturday, and packages with rental car and other activities are available.

Molokini and South Shore Maui

Molokini is accessible by boat only. It sits three miles off-shore and almost daily tradewinds make kayaking out to it too dangerous. Most boats go out to Molokini early, with check-in times between 6:00 a.m. and 6:30 a.m. to avoid the wind, which invariably increases in late morning. 2-tank dives typically include one dive off Molokini and one dive off Maui, but of course this varies. Factors such as swell direction, wind and current determine where the best diving that day will be.

DIVE OPERATORS

Molokini operators leave from all three of Maui's commercial launching areas, but the trip is shortest (about 15 minutes) from the Kihei Boat Ramp. **Dive and Sea Maui** (est. 1989) 1975 S. Kihei Rd., Kihei, HI 96753. ©874-1952. Web: www.diveandseamaui.com. Email: captron@maui.net. 26-foot boat. 6 passengers. 2-tank dive incl. equipment $115. This is a small owner-operated dive shop that caters to all levels of divers. 2-tank certified divers only on Mon., Sat., and Sun. Certified and introductory divers Tues., Wed., Thurs., Fri. Service is very personalized and certified divers are welcome to stay down as long as their air lasts.

Mike Severns Diving (est. 1979) P.O. Box 627, Kihei, HI 96753. ©879-6596. Web: www.mikesevernsdiving.com. Email: severns@mauigateway.com. 38-foot boat. 13-passengers divided into two groups. Certified divers only. 2-tank dive incl. equipment/computer $120. Owned by the authors of this book. [Editor: It is awkward in a situation like this to promote one's own business, and Mike and Pauline's operation has been around so long, and its reputation is so strong, that it isn't even really necessary. For the record, this is a very well-run operation, and they almost certainly have the most enthusiastic and knowledge-able guides on the island.]

DIVE SHOP

B&B Scuba (est. 1988) Azeka Place Shopping Center, 1280 S. Kihei Rd., Kihei, HI 96753. ©875-2861. Web: www.bbscuba.com//bbcentral.htm. Email: bvarney333@aol.com. PADI. Very friendly, down-to-earth people run this shop which is also the shop frequented by local divers. Full range of services including PADI courses, gear rental and repair, Nitrox, guided shore dives. Sea & Sea MX10 w/external strobe $35/day incl. film.

ACCOMMODATIONS

These are all in the Kihei and Wailea area.
Ann and Bob Babson's B&B

3371 Keha Dr., Kihei, HI 96753. ©(800)824-6409, 874-1166. Web: www.mauibnb.com. Email: babson@mauibnb.com. Rooms, 2-room suites and a separate 2 BR cottage are located in a quiet residential neighborhood up on a hill overlooking the ocean. A five-minute drive downhill to the Kihei Boat Ramp. $100 room to $135 cottage, 5–7 night minimum.
Kihei Kai Nani 2495 N. Kihei Rd., Kihei, HI 96753. ©879-9088. One-bedroom condos in low-rise buildings across

the street from nice beaches and within walking distance of shops and parks. A ten-minute walk to the Kihei Boat Ramp. $69 April-Nov. to $94 Dec.-Mar.
Mana Kai Maui Resort 2960 S. Kihei Road, Kihei, HI 96753. ©879-1561, Rental office (800)367-5242. Web: www.crhmaui.com. Email: res@crhmaui.com. An older hotel on one of Maui's most scenic beaches. The 8-story building has some hotel-type rooms and some condo units. About a 5-minute walk to the Kihei Boat Ramp. $95 room low-season to $300 2 BR deluxe ocean view high-season.

Renaissance Wailea Beach Resort 3550 Wailea Alanui Dr., Wailea, HI 96753. ©879-4900. Web: www.marriott.com. A medium-size hotel right on a beautiful, clean beach. A 3-minute drive to the Kihei Boat Ramp. $249 terrace view to $359 beachfront, including breakfast.
Four Seasons Resort Maui 3900 Wailea Alanui Dr., Wailea, HI 96753. © (800) 334-6284, 874-8000. Web: www.fourseasonsmaui.com. Award-winning luxury hotel on a beautiful beach with

views of the ocean and the West Maui mountains. About a 5-minute drive to the Kihei Boat Ramp. $310 mountain view to $625 ocean view.

RESTAURANTS

A Pacific Cafe 1279 S. Kihei Rd., Kihei (in Azeka Place II Shopping Center). © 879-0069. A tandoori (clay) oven and open kitchen are the centerpiece of this restaurant which specializes in Hawaiian Regional Cuisine. The two large rooms can get noisy, but the food is exceptional.
Maalea Grill Maalaea Harbor Village, 300 Maalaea Rd., Maalaea. (No telephone yet). This fun, newly opened, and

locally owned bar and grill overlooking quaint Maalea Harbor serves salads, sandwiches, seafood, and steaks at very reasonable prices. Enjoy the picturesque view now, as it will surely change in the future when the harbor expands. Lunch $5–$10 and dinner $9–$19.

Maui Tacos 2411 S. Kihei Rd., Kihei (in Kamaole Beach Center). ✆879-5005. Gourmet tacos and other Mexican fast food. You can eat inside but Kamaole Beach Park is right across the street.

Royal Thai Cuisine 1280 S. Kihei Rd., Kihei (in Azeka Place I Shopping Center). ✆ 874-0813. A quiet family-run restaurant that attracts locals and travelers. They serve lunch and dinner.

FILM PROCESSING

Pro Photo Lab 2395 S. Kihei Rd., Kihei (in Dolphin Plaza). ✆879-1508. In-house print processing and 2-hour E-6 slide processing.

Lanai and West End Maui

The vast majority of diving on Lanai is from day boats that leave from Maui and cross the Auau Channel. Normally the morning crossing is calm and the trip back a little rougher. Because of this channel crossing, dive operators going to Lanai are forced to cancel their Lanai trip more often, though still infrequently, than the Maui/Molokini operators.

On these days, the dive operators offer alternative dives off the west coast of Maui. Don't pass up the dive just because it isn't going to a listing on a brochure. You will still have good dives! On the other hand, sometimes the weather is unreasonaby *calm*. There are only a handful of these

days in a whole year. If the dive boat operators tell you that they would like to take you someplace they can't normally go, such as Molokai, don't say no just because you've signed up for a Cathedral dive that can be visited 350 days a year. Take advantage and go with the crew's suggestion of the less-traveled spot.

DIVE OPERATORS

Extended Horizons (est. 1984) 277 Wili Ko Place ✆236, Lahaina, HI 96761. ✆ 667-0611 Web: www. scubadivemaui.com. Email: info@scubadivemaui.com. 36-foot boat. 13 passengers divided into two groups. Certified divers only. 2-tank dive incl. equipment $125. An experienced dive boat operation that offers daily trips to Lanai, but they also dive West Maui and, when the wind shifts, Molokai. Their range of sites is extensive and trips are tailored to the requests of each day's divers. Depart from Mala Wharf.

Kapalua Dive Company (est. 1989) P.O. Box 11161, Lahaina, HI 96761. ✆ (877) 669-3448, 669-3448. Web: w w w . k a p a l u a d i v e . c o m . Email: info@kapaluadive. com. A small company that offers many different shore diving excursions around the west end, from scooter and kayak dives to custom beach and night dives.

DIVE SHOP

Pacific Dive (est. 1989) 150 Dickenson St. Lahaina, HI 96761. ✆(877)667-7331, 667-5331. Web: pacificdive. com. Email: pacificdive@ tiki.net. *One* of the owners of this store is a serious shopper! In addition to offering the fullest range of services including Nitrox, this 5-star PADI shop has *everything*

from rebreathers down to computer batteries. Tons of gadgets, wetsuits and children's water toys. They also have the best selection of books we've ever seen in a dive shop. Sea and Sea MX10 w/ external strobe $35/day incl. film.

ACCOMMODATIONS

All of the below are in Lahaina and Kaanapali.

Pioneer Inn 658 Wharf Street, Lahaina, HI 96761. ✆(800)457-5457, 661-3636. Web: www.pioneerinn-maui.com. Email: info@pio-neerinnmaui.com. A Victorian-style hotel built in 1901 and added to in 1966, right in the heart of Lahaina and fronting the harbor. Rooms at this historic hotel have received much-needed renovation, but that means pets are no longer allowed. A 10-minute drive to Mala Wharf. $110 to $130 depending on the season.

Kaanapali Beach Hotel 2525 Kaanapali Parkway, Kaanapali, HI 96761 ✆(800)262-8450, 661-0011. Web: www.kbhmaui.com. Email: res@kbhmaui.com. Awarded Hawaii's most Hawaiian Hotel, KBH strives to educate every one of its employees in Hawaiian culture and values and to pass this along to guests. Complementary classes in Hawaiian arts and crafts are offered daily. About a 10-minute drive to Mala Wharf. $180 garden view to $275 oceanfront, including breakfast.

Napili Kai Beach Resort 5900 Honoapiilani Rd., Napili, HI 96761. ✆(800) 367-5030, 669-6271. Web: www.napilikai.com. Email: nkbc@maui.net. 165 hotel rooms and condo units make up this complex on beautiful Napili Bay where according to a zoning bylaw no buildings may be higher than a coconut palm. The location is just stunning. A 20-minute drive to Mala Wharf. $190 garden view hotel room to $700 3-room suite ocean view.

Kapalua Bay Hotel 1 Bay Drive, Kapalua, HI 96761. ℘(800)367-8000, 669-5656. Web: www.luxurycollection.com. Part of the Kapalua Resort Development which includes three golf courses, this is a luxury hotel at the quiet, exclusive northwest end of the island. A 20-minute drive to Mala Wharf. $253–$390 garden view, $318–$490 full ocean view depending on the season.

RESTAURANTS

Cheeseburger in Paradise 811 Front St., Lahaina. ℘661-4855. Right on the water with views of Lanai this is a great place to go for juicy burgers, onion rings and other filling American food.

David Paul's Lahaina Grill 127 Lahainaluna Rd., Lahaina. ℘ 667-5117. Regularly voted Maui's Best Restaurant, David Paul's classy restaurant is located in historic Lahaina and serves delicious, creative Hawaiian regional cuisine.

Gazebo Restaurant 5315 Lower Honoapiilani Rd. Napili (next to the Napili Shores Resort). ℘ 669-5621. A tiny open-air gazebo-shaped restaurant on the southern point of serene Napili Bay. Serving both breakfast and lunch from 7:30 AM until 2 PM every day, their specialty is macadamia nut pancakes—basically a dessert!

Longhis 888 Front St., Lahaina. ℘667-2288. An open-air restaurant right on busy Front Street, Longhi's is a Lahaina institution. Known for their pasta, fish and extensive verbal menu, they serve break-

fast, lunch and dinner.

FILM PROCESSING

Wolf Camera 139 Lahainaluna Rd., Lahaina, HI 96761. ℘667-6255. In-house print

AT A GLANCE
Lanai

NICKNAME The Private Isle
LAND AREA 140.6 sq. mi. (364.0 sq. km.)
COASTLINE 47 mi. (76 km.)
HIGHEST POINT Lanaihale, 3,366 ft. (1,026 m.)
POPULATION 2,426 (1994)
YEARLY VISITORS 105,260 (1997)
BIGGEST TOWN Lanai City, pop. 2,400 (1990)
AIRPORT Lanai Airport
AIRPORT DISTANCE FROM HONOLULU 72 mi. (116 km.)
PER CAPITA INCOME $13,584 (1993)

processing only. Out-lab E-6 slide processing takes about 3 days.

Lanai

MEDICAL SERVICES

Lanai Community Hospital 628 7th St., Lanai City. ℘565-6411. 24-hour emergency service.

DIVE OPERATORS

While there are no Lanai-based dive operators, limited diving is offered for guests staying at the Manele Bay Hotel which has contracted with Maui-based snorkel/sail company Trilogy Excursions to pick up divers at the hotel for 1- or 2-tank boat dives and to meet divers at Manele Beach for a guided shore dive. Trilogy readily admits that it specializes in snorkelers and first-time divers. Bottom time and sites are limited, but if you are stuck on Lanai with a golfer and you want to dive,

this may satisfy your craving. **Trilogy Excursions** (est. 1973) P.O. Box 1119, Lahaina, Maui, Hawaii 96767. ℘(888) 225-MAUI, 661-4743. Web: www.sailtrilogy.com. Email: trilogy@maui.net. 2-tank dive Tues. and Thurs. certified divers only $160 incl/ equip. and hotel pickup. 6 diver minimum to confirm trip. 1-tank dive Mon., Wed., Fri., Sat., divers and snorkelers $160 (this is not a typo) incl. equip. 8:30 a.m. to 12:30 p.m.

ACCOMMODATIONS

Manele Bay Hotel Box 310, Lanai City, HI 96763, ℘(800) 321-4666, 565-7700. Web: www.lanai-resorts.com. This luxury hotel overlooks Hulopoe Bay, a marine preserve with excellent snorkeling. Golf is the main attraction on this island however. $375 terrace room to $1,100 oceanfront suite (and we're not even getting into the "Butler Suites").

RESTAURANTS

Blue Ginger Cafe 409 7th Street, Lanai City. ℘565-6363. A casual home-style restaurant and bakery serving breakfast ~$5, lunch ~$6, and dinner ~$12. **Henry Clay's Rotisserie** (in the Hotel Lanai). ℂ565-4700. The hardwood floors and high ceilings of this older hotel create a fine setting for

dinner. The chef is a New Orleans native and some of the dishes reflect his origins. Dinner only $18–$40. **Tanigawa's** 419 7th St., Lanai City. ℂ565-6537. Basic local food such as teriyaki beef, friend chicken and burgers. The grill is kept sizzling by its local following. Breakfast, lunch and dinner $2–$6. Closed Wednesdays.

Molokai

MEDICAL SERVICES

Molokai General Hospital Kaunakakai. ℂ553-5331. 24-hour emergency service.

DIVE OPERATORS

If you are staying on Molokai, boat diving tours are offered by only one operation. Molokai is also dived by divers on day boats out of Lahaina. **Bill Kapuni's Snorkel and Scuba Adventures** (est. 1991) P.O. Box 1945, Kau-

nakakai, HI 96748. ℂ553-9867. Web: www.molokai.com/kapuni. E-mail: cpgroup@aloha.net. 22-foot Boston Whaler. 6 divers. Bill Kapuni's boat dives are a rare opportunity to dive with and be guided by a full-blooded Hawaiian. The small family-run operation and group size means there is much personal attention and plenty of time to absorb his local knowledge and share his culture. 2-tank dive incl. equipment $95. Tank rentals for shore diving are also available.

ACCOMMODATIONS

These are all about 5 minutes from Kaunakakai Harbor.
Aahi Place B&B Box 528, Kaunakakai, HI 96748. ℂ(406) 549-8345, 553-5860. Web: www.molokai-aloha.com/aahi. Email: mitty@aloha.net. Private 1BR cedar cottage nestled in a tropical garden. No TV or phone. $85 incl. continental breakfast, minimum 2-night stay.
Hotel Molokai Box 1020, Kaunakakai, HI 96748. ℂ(800) 367-5004, 553-5347. Web: www.hotelmolokai.com. Email: info@hotelmolokai.com. Recently refurbished, this laid-back complex of two-

story buildings on a palm-tree lined beach has comfortable rooms, some with kitchenettes. It doesn't get much more "old Hawaii" than this. $80–$135 depending on room size and view.
Ka Hale Mala B&B Box 1582, Kaunakakai, HI 96748. ℂ553-9009. Web: molokai-bnb.com. Email: cpgroup@aloha.net. A quiet 4-room ground floor apartment with lanai overlooking the garden. $80 incl. freshly prepared gourmet Hawaiian breakfast, $70 without.
Molokai Shores Box 1037, Kaunakakai, HI 96748. ℂ(800) 535-0085. Web: www.marcresorts.com. Email: marc@aloha.net. A nice 100-unit condo with everything you'd need. Units on the third floor have high cathedral ceilings. $144 1 BR to $189 2 BR.

RESTAURANTS

Kanemitsu Bakery 79 Ala Malama St., Kaunakakai. ℂ553-5855. Famous throughout the islands for their fresh-baked sweet bread, they also, strangely, serve a variety of Danish pasties. The restaurant in the back serves local-style breakfasts and plate lunches for about $6. Closed Tuesdays.
Hotel Molokai Restaurant (in the Hotel Molokai) ℂ553-5347. An open-air restaurant right on the beach ideal for watching sunset and surf. Lunch is burgers and sandwiches for about $8, dinner is fish and steak from $12–$18.

Pocillopora meandrina

Oahu

Few divers think of Oahu as a dive destination, and truthfully many of the operators here concentrate on beginners and casual divers (and making money). Still, there are a couple of good and conscientious outfits, and some fine diving, if you look for it. The north coast, for example, still intrigues us.

MEDICAL SERVICES

Queen's Medical Center 1301 Punchbowl St. Honolulu. ©538-9011. 24-hour emergency service.

DIVE OPERATORS

Oahu, more than any other island, requires careful research when choosing a dive boat operator. Some of the oldest dive shops do not even have their own boats, some boats get divers from several shops at once, and many do quick back-to-back trips. Most cater to beginning divers.

Partly because of the constant influx of new divers from the military bases, and partly because Oahu is not typically visited as a diving destination, operators on Oahu focus more on instruction than high-quality boat dives for experienced divers. A quick check of Oahu web sites makes this clear: photos of clownfish (there are none in Hawaii) and octopus harassment, descriptions of dive sites plagiarized from guidebooks (haven't they been there themselves?), and our all-time favorite, posting the bottom time of the dive (how do they know your air consumption?).

This said, the following two dive boat operations seem to realize there are more experienced divers out there who want a quality trip, and they are willing to provide it.

Dive boats leave from Maunalua Bay Ramp (a 15-minute drive east of Waikiki), Kewalo Basin, or the Waianae Harbor (45-minute drive northwest of Waikiki). Hotel pick-ups are usually 7:30 a.m.–8:00 a.m., and dive sites are reached within 20 minutes.

Aquazone (est. 1986) at the Outrigger Waikiki Hotel 2335 Kalakaua Ave. #112, Honolulu, HI 96815. ©923-3483 Web: www. aquazone.net. Email: aquazonehawaii@aol.com. Two 27-foot boats. One 12-passenger, one 6-passenger. 2-tank dive incl. equipment $120. Owner Devon Merrifield is still excited and enthusiastic about the animals after 15 years in the business, and takes divers to the best dive sites available, not just the closest. But do request the 6-passenger boat.

Camera rental $25 incl. film. **Captain Bruce's Scuba Charters** (est. 1990) P.O. Box 240451, Honolulu, HI, 96824. ©(800)535-2487, 373-3590. Web: www.captainbruce.com. Email: info@captainbruce.com. Two boats: 42-foot boat, 16 passengers including introductory divers, snorkelers and riders, and a 6-passenger boat for private charters or more experienced divers. 2-tank dive incl. equipment $122. Owner Fritz Sandoz is trying hard to raise the level of diving provided on Oahu. One of his boats is reserved for more experienced divers and natural history briefings are given before the dives. This is Oahu's only dive boat operation that runs its own boats out of two sides of the island: Waianae and Hawaii Kai (Maunalua Bay

AT A GLANCE
Oahu

NICKNAME The Gathering Place
LAND AREA 597.1 sq. mi. (1,546 sq. km.)
COASTLINE 112 mi. (180 km.)
HIGHEST POINT Kaala, 4,003 ft. (1,220 m.)
POPULATION 871,800 (1996)
YEARLY VISITORS 5,002,530 (1997)
BIGGEST TOWN Honolulu, pop. 377,059 (1990)
AIRPORTS Honolulu International Airport
DISTANCE FROM SAN FRANCISCO 2,397 mi. (3,857 km.)
PER CAPITA INCOME $24,929 (1993)

Ramp). Larger 100 cu. ft. tanks are available as well as Nitrox. Camera rental $25.

DIVE SHOP

Aloha Dive Shop (est. 1970) 377 Keahole St. #101, Honolulu, HI 96825. ☏395-5922. Web: www.alohadiveshop.com Email: firstlady@lava.net. This long-established 5-star PADI dive center recently moved to a sparkling new location in Hawaii Kai Shopping Center. They have a decent selection of equipment for sale or rent and can do NAUI and SSI certifications in addition to the full range of PADI courses. Air fills and gear repair also available.

ACCOMMODATIONS

Ilima Hotel 445 Nohonani St., Honolulu, HI 96815. ☏(888)864-5462, 923-1877. Web: www.ilima.com. Email: mail@ilima.com. A relatively small (99 rooms) condo-style hotel in a little quieter section of Waikiki two blocks from the beach. Large rooms, lots of ammenities and friendly staff. $99/$109 studio, $150/$170 1 BR, $190/$210 2 BR depending on season.
Outrigger Reef Hotel 2169 Kalia Rd. Honolulu, HI 96815. ☏(800) 688-7444, 923-3111. Web: www.outrigger.com. Email: beachfront@outrigger.com. Newly renovated, this 9-story hotel sits on Waikiki beach just feet from the water's edge. $220 no-view to $450 oceanview.
Sheraton Moana Surfrider 2365 Kalakaua Ave. Honolulu, HI 96815. ☏922-3111. Web: www.sheraton-hawaii. com. This was Hawaii's first beachfront hotel in 1901, and has been renovated. $265 city view to $405 ocean view.

RESTAURANTS

Diamond Head Grill 2885 Kalakaua Ave. Waikiki. ☏922-

3734. On the 2nd floor of the W Honolulu this contemporary setting includes a wall of windows looking out over Diamond Head. Hawaiian cuisine. Dinner only, $25–$60.
Ono Hawaiian Food 726 Kapahulu Ave., Waikiki. ☏737-2275. This simple diner serving Hawaiian food is so popular that people line up outside waiting to get in. Open for lunch and dinner, about $8. Closed Sunday.
Shore Bird Beach Broiler 2169 Kalia Rd., Waikiki. ☏922-2887. Open-air beachside restaurant in the Outrigger Reef Hotel. Breakfast buffet $7, dinner buffet $8. You can cook your own mahimahi or sirloin steak or teriyaki chicken at dinner on a common grill.

FILM PROCESSING

Photo Express 1778 Ala Moana Blvd., Suite LL01, Waikiki (in the Discovery Bay building). ☏942-2644. One-hour print processing and overnight E-6.

North Shore

If you're not going to be here in the winter and you want to experience Oahu as few divers do, stay and dive on the north shore. You won't see the wrecks sunk on the south and west coasts for divers to play on (although you could drive down if you just had to see them), but you would be diving places rarely dived by non locals and getting to know the crew of the one small dive operation on this coast which only takes six divers.

DIVE SHOP/OPERATOR

Deep Ecology (est. 1996) 66-456 Kamehameha Hwy., Haleiwa, HI 96712. ☏(800) 578-3992, 637-7946. Web: deepecologyhawaii.com.

Email: dive@deepecology hawaii.com. 24-foot boat. 6 divers. 2-tank dive incl. equipment $110. Hour drive from Honolulu. Owner Ken Nichols and his staff have been involved in numerous turtle rescues and net recoveries, and are strong advocates for creating a marine preserve on the north shore. This passion carries over into their dive trips.

ACCOMMODATIONS

Backpackers 59-788 Kamehameha Hwy., Heleiwa, HI 96712. ☏638-7838. Web: www.backpackers-hawaii. com. A long established business with a variety of accommodations from $15 beds to whole cottages at $150.
Turtle Bay Golf & Tennis Resort 57-091 Kamehameha Highway, Kahuku, HI 96731. ☏(800) 774-1500, 293-8811. Web: www.hilton.com. The only hotel on the north shore, this luxury resort has 485 rooms, suites and cabanas, all with ocean views. Also pools, golf courses, tennis courts, and even horse stables. $159 1 BR to $1,950 2 BR suite.

RESTAURANTS

Cafe Haleiwa ☏637-5516. On the south side of Haleiwa. Small cafe popular with local surfers. Burritos and sandwiches with terrific fries. $5 breakfast, $9 lunch.
Kua Aina 66-214 Kamehameha Hwy., Haleiwa. ☏637-6067. In the center of town. Excellent fish sandwiches and burgers for about $5. Lunch and dinner.
Sunset Diner ☏638-7660. Opposite Sunset Beach Park in Waimea. Burgers and sandwiches for about $6.

FILM PROCESSING

Del's Photo 66-200 Kamehameha Hwy., Haleiwa. ☏637-3357. One-hour prints, two-day E-6.

Kauai and Niihau

Kauai's dripping green beauty is famous, and for many regular visitors to the islands, this one is their favorite. The diving isn't as well-known, although there are some fine sites. Niihau and Lehua, however, are legendary—if you get the opportunity, by all means go. You won't regret it.

MEDICAL SERVICES

Wilcox Memorial Hospital 3420 Kuhio Highway, Lihue. #245-1100. 24-hour emergency service.

DIVE OPERATORS/SHOP

Since the actual capsizing of one of the commercial dive boats in the summer of 2001, it is even more important that you choose your dive operation carefully. Dive boats leave from two harbors, Port Allen and Kukuiula, both on the south coast and dive sites are usually reached in less than 20 minutes. Meeting times for 2-tank morning dives are typically 7:30 a.m.–8:00 a.m.
Bubbles Below (est. 1983) P.O. Box 157, Eleele, HI 96705. ©332-7333 Web: BubblesBelowKauai.com. Email: kaimanu@aloha.net. 35-foot boat (w/ hot water shower!) 8 divers. Certified divers only. 2-tank dive incl. equipment/computer $125. This hardy team led by knowledgeable and spirited Linda Bail makes sure to describe and point out the many animals that are unique to Hawaii both before the dives using pictures and during the dives. Their leadership in reef protection over the years, and the care they exercise during their charters, makes them the top choice for boat diving on Kauai. Depart from Port Allen.
Fathom Five/OceanQuest

(est. 1980) 3450 Poipu Rd., Koloa, HI 96756. © (800) 972-3078, 742-6991. Web: w w w . o c e a n q u e s t . n e t, www.fathomfive.com. Email: fathom5@fathomfive.com. Fathom Five's Shakespearean name recognition and over 20 years in business produced a somewhat loyal following, so new owners George and Jeannette Thompson have decided to keep the name linked to theirs for awhile. Kauai's oldest dive shop is fully stocked

and they also do gear repair and pump air. Full range of PADI courses are offered. Two 25-foot boats. 6 divers. Certified divers only. 2-tank dive incl. equipment/computer $120. This down-to-earth and friendly crew loves to share the sport of diving with others. SeaLife ReefMaster cameras $60/day incl. film

and developing. Depart from Kukuiula Harbor.

ACCOMMODATIONS

Kahili Mountain Park Cabins Box 298, Koloa, HI 96756. ©742-9921. Run by the Seventh Day Adventist church, these 4–6 person cabins, some rustic, some new are spread out in a beautiful, quiet setting up on a hill beneath Mt. Kahili. All have kitchen facilities, none have TV or phone. 20 minutes to either

Port Allen or Kukuiula Harbor. $35–$45 for cabinettes (shared bath), $56–$66 for cabins (private bath).
Gloria's Spouting Horn B&B 4464 Lawai Beach Rd., Poipu, HI 96756. ©742-6995. An upscale B&B with only 3 guest rooms, all right on the ocean, each with its own balcony and deep soak-

ing tub, refrigerator, microwave, TV and phone. 5-minute drive to Kukuiula Harbor. $200 incl. breakfast, minimum 3-night stay.

Waimea Plantation Cottages 9400 Kaumualii Hwy., Waimea, HI 96796. ✆(800) 992-4632, 338-1625. Web: www.waimea-plantation.com. Email: waiple@aloha.net. 48 restored plantation worker's cottages dating from the early 1900's and nestled on a 27-acre coconut grove result in a one-of-a-kind lodging experience. All have kitchens, period furnishings and wood floors. 5-minute drive to Port Allen. $130 1 BR grove view – $385 5 BR oceanfront.
Kiahuna Plantation 2253 Poipu Rd., Poipu, HI 96756. ✆(800) 688-7444, 742-6411. Web: www.outrigger.com. Email: kpr@outrigger.com.

Built before ocean setback laws were passed, this condo complex's oceanfront units are *right* on the beach. The grounds are quiet and tropical. 5-minute drive to Kukuiula Harbor, $215–$450 1 BR units, $345–$485 2 BR units, depending on location.
Sheraton Kauai Resort 2440 Hoonani Rd., Poipu, HI 96756. ✆(800) 782-9488, 742-1661. Web: www.sheraton-hawaii.com. A luxury hotel on Poipu beach with many rooms very close to the water. Rebuilt and renovated in 2000 due to hurricane Iniki, all rooms have lanais. $265 garden view to $750 suite.

RESTAURANTS

Beach House 5022 Lawai Rd., Poipu. ✆742-1424. Right on Lawai Beach, this open air restaurant is a popular place to watch surf and the sunset. American and Hawaiian Regional Cuisine is served including steak and seafood. Dinner $25–$40.
Brick Oven Pizza 2-2555 Kaumualii Hwy., Kalaheo. ✆332-8561. Though not baked in a brick oven, the pizza here is excellent and the service friendly and attentive. You can eat in or take out, but if you eat in your kids will be given a ball of pizza dough to play with. $8–$18.
Gaylord's 1 1/2 miles south of Lihue on Hwy. 50. ✆245-9593. Located in the courtyard of the 1930s Kilohana sugar plantation estate, the tables overlook a huge lawn and the setting is peaceful and romantic. The menu includes creatively prepared fish, pasta and steak. After dinner you can wander through the restored mansion and view Hawaiian artifacts and works by local artists. The massive calabash in the entryway made from the trunk of a monkeypod tree is worth stopping by for. Insured for tens of thousands of dollars, it is one of few of this size in existence. They serve lunch ($10–$13) and dinner ($19–$32).
Shells In the Sheraton Kauai Resort. ✆742-1661. A great view overlooking Poipu Beach is the reason to eat here. They have a breakfast buffet for $18.95 in addition to ala carte. Dinner menu items range from pasta and steak to fish and lobster, $16 to $34.

FILM DEVELOPING
Koloa One-Hour Photo 3450C Poipu Rd., Koloa. ✆742-8919. In-house print processing only.
Camera Lab 733 Kuhio Hwy., Kapaa. ✆822-7338. In-house overnight print and E-6 processing.

Eretmochelys imbricata ssp. bissa

The hawksbill turtle is far less commonly seen in Hawaii than the green turtle.

Midway

Our only real advice about Midway is... Go! It's not cheap (figure at least $2,300 for a week on the island with diving) but this place offers a rare taste of the wild Pacific. If you like sharks you'll be in heaven. The nesting birds are a hoot, and eating in a mess hall is just like being back in school.

Diving is offered at Midway from May through September as sea conditions are just too rough during the winter. The normal schedule at Midway is a 2-tank dive in the morning, meeting at 8 a.m. followed by a one-tank dive after lunch.

GETTING THERE

Weekly flights to Midway are aboard a chartered Aloha Airlines 737 with some additional Wednesday flights from February through September. ($590 RT from Honolulu). The 2.5–3 hour flights are scheduled to depart Midway and arrive on Midway at night so as not to interfere with the hundreds of thousands of seabirds leaving the atoll to feed and returning to feed their chicks during daylight. This makes it rather inconvenient on the return flight which arrives in Honolulu too late to connect to other flights, so divers usually stay near the airport at the Honolulu Airport Hotel which provides free shuttle service and offers a discount to Midway guests.

Midway Atoll is an unincorporated possession of the United States but is outside the United States Customs Service, Immigration Service, and Agriculture Department boundaries. Therefore when you re-enter the United States in Honolulu, you must go through the federal port facility there and show valid proof of citizenship such as a current passport, certified birth certificate (if you are a U.S. citizen), or one of several other approved proofs. You will also be required to go through U.S. Customs.

RESERVATIONS

Reservations are handled by Destination: PACIFIC. ℂ1(888) BIG-ULUA. Web: www.fishdive.com/

AT A GLANCE

Midway

LAND AREA 2.5 sq. mi. (6.4 sq. km.)
HIGHEST POINT 12 ft. (4 m.)
POPULATION 230 (est. 2001)
YEARLY VISITORS ca. 800,000 (albatrosses, of course)
DISTANCE FROM HONOLULU 1,309 mi. (2.106 km.)

midwayatoll.htm. Email: dest-pacific@hawaii.rr.com. These people have been to Midway and know the answers to your questions. The beauty of making arrangements for a trip to Midway is that Destination: PACIFIC can handle every aspect of your trip.

ON-ISLAND TRANSPORTATION

One of the many aspects that make Midway just plain fun is how you get around the island. You could walk to get around the entire time you are on Midway and you would never tire of it due to scenery and birds, but if you have a heavy social schedule or want to see every corner of the atoll, then renting a bicycle for $5 a day makes more sense. If you want to be popular with your fellow divers, rent a golf cart for $30 a day. You can charge the battery at the barracks.

WEATHER

During the months that divers are typically on-island the temperature ranges from 70 to 85 degrees with cooler nights. Rain during this time is not common with about 2 inches falling per month. Water temperature ranges from the high 60s in the spring to the high 70s in the summer/fall.

MEDICAL TREATMENT

A medical clinic is staffed by a full-time licensed physician who can provide limited medical care on a fee for service basis. There is no hyperbaric chamber on Midway, and the diving is conservative partly for this reason.

DIVE OPERATOR/SHOP

Dive Midway is the name of Midway's one and only dive operation. They have two boats: a brand new Custom Dive Boat Pro 48 named *Sea Angel* and a refurbished 40-foot boat of military origin named the *Spinner D*. Both typically take 12 divers, although the *Sea Angel* will sometimes take more. All dives are guided and sites are varied so that repeating divers see as many different sites as possible. The normal schedule is a 2-tank dive in the morning and a 1-tank dive after lunch for $195, including gear if needed. They offer a 6-day, 10-tank package for $650.

Although we were once able to have a gear for a camera housing fabricated by the local workers using the big shipyard lathe, you had better bring every-thing you will need in the way of camera equipment and then some. There is nothing here to fall back on, so make sure everything is on order and bring spares. Film processing is not available.

ACCOMMODATIONS

Renovated in 1996, the Bachelors Officers Quarters, either Bravo or Charlie, are where you'll stay. All rooms have air conditioning, maid service, satellite TV and HBO and there are laundry facilities on each floor. Rooms range from $125 for one-room w/ shared bath to $300 for a three-room suite w/ private bath, with various levels in between.

DINING

The Galley Cafeteria is the former Navy Galley and serves a huge variety of food at every meal. People who live on the island eat here almost every meal in the cafeteria-style setting. It's just a fun place to eat—you'll feel like you're back in school! Breakfast $8, lunch $10, dinner $12.

The Clipper House is Midway's fine dining restaurant and this is no hype. It overlooks the fine white sand beach on the north side of the island. The food is prepared by an actual French chef, and is delicious! There is even a wine list. They serve breakfast ($10) and dinner ($35) only.

The All Hands Club kept its name from Midway's days as a Navy base. The local pub, it has a full bar and burgers and excellent burritos, plus pool tables and other table games.

RECREATION

Midway is a beautiful place for running (and it's flat!) but the birds can make it challenging. Indoor facilities such as a gym, weight room, basketball courts, handball/raquetball courts, and a bowling alley are available and are a great way to mix with the locals. Outdoors there are tennis courts, a volleyball court on the beach, and at night incredible star-gazing (there is zero light pollution here).

Videos are played at the "big screen" Station Theatre at 8:00 p.m. on weekends and occasionally wildlife presentations are given by visiting scientists or residents.

There is also a library with the kind of wild selection that you'd expect on an atoll in the middle of the Pacific Ocean. Pool, darts, and table tennis can be played at the All Hands Club.

SHOPPING

T-shirts, postcards, Midway books and other Midway souveniers are sold at The Ship's Store in "The Midway Mall."

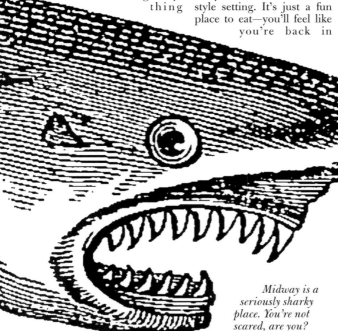

Midway is a seriously sharky place. You're not scared, are you?

Further Reading

Bertsch, Hans, and Scott Johnson, 1981. *Hawaiian Nudibranchs*. Honolulu: Oriental Publishing. Softcover, 112 pages.

This is the only nudibranch guide currently available. Although many of the scientific names have changed since it came out, it is a good basic introduction to Hawaiian nudibranchs by two of Hawaii's pioneer " 'branchers."

Carpenter, Russell & Blyth, 1981. *Fish Watching in Hawaii* San Mateo, California: Natural World Press. Softcover, 199 pages.

A good introduction to watching and understanding fish behavior in Hawaii. Answers a lot of "whys?" regarding fish and their varied forms. Although paintings of some Hawaiian fish are included, this is not an identification guide.

Gulko, David, 1998. *Hawaiian Coral Reef Ecology*. Honolulu: Mutual Publishing. Softcover, 245 pages.

This book defies characterization. Using photos, diagrams and cartoon-type pictures, Gulko explains many complex reef associations and processes in entertaining and easy to understand language. If you have an above average interest in life on the reef this will make all your dives, not just those in Hawaii, infinitely more enjoyable.

Hoover, John P., 1996. *Hawaii's Fishes: A Guide for Snorkelers, Divers and Aquarists*. Honolulu: Mutual Publishing. Softcover, 183 pages.

An excellent identification guide to 230 species of Hawaii's reef fish. Includes many interesting stories and tidbits from Hawaiian folklore and scientific fish studies.

Hoover, John P., 1998. *Hawaii's Sea Creatures. A Guide to Hawaii's Marine Invertebrates*. Honolulu: Mutual Publishing. Softcover, 366 pages.

This is the best resource available for identifying Hawaii's invertebrates, beginning with sponges and ending with tunicates. Well-researched with excellent photos, it is a must for anyone who cares about what they are seeing in Hawaiian waters. Get a copy.

Juvik, Sonia P. and James O. Juvik, eds. *Atlas of Hawaii*, 3d edition. Chief cartographer: Thomas R. Paradise. Honolulu: University of Hawaii Press. Limpbound, 333 pages.

A very complete reference and gazetteer to Hawaii, covering everything from agriculture to zoogeography. Even if you are just interested in diving subjects, the sections on physical oceanography, marine ecosystems, climate, biogeography, etc. make this book worth having. Oddly, the main reference maps are the weakest part of an otherwise impressive effort.—ed.

Kaufman, Gregory D. and Paul H. Forestell, 1995. *Hawaii's Humpback Whales*. 2nd. ed. Honolulu: Island Heritage Publishing. Softcover, 176 pages.

An excellent introduction

to humpback whales that migrate to Hawaii during the winter. In addition to information on their social dynamics, biology and song, there are photos depicting behavior and advice on how to interpret that behavior. This is helpful when viewing whales from shore or from a boat.

Randall, John E. 1998. *Shore Fishes of Hawaii*. Honolulu: University of Hawaii Press. Softcover, 216 pages.

Written by the top expert in the field of Hawaiian fish, Dr. Randall has produced a compact guidebook with excellent photographs covering 342 species. [*The* Hawaiian fish I.D. book to have—ed.]

Severns, Mike, 2000. *Hawaiian Seashells*. Honolulu: Island Heritage. Spiral hardcover, 277 pages.

The most comprehensive color identification guide to Hawaii's shells. Every species photograph shows both the back and underside of the same shell making identification crystal clear. Covers 360 species, about 30 of which are found only in Hawaii.

Taylor, Leighton, 1993. *Sharks of Hawaii*. Honolulu: University Of Hawaii Press. Hardcover, 125 pages.

A comprehensive guide to the shark species found in Hawaiian waters including the biology so-far known for each. An added bonus is a fascinating appendix that gives a case by case account of all recorded shark attacks in Hawaii since 1779.

Index

Page numbers in boldface indicate the main section on that topic; page numbers in italic indicate photographs